My Healing

MINISTRY/ANTHOLOGIES of
POETIC SPIRITUAL
MEDITATIONS

Didatic Teachings Through Versemeter

My Healing

MINISTRY/ANTHOLOGIES *of*
POETIC SPIRITUAL
MEDITATIONS

TEACHING AND LEARNING COMES BY HEARING THE WORDS OF GOD

Gloria Solomon

XULON PRESS

Xulon Press
2301 Lucien Way #415
Maitland, FL 32751
407.339.4217
www.xulonpress.com

Unless otherwise indicated, Scripture quotations taken from the King James Version (KJV)–*public domain*.

Paperback ISBN-13: 978-1-6628-2590-3
Ebook ISBN-13: 978-1-6628-2591-0

TABLE OF CONTENTS

GOD CREATED THE HEAVENS/EARTH WITH AN ECUMENICAL BASIS FOR MANKIND

God perfectly planned humanity and initiated soteriology, to be through his son as, the vessel, and initiator of the redemptive goodwill for all mankind. God's words are laws, laws are to be adhered to. God's promises are like promissory notes, upon fulfillment of his commandments and right living we are heirs to his Kingdom and the promises of eternal life.

A blessed life without disease and plagues of physical inferiorities, and fruits of the flesh. We will be perpetuated by the fruits of the HOLY SPIRIT, in a divine realm without the vicissitudes of physical abnormalities.

In God's word, ("John 5:36-39, KJV) - But I have greater witness than that of John: for the works which the Father hath given me to finish, the same works that I do, bear witness of me, that the Father hath sent me.

37 And the Father himself, which hath sent me, hath borne witness of me. Ye have neither heard his voice at any time, nor seen his shape.

39 Search the scriptures; for in them ye think ye have eternal life: and they are they which testify of me.

PAGE DEDICATED TO:

BISHOP EDDIE LEE & CHARLENE THOMAS

DEDICATION

First and foremost, this book is dedicated to the most-high God, who has given me an innate gift that I have composed into a form ascertainable by others. This is my way of Kingdom building for God through my works and opening my door to those interested in my views. I would like to dedicate this book to the late Dr. Martin Luther King Jr., who was the driving force in black America, at a time when the need for equality was at the doorsteps of the White House.

The birth of the civil rights bill was initiated and it was his destiny to bring it to fruition. He was prepared for the task and so eloquently took the helm to direct and introduce the civil rights bills into the annals of history. For the sake of justice, equality, and ethics, due to all black Americans.

To my son De Andre' Thomas, my grandson De Andre' Thomas Jr., my granddaughter Destiny Thomas and my granddaughter Andrea Berardi- Thomas. Also to my immediate family: The late Bishop Eddie L. Thomas, my loving mother Charlene Thomas, sisters and brothers, Mary L. Thomas-Pittman, James Thomas, Joannah Thomas-Jackson, Jesse Thomas, Isaiah Thomas, Charlene Thomas-Dunn, Geraldine Thomas-King, Timothy Thomas, Patricia A. Thomas-Garrett, Willie Thomas and Eddie L. Simpson. To my church family, Church of God, Faith Tabernacle, Jesus Name Temple in Oakland, CA, the presiding Bishop Robert W. Harrison and first lady Barbara Harrison. To a beloved friend, Keith Thomas, may your flight be blessed with wings of Grace

I HAVE SOMETHING TO SAY

Don't try to silence, the fullness of my mouth, that roars with the sounds of rushing tides,

When I speak, I draw my breadth deeply from the seven seas,

Don't try to hide or bury me, in your whimsical tactics of deceitful games, Seeking, to ravish an unsuspecting soul, because I have something to say,

How can you hide what can't be hidden, for I am born of the bluest of skies,

I am laden with the ether of the heavens, I have no end,

How can you bury the earth, for she encompasses herself, in all her depths,

You can't because I have something to say,

Why do you change my pathways, and try to divert my footsteps?

I am a path within a path, my footsteps are set by my King,

I was present when he ordered them,

I have much to say!

With all your meddling, changing, robbing, stealing and killing,

You still have not heard!

I am here,

I have been here and I have returned here and will continue to be here until,

I say what God has given me to say...

GLORIA SOLOMON
AUTHOR

HEALING POETRY

(FOR VARIOUS DISEASES)

CANCER

IN LIFE EVERYTHING HAS A NAME, IN THE SPIRIT WORLD EVERYTHING HAS BEEN FRAMED,

WE KNOW THAT GOD HAS IT ALL IN HIS CONTROL AND VIEW, EVEN DISEASE HAS A REFERENCE POINT TO GOD NONE OF IT IS NEW,

BEHOLD TO ALL DISEASE, GOD IS THE ANSWER, HE HEALETH ALL OUR INFIRMATIES AND DISPELLS EVERY FORM OF CANCER,

Please read these three (3) scriptures on healing, each day that you pray. Believe and know that God wants you whole and healed. It has already been paid for by CHRIST.

Isaiah 53:4-5,

Exodus 23:25, Exodus 23:25 And you shall serve the LORD your God, and he shall bless your bread, and your water; and I will take sickness away from the middle of you.

Ecclesiastes 3:3 3a time to kill and a time to heal, a time to tear down and a time to build,

KNOW THAT WHEN JESUS DIED HE OPENED UP A COMPLETED/ ACCOMPLISHED PATH AND TIME FOR PERFECTED HEALING IN THE FUTURE TENSE, PRESENT TENSE AND PAST TENSE, FOR YOUR HEALING.

YESTERDAY, TODAY, AND TOMORROW, HE WILL ALWAYS BE THE SAME.

ARTHRITIS

IN THE NAME OF JESUS CHRIST, WE KNOW THAT HE PAID THE PRICE,

FOR OUR COMPLETE BODY TO BE HEALED,

IT WAS HIS PROMISE AND IT WAS HIS WILL,

IN THE NAME OF HIM WHO BORE OUR SINS, SO THAT SICKNESS,

SIN AND EVIL COULD NOT WIN,

WE CALL OUT THE NAME OF ATHRITIS,

WE COMMAND IT TO GO GOD NEVER PROMISED US THIS,

THANK YOU, LORD, FOR YOUR HEALING PRESENCE,

AND FOR RENEWING MY BODY WITH YOUR HEALING ESSENCE,

Please read these three (3) scriptures on healing, each day that you pray. Believe and know that God wants you whole and healed. It has already been paid for by CHRIST.

(2 Deuteronomy 32, 39,).See now that I, even I, am he, and there is no god with me: I kill, and I make alive; I wound, and I heal: neither is there any that can deliver out of my hand.

(Psalms 41,) I said, LORD, be merciful unto me: heal my soul; for I have sinned against thee.

(Psalms 103:2-3) Bless the Lord, O my soul, and forget not all His benefits: Who forgives all your iniquities, who heals all your diseases,

HEART TROUBLES

GOD MADE THE HEART SPECIAL FOR HIM TO DWELL IN,

BUT WE MUST KEEP IT PURE AND FREE ABOMINIMAL SINS,

I THINK WHEN WE SIN AGAINST GOD OUR SINS DOUBLE,

ONE OF THE WAGES OF SIN IS HEART TROUBLE,

WE PRAY LORD THAT YOU HELP US KEEP YOU IN OUR HEART,

THAT WE MAY EACH DAY HAVE A PERFECT START,

YOUR LOVE IS THE RHYTHM THAT KEEPS ME IN STEP WITH EVERY BEAT,

AS MY FATHER, WITH THE SON, IN MY SOUL YOU MAKE ME DIVINE/AWESOMELY COMPLETE,

Please read these three (3) scriptures on healing, each day that you pray. Believe and know that God wants you whole and healed. It has already been paid for by CHRIST.

(Psalms 107:19-21), Then they cried out to the Lord in their trouble, And He saved them out of their distresses. 20 He sent His word and healed them,

(Proverbs 4:20-22), - My son, pay attention to what I say; turn your ear to my words. 21 Do not let them out of your sight, keep them within your heart; 22 for they are life to those who find them and health to one's whole body.

(Matthew 4:23), And Jesus went about all Galilee, teaching in their synagogues, and preaching the gospel of the kingdom, and healing all manner of sickness and all manner of disease among the people."

LEPROSY

GOD HEALS ALL DISEASES CROSS-OVER AND OLD,

HIS HOLY WORD REVELS HOW HE PROTECTS AND PERFECTS OUR SOULS,

SIN HAS BOUND SOME TO UNHEALTHY WAYS, PLAGUED THEIR LIVES AND SHORTENED THEIR DAYS,

JESUS WAS A PROMISE AND SALVATION FOR ME,

HE CASTED OUT THE EVILS OF SIN AND DESTROYED LEPROSY,

THANK YOU, FATHER, FOR ALL YOUR CARE, TAKING THE PENALTIES OF SIN WE COULD NOT BEAR,

YOU CLEANED UP OUR LIVES AND MADE US WHOLE, GAVE US ANEW DAY AND A BRAND-NEW SOUL.

Please read these three (3) scriptures on healing, each day that you pray. Believe and know that God wants you whole and healed. It has already been paid for by CHRIST.

(Matthew 9:35), Jesus went through all the towns and villages, teaching in their synagogues, proclaiming the good news of the kingdom and healing every disease and sickness.

LUPUS

SOME DISEASES ARE FROM UNNATURAL SOURCES,
ESPECIALLY WHEN YOU ARE DEALING WITH AN EVIL FORCES,

THERE IS GOOD AND EVIL POWERS, WE NEED TO LEARN
WHICH SIDE IT IS WE EMPOWER,

I BELIEVE THIS IS ONE OF THOSE RARE AND ANCIENT
CONDITIONS, THAT IS SURROUNDED BY DEVILS AND UNHOLY
TRADITIONS,

THEY WANT TO TAKE CONTROL, AND DECEIVE AN
UNSUSPECTING SOUL,

WHEN WE ARE NOT IN GOD'S GRACE, WE FALL PREY TO
ALL THAT TRIES TO TAKE ITS PLACE,

THE MOST IMPORTANT THING IS TO BELIEVE AND TRUST,

THAT GOD HAS ALREADY DELIVERED AND HEALED YOU
FROM LUPUS,

Please read these three (3) scriptures on healing, each day
that you pray. Believe and know that God wants you whole
and healed. It has already been paid for by CHRIST.

(Matthew 8:13), Then Jesus said to the centurion, "Go
your way; and as you have believed, so let it be done
for you." And his servant was healed that same hour.

(Matthew 10:1), And when He had called His twelve
disciples to Him, He gave them power over unclean
spirits, to cast them out, and to heal all kinds of sickness
and all kinds of disease.

(Luke 5:17), Now it happened on a certain day, as He was teaching, that there were Pharisees and teachers of the law sitting by, who had come out of every town of Galilee, Judea, and Jerusalem. And the power of the Lord was present to heal them.

DIVINE POETRY

ONE TRILLION CELLS IN ME

GOD MADE ME WITH MY OWN WEALTH, HE GAVE ME THE ABILITY TO HEAL MY OWN SELF,

HE SET ME IN THE CENTER OF MY OWN BEING AND TIME, HE GAVE ME THE VISION TO DEVELOP MY OWN MIND,

HE GAVE ME THE CHARACTER, TO BE WHATEVER I WANTED TO BE, SO HE PUT ONE TRILLION CELLS INSIDE OF ME,

GOD MADE ME THREE ENTITIES IN ONE, MY SPIRIT, MY MIND AND MY SOUL, ALL WORK TOGETHER TO KEEP ME WHOLE,

IN ESSENCE I AM SO MUCH MORE THAN YOU CAN SEE, GOD HAS PUT MORE THAN ONE TRILLION CELLS INSIDE OF ME,

EACH CELL BELONGS TO MY SPECIAL DAY, WHEREVER I CHOOSE TO PUT MY DNA,

WHATEVER I CHOOSE AS MY SPECIALTY, I HAVE MORE THAN A TRILLION CELLS TO PERFECT ANY PART OF ME,

SO YES, I AM VERY RICH INDEED, I HAVE A HUMONGOUS AMOUNT OF GENETIC SEED,

AS A MATTER OF FACT, INSIDE OF ME THERE ARE MANY CREATED WORLDS,

THEY ARE ALL A PART OF ME THE WEALTH OF MY POTENTIAL CHARACTERS, INNATELY UNFURLED,

THANK GOD WHAT'S INSIDE DOES NOT SHOW, THEN THE WHOLE UNIVERSE COULD SEE THE TRUTH THAT I KNOW,

WHAT EVER I CHOOSE MY DESTINY TO BE, THERE WILL BE A TRILLION OTHER GENETIC CELLS GETTING THEIR LIFE FROM ME,

THE MYSTERY IS INTELLECT AND WISDOM, DOES NOT ALWAYS STAY THE SAME, INSIDE OF EACH ONE OF US IS AN ETHNIC CHANGE,

SEEK OUT GOD, AND ATTAIN YOUR VERY BEST, KNOWING HIS TRUTH WILL MAKE YOU SO MUCH BETTER THAN THE REST,

GOD GAVE ME THE CHARACTER, TO BE WHATEVER I WANTED TO BE, SO HE PUT ONE TRILLION CELLS INSIDE OF ME,

IN ESSENCE I AM SO MUCH MORE THAN YOU CAN SEE, GOD HAS PUT MORE THAN ONE TRILLION CELLS INSIDE OF ME,

I REALIZE

NATURE WAS CONSTRUCTED TO WORK WITHIN SPECIFIC LAWS OF MAN, MEASURING EVERYTHING IT NEEDED TO ENCUMBER WITHIN THE LAND,

GOD GAVE US NATURE FOR ALL PURPOSES AND INTENTS, GOD GAVE US NATURE TO WORK WITHIN THE ELEMENTS,

AS I GROW OLDER, I REALIZE, WHY AND HOW NATURE PUT THE BIRDS IN THE SKIES,

NATURE SAW FIT TO MAKE THE EARTH, A PLACE FOR MAMALS, FLOWERS AND TREES TO HAVE A BIRTH,

NATURE ASSISSTED WITHIN GOD'S PLAN FOR MAN, THE WATER WOULD BE ESSENTIAL TO MAN AND THE LAND,

GOD DESIGNATED THE WATER AS SACRED AND LIVING, FULFILLING HIS LAWS FOR CLEANSING AND SPIRITUAL GIVING,

GOD GAVE THE BREATH OF LIFE TO MAN WITHIN THE AIR, WHEREVER GOD'S BREADTH WAS HE WOULD BE THERE,

I THANK GOD THAT I REALIZE, THE HOLY AND SACRED THINGS I COULD NOT RECOGNIZE,

IT WAS ALL FOR MY GROWTH AND PERFECTION, SPIRITUALITY, AND GOD'S DIVINE PROTECTION,

MY FATHER'S COAT

I HAVE BEEN GIVEN A GIFT BEYOND MEASURE, A GIFT THAT IS ABOVE ALL TREASURES,

MY FATHER VESTED IN ME HIS HEALTH, WHICH INCLUDED ALL HIS WEALTH,

MY FATHER GENERATED ALL BIRTHS, MY FATHER CREATED THE UNIVERSE AND THE EARTH,

ALL LIFE AND PEOPLE YOU SEE AND LOVE, HAS BEEN CREATED DIVINELY FROM GOD UP ABOVE,

NOTHING EXIST WITHOUT HIS CREATION, ALL OTHER THINGS ARE JUST IMITATIONS,

MY FATHERS COAT IS THE COLOR OF ALL NATIONS, IT IS THE LIFE AND SUBSTANCE OF ALL GENERATIONS,

IN GOD'S SACRED BOOKS, IT IS CALLED THE COAT OF MANY COLORS AND MANY HUES, IT IS THE TOOL TO BRING FORTH MANY ME'S AND MANY YOU'S,

THE MYSTERY AND THE SECRET WITHIN EVERY NATION, AND EVERY SINGLE DAY IS HIDDEN WITHIN IT'S DNA,

EVERY NATION HAS A SEED, PRODUCING AFTER IT'S OWN KIND, SOME ARE RARE SOME ARE HARD TO FIND,

MY FATHER DRESSED ME FOR ALL I INHERITED, ALL THE THINGS IN LIFE HE HAD ALREADY MERITED,

HIS LEGACY, HIS LAND, HIS PEOPLE, WOULD BE MINE, HIS BIBLE, HIS JEWELS, AND HIS ETERNAL TIME,

MY FATHERS COAT IS THE COLOR OF ALL NATIONS, IT IS THE LIFE AND SUBSTANCE OF ALL GENERATIONS,

THEY NEVER REPAIRED ME

I LOOK AT THIS WORLD WITH NO ANTICIPATIONS,

ALL THEY EVER GAVE YOU AND ME WAS DENIGRATIONS,

THEY FORCED ME AND MY PEOPLE INTO LABOR,

AND DENIDED US OUR RIGHTS TO OUR GOD, AND HIS DIVINE FAVOR,

THEY'RE EVILS NEVER SEEMED TO CEASE, LOOK WHAT THEY DID TO THE JAPANESE,

80 YEARS LATER THEY CAN FINALLY SEE, THEY ARE OFFERING JAPAN AN OFFICIAL APOLOGY,

THEY NEVER ONCE OFFERED THAT TO MY PEOPLE OR TO ME,

THEY NEVER EVEN CONSIDERED AN APOLOGY, THE PROMISE TO US IS STILL ON THE BOOKS FOR ALL PEOPLE TO SEE,

THEY USED ALL MY PEOPLE AS THEIR BUILDING TOOLS, WE BUILT AMERICA, AND THEY OFFER US 40 ACRES AND A MULE,

THEY RAPED AND STOLE THEIR WAY THROUGH OUR HERITAGE AND OUR LIVES, TRYING TO CAST OUT OUR HISTORY HOPING WE DON'T REALIZE,

THE ULTIMATE CONTRIBUTIONS TO AMERICA MADE BY BLOOD SWEAT AND TEARS,

THE CONSUMPTION OF TOO MANY LIVES FOR TOO MANY YEARS,

DESERVERS MUCH MORE THAN 40 ACRESE AND A MULE, FOR USING A NATION'S MIND, BODY, AND SOUL AS A TOOL,

IN WRITING THIS MASTER'S PIECE OF WORDS AND DEEDS, I CAN TRULY SAY THEY NEVER FULFILLED ME OR MY PEOPLE'S NEEDS,

AS I WRITE, BROKEN HEARTED, BROKEN SPIRITED, AS YOU CAN SEE,

I CAN HONESTLY AND TRULY SAY THEY NEVER REPAIRED ME,

I AWAIT THE DAY JUDGEMENT AND REPARATIONS, BY THAT TIME GOD WILL BE MAKING DIVINE SEPARATIONS,

WE MUST LOVE ONE ANOTHER

GOD LEFT US AN EXAMPLE OF HIS GIFT OF LOVE WE MUST FOLLOW, IF YOU ARE A TRUE CHILD OF HIS CHRIST YOU MUST KNOW,

IT WAS THE SACRIFICE OF HIS SON, THAT MADE A PATHWAY FOR YOU AND ME, HIS BLOOD PAVED THE FOUNDATION THAT SET US ALL FREE,

GOD JUST ASKED US TO LOVE ONE ANOTHER, LIKE THEY ARE YOUR HEAVENLY SISTERS AND BROTHERS,

GOD DID NOT GIVE US A HEART OF STONE, ALLOWING US TO TREAT OUR SISTERS AND BROTHERS WRONG,

WE ARE SUPPOSE TO BE THE TRUE ESSENCE OF GOD'S SPIRIT, IF WE CAN'T SHOW HIS LOVE WISDOM SAYS THEN WE SHOULD SURLY FEAR IT,

THE SAGES HAVE WRITTEN, IT IS THE BEGINNING OF WISDOM TO FEAR THE LORD, TO KICK AGAINST HIS PRICKS, WOULD BE PHYSICALLY, AND SPIRITUALLY HARD,

WE ARE THE EXAMPLES OF HEAVEN'S BEST, SURLY WE CAN LOVE EACH OTHER AS WE SHOULD, THEN THE WORLD WE CAN BLESS,

WE CAN SHARE GOD'S LOVE NATION WIDE, PUTTING HATRED ON THE RUN WITH NO WHERE TO HIDE,

I APPEAL TO YOUR HEART AND SPIRIT, MY SISTER, MY BROTHER, LET'S LET THE WORLD SEE AND KNOW WE ARE GOD'S CHILDREN LET'S LOVE ONE ANOTHER,

WHILE I AM AGING

GOD MEANT FOR ALL THINGS HE CREATED TO HAVE Its PLACE, HE INCORPORATED GENERATIONS WITHIN OUR HUMAN RACE,

ONE GENERATION SHOULD NOT PRECEED ANOTHER, THERE IS A SEQUENCE AND ORDER SO THAT WE DON'T OVER-STEP ONE ANOTHER,

A GOOD EXAMPLE IS CHILDREN SHOULD NOT EXIST BEFORE THEIR PARENTS, THEN HISTORY WOULD BE FULL OF HISTORICAL, BIOLOGICAL ERRENTS,

GOD IS VERY ORDERLY EVERYTHING HE DOES IS WITHIN LAWS, HE IS PERFECT AND KNOWS NO FLAWS,

ALL THINGS HAVE THEIR OWN BEAUTY TO THE EYE, EVEN THE HONORED ROSE LOSES ITS BEAUTY, LUSTER AND ONE DAY MUST DIE,

ONE FUNCTION GOD CREATED WITHIN THE EARTH, SPECIFIC PLANTS, FLOWERS, VINES AND TREES ANNUALY WOULD HAVE NEW BIRTHS,

WHILE I AM AGING ARE NO LONGER ARE MY HIPS DANGEROUS CURVES, I NO LONGER FEEL LIKE A BUNDLE OF JOY, BUT A BUNDLE OF NERVES,

MY LIPS WERE FIRM AND MY WORDS SMOOTH AS OIL, MY SWEETNESS AND MY PURENESS, OTHERS HAVE SPOILED,

MY EYES GROW DIM, MY VISION IS BLEAK, MY ABILITY TO SUSTAIN MYSELF YEARLY GROWS WEAK,

NO LONGER ARE MY HORMONS RAGING, I HAVE COME TO
THE CONCLUSION IT IS BECAUSE I AM AGING,

I AM NOT AFRAID OF GROWING OLD, SOME THINGS ARE
BETTER I AM TOLD,

WHEN THEY HAVE BEEN PROPERLY CULTIVATED, THEN THEY
CAN BE FULLY AND MASTERFULLY MANIPULATED,

NO-ONE IS OLDER THAN GOD, WITH HIM IT IS A BLESSING,
A PRIVELEDGE TO KNOW HIM WITHOUT GUESSING,

IT IS AN HONOR TO BE A SERVANT OF THE KING, HE IS THE
EPITOME OF ALL LIFE HE IS EVERYTHING,

WHILE I AM AGING, I CAN SAY I TRULY KNOW, THAT GOD
WILL HAVE MY BACK WHEREVER I MAY GO,

CHRIST LIFE IS OUR DEFENSE

LOOKING BACK OVER THE ANNALS OF TIME AND HISTORY,

I REALIZE MY LIFE AND EXISTENCE IS BOUND TO YOUR SACRED STORY,

THERE IS REALLY NOTHING OUTSIDE OF YOUR WORD,

OUR ANCESTORS AND PARENTS, TAUGHT US EVERYTHING WE'VE HEARD,

YOUR WORD MANIFEST EVERYTHING WE HEAR AND SEE,

YOUR WORDS ARE THE EPITOME OF ALL DESTINY,

YOUR WORDS KEEPS US HEALTHY, UPRIGHT, WISE, AND STRONG,

YOUR WORDS MAKES US WEALTHY, WORTHY,

GIVING ALL OUR HEARTS NEW SONGS,

WHO WOULD KNOW AND BELIEVE THE LIFE AND HEALING PROPERTY,

OF JUST YOUR UTTERED AND WRITTEN HOLY WORDS FOR ALL HUMANITY,

SOMETIMES TO THE NATURAL MIND IT DOESEN'T MAKE SENSE,

HOW A HOLY GODS'S LIFE CAN BE OUR ULTIMATE DEFENSE,

YES, YOUR WORDS GIVE LIFE EVERY SINGLE DAY,

IT PROTECTS AND KEEPS US WHILE WE ARE ASLEEP, ESPECIALLY WHEN WE PRAY,

YOUR WORDS ARE THE KEYS TO ALL OUR NEEDS,

THEY ARE THE DETERMINANTES TO ALL OUR HOLY DEEDS,

THEY ARE THE WISDOMS OF ALL TIME,

THEY HOLD THE ANSWER TO THE DEEPEST OF ALL OUR MINDS,

CHRIST WORDS ARE DIFFUSED THROUGHOUT THE LAND,

IN THE END ONLY WHAT YOU DO FOR CHRIST WILL STAND,

TO A NATURAL MAN IT DOSEN'T MAKE SENSE,

HOW A HOLY GOD'S LIFE CAN BE A NATIONS ULTIMATE DEFENSE,

YESTERDAY, TODAY, OR TOMORROW, HE IS STILL THE SAME,

ALL THE POWER AND SECRETS ARE IN JESUS NAME,

NOBODY'S FOOL

I KNOW THE LIES YOU TELL AND I KNOW YOUR WRATH,

I HAVE SEEN YOU DISTORT MY PRESENT, AND TRY TO ERASE MY PAST,

YOU RAVISHED MY HEART AND ALTERED MY WAY, NOW YOU'RE TRYING POSSESS MY YESTERDAY,

IN MY COMPUTER YOU ARE AN OMINOUS GLITCH,

ALL YOUR ACTIONS ARE TO PERFORM, PRODUCE, AND START AN EVIL SWITCH,

A SWITCH TO DENIE MY LIFE, AND PURPOSE ME TO LIVE, IN ILLUSIONS AND TO SUFFER STRIFE,

I AM HERE TO WRITE AND TELL YOU I AM NOBODY'S FOOL,

WITH ALL YOUR DECEIT, LIES AND UNTRUTH, YOU STILL WILL BE JUDGED BY MY GOD'S RULES,

GOD NEVER GAVE YOU THE RIGHT TO CHANGE ME,

NOR DID HE GIVE YOU THE RIGHT TO REARRANGE OR MAIM ME,

AGAIN, I SAY I AM NOBODY'S FOOL, SOME OF THE EVILS YOU ARE COMMITTING, GOD HAS ALREADY JUDGED, SENTENCED AND RULED,

NO MATTER WHAT YOU SAY OR WHAT YOU DO, ONLY WHAT GOD HAS MADE WILL REMAIN TRUE,

YOU MAY HAVE STOLEN SOME THINGS, AND THINK YOU HAVE GOTTEN AWAY, YOU MUST REMEMBER GOD USES ALL YESTERDAYS,

TO PERFECT OUR LIVES SO WE WON'T BE LAST, "GOD" CONSTRUCTS AND REBUILDS US NEW LIVES FROM THE PAST,

I MUST CONFESS IN GOD I AM NOBODY'S FOOL, WE ARE ALL JUDGED, SENTENCED, AND MANDATED BY GOD'S RULE,

ALL CLEANED UP

WHEN MY LIFE WAS A MESS AND I WAS IN SIN, THAT WAS THE TIME I LET JESUS IN,

WHEN I DID'T KNOW WHAT TO DO OR WHERE TO GO, JESUS WAS THE ONLY FRIEND I NEEDED TO KNOW,

I COULD GO IN MY BATHROOM AND TAKE A SHOWER, THAT WASN'T THE KIND OF CLEANING THAT HAD SOUL SAVING POWER,

JESUS CLEANS US UP INSIDE AND OUTSIDE, HE RIDS US OF THE DEEP INTERNAL GERMS THAT THE DEVILS TRY TO HIDE,

I CAN TRULY SAY TODAY, I AM ALL CLEANED UP, I DON'T WANT TO RELAPSE AND ENDANGER MY SOUL NO MATTER WHAT,

GOD LET ME SEE MY DEGRADATED SOUL, SO I COULD KNOW HE WAS THE ONLY ONE TO MAKE ME WHOLE,

THANK YOU FATHER FOR CLEANING MY LIFE, REMOVING ME FROM SIN AND DECEITFULNESS, AND STRIFES,

I FEEL LIKE I COULD WEAR A ONE THOUSAND PAIRS OF WINGS, CAUSE I KNOW TODAY I HAVE BEEN DIVINELY CLEANED.

ALTERED STATE

FOR A VERY LONG TIME, I HAVE BEEN HIDDEN IN THE BACKGROUND, BECAUSE INSECURE PEOPLE DIDN'T WANT ME AROUND,

THEY KEPT ME DRUGGED AND SEDATED, IN AN ALTERED STATE TO JUSTIFY THEIR EVILNESS AND HATE,

THEY COPIED MY LIFE AND LIVED IN MY WEALTH, THEY REMOVED MY CHILDREN AND STOLE MY HEALTH,

CLONING AND TRANSFERRING MY GOD GIVEN RIGHTS, THROUGH BREECHING ME AND MY LIFE HAS TAKEN SCIENCE TO NEW HEIGHTS,

THEY CHANGED MY WORLD FROM THE INSIDE OUT, THEY MENTALY TRAINED ALL MY CELLS TO TRUST AND NEVER DOUBT,

THEY WERE ALSO HELD CAPTIVE WITHIN THEIR OWN MINDS, NOT KNOWING THEY WERE A PART OF ALTERED TIME,

THEY USED THE DEEPEST RECESSESS OF THE HUMAN FOUNDATION, THEY USED HYPNOSIS AND REGRESSIVE THERAPY TO ERASE THEIR CREATION,

THEY USED DREAMS STATES TO CREATE FALSE REALITIES, TO TEACH MY OWN PEOPLE HOW TO HATE ME,

IF YOU EVER QUESTION WHERE YOU ARE AND WHY SO MUCH HATE, IT MAY BE THAT YOU ARE CAPTIVE IN AN ALTERED STATE,

NO MATTER HOW THEY DRUG AND SEDATE ME, I KNOW THAT MY GOD HAS MADE ME,

THERE IS NO STATE WHERE GOD CANNOT GO, HE CREATED THE FIFTY STATES WE NOW KNOW,

THAT'S ONLY TO MENTION A FEW, I AM SURE THERE ARE OTHER STATES WITHIN YOU,

OUT OF JEALOUSY, FEAR, EVILNESS AND HATE, THEY MADE ME LIVE IN AN ALTERED STATE,

GOD GAVE ME ENOUGH TO MAKE THE BEST OUT OF WHAT HAS BEEN DONE, EVEN TO CHANGE THIS ALTERED STATE INTO AN UNALTERED ONE,

SO IN THIS PLACE, I AM GOD AND GOD IS IN ME, ALTERED OR NOT WE CAN BE ANYTHING WE WANT TO BE,

IN THE WAKING OF MY NEW FOUNDATION, I REALIZE I AM A VERY GREAT PART OF THIS CREATION,

I COULD NEVER BUILD UPON HATE, I CAN HOWEVER CREAT A NEW ALTERED STATE,

BEARING GOD'S THE LIGHT

SOME THINGS WERE MADE FOR US TO BEAR, JESUS CHRIST BEARED IT ALL TO SHOW THAT HE CARED,

HE KNEW THIS PHYSICAL WORLD, NEEDED HIS DIVINE RITES, IF THEIR SOULS WERE TO BE REDEEMED BACK TO GOD'S LIGHT,

WE TAKE PRIDE IN CERTAIN THINGS WE DO, GOD IS PLEASED IN MAKING US ANEW,

GOD GAVE EACH ONE OF US A SOUL, COMPRABLE TO WHAT HE KNEW WOULD MAKE US WHOLE,

IF YOU WANT YOUR LIFE TO TURN OUT RIGHT, PRAY, REPENT, REASSESS YOURSELF AND BEAR GOD'S LIGHT,

I KNOW NOW THAT FOR ME TO RETAIN GOD'S LIGHT,

FOR THE REST OF MY LIFE I WILL BE IN A SPIRITUAL FIGHT,

THIS FIGHT HAS BEEN FOUGHT WAY BEFORE MY TIME,

IT IS THE PURPOSE OF THOSE OF JESUS CHRIST'S DIVINE LINE,

PRODUCING EVERY BLOOD BOUGHT SON OF JESUS CHRIST,

FIGHTING FOR THE FREE GIFT GOD HAS GIVEN TO OUR LIFE,

TO WAR AGAINST THE EVILS THAT PLAGUE AND CORRUPT WHAT IS RIGHT,

KEEPING THE DARKNESS SEPARATED FROM THE DIVINE LIGHT,

AS WE GROW, WE LEARN NOT TO FAINT, WE GO UP IN RANK AND BE COME ONE OF GOD'S SAINTS,

WE ARE TRULY SOLIDERS IN THE ARMY OF THE LORD, FIGHTING WITH JESUS CHRIST, HOLY DIVINE SWORD,

KEEPING HIS NAME AND WORDS LIFTED HIGH, IN THIS FIGHT FOR LIFE UNTIL WE DIE,

KNOWING THAT IN THE END WHEN ALL IS SAID AND DONE,

WE GET A NEW LIFE IN CHRIST BECAUSE ON THE CROSS, ALL OF OUR LIVES HE WON,

JUST REMEMBER THE FIGHT IS ALREADY WON, SATAN IS ALWAYS TRYING TO CONFUSE OUR MINDS TO CONFUSE WHAT JESUS HAS ALREADY DONE,

IF SATAN CAN POSSESS YOUR MIND, HE WILL CHANGE YOUR TRUTH, TO ALTER EVERYTHING YOU EVER KNEW FROM YOUR YOUTH,

REMEMBER TO GUARD YOUR GATES, AGAINST SATANS ILLUSIONS, DELLUSIONS, PRIDE AND HATE,

IF YOU WANT YOUR LIFE TO TURN OUT RIGHT, PRAY, REPENT, REASSESS YOURSELF AND BEAR GOD'S LIGHT.

BREECHED

Lord, so many evils have come against my mind, So many evils has tried to steal my time,

So many evils are prevalent in the land, They desired to placed their falsehoods and lies within every man,

Regardless to all their evil intents, I know you conquered, them by what was Heaven sent,

You sent the word of Jesus, as our comforter to teach, For all of us who were sin bound and deceitfully breeched,

They breeched, my mind body and my vision, They distorted all you instilled in me, I could no longer make understandable decisions,

Many days I felt I was hypnotized, I knew I was not who you made me I was dehumanized,

My only solace was to remember what, Jesus teached, to find my soul's depth and pray for a divine release/relief,

Lord you are the master of my soul, without you I cannot become whole,

You promised to keep me and never to leave, on those promises I am still standing and believe,

One day I am saying to myself, I will no longer be breeched, Jesus spirit will come in and I will be spiritually reached,

CANNIBALS

I COME FROM A LONG LINE OF LEADERS, NOT PEOPLE WHO SELL OUT AND BECOME SATANIC PLEADERS,

WE RESPECT AND RELISH THE FAMILY WE ARE IN, WE LOVE AND DEPEND ON OUR GOD AND ESCHEW EVIL AND SIN,

ALL THE THINGS WE WERE EVER TAUGHT, YOU CANNOT FIND ON A SHELF, AND THEY CANNOT BE BOUGHT,

ONE THING FOR SURE, THAT GOD CONSIDERS LETHAL, DO NOT PREPARE AND TRY TO EAT UP ALL GOD'S PEOPLE,

I NEVER KNEW ALL THIS TIME PEOPLE COULD BE LIKE ANIMALS, I FOUND OUT THEY REALLY ARE LIKE HUMAN CANNIBALS,

THE PSALMIST, IN THE BIBLE I REMEMBER HE SAID, WICKED ONES, THEY EAT UP GOD'S PEOPLE LIKE A PIECE OF BREAD,

I NEVER KNEW PEOPLE HAD SUCH AN APPETITE, I GUESS WHEN YOU ARE OUTSIDE OF GOD NOTHING IN YOU IS REALLY RIGHT,

FOR ME I HUNGER FOR THE PURE WORD, I TRY TO HIDE IT IN MY HEART, AND TREASURE WHAT I'VE HEARD,

EATING GOD'S PEOPLE WON'T BRING ANYONE SALVATION, WE NEED JESUS INSIDE OF US, FOR US TO REACH GOD'S DESTINATION,

I NEVER KNEW PEOPLE COULD BE LIKE ANIMALS, I FOUND OUT THEY REALLY ARE LIKE HUMAN CANNIBALS,

CHANGE OUR COURSE

LORD YOU KNOW EVERYTHING THAT WE NEED, FROM OUR DAILY, RATIONS TO OUR GENETIC SEED,

WHEN WE FALTER AND ERR IN LIFE AND GET OFF TRACK, WE EXPECT YOUR WISDOM AND GUIDANCE TO BRING US BACK,

NO MAN IS ENTIRE OF HIMSELF, WE NEED YOUR LOVE, STRENGTH, LIFE AND HEALTH,

IF FOR SOME REASON FATHER, WE DON'T MAKE YOUR EXPECTED GRADE,

REMEMBER WE ARE ONE OF THE VESSELS YOU MADE,

NO MATTER WHAT WE DO OR WHATEVER THE COURSE, YOU ARE OUR BEING YOU ARE OUR SOURCE,

IF FOR SOME REASON WE GET OFF COURSE, WE EXPECT YOU FATHER TO REDIRECT AND CHANGE OUR COURSE,

WE ARE ONLY SENTIMENTS OF YOUR TRUTH AND GRACE, TRYING TO REACH A SACRED AND DESTINED PLACE,

WE PRAY THAT WE MOVE BEYOND OUR PAST, THAT WE WILL RECOGNIZE YOU MADE US FIRST AND NOT LAST,

IN THIS LIFE OF CHANGING COURSES, WE REALIZE THERE ARE NOT MANY DIVINE SOURCES,

IF FOR SOME REASON WE GET OFF COURSE, WE EXPECT YOU FATHER TO REDIRECT AND CHANGE OUR COURSE,

CHRIST'S ARMY OF ONE

I AM A SOLIDER IN THE ARMY FOR MY GOD, TO KEEP UP HIS BANNER WITH HIS NAME IS NOT SO HARD,

WITH MY SHIELD AND SWORD IN MY HAND, I WARN ALL ENEMIES THIS IS MY GOD'S LAND,

THERE WERE LEGIONS OF ANGELS, FIGHTING IN ARMAGGETON, IN MY WORLD I AM ONLY AN ARMY OF ONE,

I LEARNED HOW TO FIGHT WITH GOD'S WORD, I LEARNED HOW TO STAND ON GOD'S FAITH, I LEARNED HOW TO UTILIZED GOD'S AMAZING GRACE,

I LEARNED HOW TO PRAY TO THE ONLY BEGOTTON SON, AND REQUEST HELP FOR, NO MATTER WHAT YOU SAY NO MATTER WHAT YOU DONE,

THERE WERE LEGIONS OF ANGELS, FIGHTING IN ARMAGGETON, IN MY WORLD I AM ONLY AN ARMY IF ONE,

CROSSED UP

GOD GAVE ME MANY PATHWAYS TO CHOOSE, NOT ONE OF THEM WAS MEANT FOR ME TO LOSE,

GOD DID NOT CREATE US JUST TO LAMENT, GOD DESIGNED US TO HAVE HIS CONFIDENCE,

SOMETIMES IN THIS WORLD WE LOSE OUR WAY, IT'S OKAY GOD WOULD NEVER LET US LOSE OUR DAY,

WE GET CROSSED UP AND TOSSED UP TURNED INSIDE OUT, THAT'S HOW WE LEARN WHAT GOD IS ALL ABOUT,

WHEN HE PUTS US BACK ON THE RIGHT TRACK, WE REALLY REALIZE HOW MUCH GOD HAS OUR BACK,

SO MANY THINGS IN LIFE SEEM TO BE PARALLELS, RUNNING SIDE BY SIDE, OUT OF CONTROL WITHOUT A GUIDE,

WHAT I LIKE MOST ABOUT PARALLELS, THEY DON'T CROSS PATH, THEY WON'T MAKE YOU FAIL,

SOMETIMES IN LIFE WE DON'T KNOW WHICH WAY TO GO, THAT'S WHEN IT IS JESUS WE NEED TO KNOW,

WHEN YOUR THOUGHTS AND WORDS NEGATIVLY COMPEL YOU,

THINK OF JESUS ANYWAY HE WON'T FAIL YOU,

SATAN WANTS TO KEEP YOUR MIND CONFUSED, SO YOU WON'T BE GODLY AND DIVINELY USED,

WHEN IN DOUBT THINK ABOUT GOD AND WHAT'S UP,

HE WILL KEEP YOUR PATHS FROM BEING CROSSED UP,

CULTIVATED SPIRIT

Man cultivates organisms and cells, he creates them in a flask what some would call heaven or hell,

Trying to play the role of a supreme God, by creating, forms of life is a task really hard,

I know that man really don't want to hear it,

But my God cultivates all, mind, body and spirit,

God knew he would need a special seed, so he CULTIVATED the disciples twelve, to fulfill ministry his needs,

He CULTIVATED the Apostles too, so that, they would witness to who the disciples didn't witness to,

All spirits are special in some form in God's, great book, certain spirits were given extra meritorious powers within this great book,

Some spirits were universal and could only be God sent, God gave us Father Abraham, whose cell was totipotent,

Through Father Abraham, God created all nations, so that all life, gentile and Jew could have a Godly relation,

The greatest spirit, had to be Soteristic, to complete the plan, of salvation and redemption for every child and every man,

Just remember while your body is being made of a grade, God has already chosen how you will be mentally and spiritually made,

Jesus Christ, was God's most precious created spiritual essence,

The only recognizable way to God, through true repentance,

DEVIL IN DISGUISE

THE DEVIL HAS BEEN GONE FOR AGES, YET HIS ANGER STILL RAGES,

RAGE THAT REACHES OUT TO CAPTURE, UNSUSPECTING MINDS TO DEFILE THEIR LIVES AND STEAL THEIR TIME,

THE DEVIL AND HIS KINGDOM ARE ALL SHADOWS AND PHANTOMS, AND GHOST,

THE REMENANTS OF YESTER YEAR OF SATAN AS A DEFEATED HOST,

YOU CANNOT FALL FOR ANY OF SATAN'S LIES, HE IS ALWAYS CHANGING HE IS THE DEVIL IN MANY A DISGUISE,

HE WILL PROMISE YOU THE MOON, BUT WILL DELIVER YOU TO A TOMB,

ALL THE THINGS HE PROMISES TO GIVE, IS JUST TO DECEIVE YOU SO HE CAN MENTALLY LIVE,

HE LIVES IN YOUR MIND AND YOUR DREAMS, ROBBING YOUR MEMORY BANK OF YOUR EVERYTHING,

SATAN IS THE MASTER OF TRICKERY AND IS VERY FAST, WITH THE BLINK OF YOUR EYE LASH, HE HAS CHANGED AIR INTO CASH,

YOU CANNOT FALL FOR ANY OF SATAN'S LIES, HE IS ALWAYS CHANGING HE IS THE DEVIL IN MANY A DISGUISE,

SATAN WILL TRY TO MAKE YOU THINK YOU ARE LOST, HE WILL TELL YOU JESUS DIDN'T DIE ON THE CROSS,

HE WILL TELL YOU THAT YOU SOUL IS LOST, AND THAT HE SHED HIS BLOOD AND PAID YOUR COST,

YOU CANNOT FALL FOR ANY OF SATAN'S LIES, HE IS ALWAYS CHANGING HE IS THE DEVIL IN MANY A DISGUISE,

DON'T CHOOSE HELL, WHEN YOU CAN REFUSE HELL

YOU MAY NOT ALWAYS BE WHERE YOU WANT TO BE, GOD GAVE YOU TWO EYES FOR YOU TO SEE,

HELL IS NOTHING LIKE HEAVEN, YOU CAN'T MAKE A MISTAKE IN THIS RACE, THERE IS ONLY ONE PLACE FOR GOD'S AMAZING GRACE,

DON'T CHOOSE HELL, WHEN YOU CAN REFUSE HELL,

GOD SAID RESIST THE DEVIL AND HE WILL FLEE, YOU WILL NOT KNOW THIS POWER UNTIL YOU TEST IT TO SEE,

YOU ARE A BLOOD BORN CHILD OF THE KING, BECAUSE OF GOD YOU ARE A HEIR OF EVERYTHING,

BEING A CHILD OF GOD'S YOU HAVE A SPECIAL TIME,

YOU ARE A PART OF ROYALTY AND A ROYAL BLOOD LINE,

DON'T LET THE DEVILS FOOL YOU MAKE YOU BELIEVE, THEIR PURPOSE IS NOT TO THIEVE AND DECEIVE,

LIFE SOMETIMES IS FULL OF STORMS, DON'T WORRY GOD CHOSE YOU BEFORE YOU WERE BORN,

I AM TELLING YOU DON'T CHOOSE HELL WHEN YOU CAN REFUSE HELL,

YOU ALREADY HAVE A KEY TO HEAVENS GATE, KEEP YOUR

APPOINTMENT WITH GOD AND DON'T BE LATE,

YOU AND YOUR FAMILY WILL BE FINE, NONE OF US CAN EVER BE LATE, CAUSE GOD IS THE MAKER OF ALL TIME,

SO BE PROUD OF WHO YOU ARE AND WHO GOD MADE YOU,

THE DEVIL WILL ALWAYS BE MAD AT YOU,

BECAUSE WHAT THE BIBLE SAYS ABOUT YOU IS TRUE,

CHOOSE THE HEAVENLY STATE, THAT'S THE PLACE WHERE YOU ARE GREAT,

WHEN YOU GET TO HEAVENS INN, YOU WILL FIND JESUS WAITING THERE HE WAS ALWAYS YOUR FRIEND,

ETERNITY

WHY TRY TO DISCREDIT AND BURY ME, WHEN MY GOD MADE ME APART OF ETERNITY,

WHEN YOU TRY TO COVER ME WITH SOIL AND EARTH, EARTH WILL BE COVERING MY DIVINE BIRTH,

EARTH'S SOIL WILL BE LIKE A BLANKET TO COVER ME, BECAUSE SHE KNOWS WHERE GOD MEANT FOR ETERNITY TO BE,

I KNOW WHERE ETERNITY WAS MEANT TO BE, IT IS FOR THE EARTH TO GROW LIKE A PLANT, GRASS, OR A TREE,

THAT IS NOT WHERE ETERNITY WAS MEANT TO BE,

IT IS A HOLY PLACE A HOLY CITY FOR YOU AND FOR ME,

NO MATTER HOW MUCH YOU TRY TO STEAL SUPPLANT AND HIDE,

MY SPIRITUAL ESSENCE, WILL STILL BE MY GUIDE,

I KNOW WHAT YOU USE TO COVET MY WORTH, GOD NEVER GAVE YOU CHARGE AND CONTROL OVER MY BIRTH,

ALWAYS TRYING TO BERATE ME, ONE DAY YOU WILL REALIZE, IT IS TRULY GOD THAT IS ON MY SIDE,

GOD HAS A PLACE FOR ME CALLED ETERNITY, THAT ALL THINGS EVIL DON'T ME WANT ME TO SEE,

NO MATTER WHAT GOD HAS SPOKEN HIS WORD, ALL LIFE FORMS, TREES, CLOUDS, AND ANIMALS HAS HEARD,

I AM A PART OF THE MAIN, THAT GOD HAS CREATED, I AM A PART OF ETERNITY, NOT TO BE BERATED,

EVERY PART OF ME

GOD DOES NOT PARTICIPATE IN HATE, NOR DOES HE MAKE A HATEFUL MISTAKES,

GOD KNOWS EVERY BEAT OF YOUR HEART, HE HAS DESIGNED AND CRAFTED YOUR EVERY SINGLE PART,

YOU MAY NOT KNOW NOR YOU MAY NOT REMEMBER, BUT GOD HAS PLACED AND DESIGNATED ALL OF YOUR MEMBERS,

BEST THING I CAN SAY, GOD CRAFTED EVERY PART OF ME, IN SPITE OF ALL THE PEOPLE DECEIVING ME,

I AM GOD SPAWNED, HEAVEN BOUND, I POSSESS A HOLY GHOST FILLED ANATOMY,

A CHILD OF GOD'S HE IS EVERY PART OF ME, EVEN WHEN I DON'T UNDERSTAND AND CANNOT SEE,

GOD MADE ME AND GAVE ME A DAY, TO CHOSE MY LIFE AND TO CHOSE ME A WAY,

HE ADMONISHED WHATEVER IT WAS I WOULD DO, MAKE SURE I UPHELD HIS INEFFABLE TRUTH,

NO MATTER WHAT GETS INSIDE OF ME, GOD WILL STILL RESIDE AND ABIDE IN ME,

EVEN DOWN TO THE VERY LAST CELL, THAT CELL WILL NEVER COMPLETELY BELONG TO HELL,

SINCE GOD IS IN EVERY PART OF ME, MY VERY LAST CELL BELONGS TO GOD AND HIS DIVINITY,

EVERYTHING YOU DO TO ME COMES BACK TO YOU

SOMETHINGS YOU SHOULD NOT HURT, HARM OR STEAL, ESPECIALLY IF ITS AGAINST THE FATHERS WILL,

IT IS NOT TO BE LABELED, MARKED OR CURSED, ONLY MAKES YOUR OWN LIFE WORSE,

GOD SEES EVERYTHING YOU DO, SO THAT EVERYTHING YOU DO TO ME COMES BACK TO YOU,

HOW CAN YOU AVOID AN INEVITABLE FATE, THAT YOU MADE EVIL AND WILL NEVER BE GREAT,

YOU WILL BE LEFT IN A TIME AND PLACE, WITHOUT LOVE, ENTERTAINMENT, CARE OR GRACE,

EVERY PLIGHT YOU DEVISE FOR ME, IS THE PLACE WHERE YOU ARE GOING TO BE,

SO BE VERY CAREFUL OF WHAT YOU SAY AND WHAT YOU DO, A HIGHER POWER IS WATCHING YOU,

YOU SHOULD KNOW BY NOW YOU ARE NOT GREAT, EVERYTHING YOU HAVE YOU STOLE AND YOU EVEN RAPED,

TRYING TO MAKE A LIFE FIT THAT WILL NOT CHANGE, EVIL LOOKS CONSPICIOUS, TRYING WEAR GODS PROPERTY, IT LOOKS VERY STRANGE,

YOU MAY STEAL GOODNESS, AND EVEN HAVE IT FOR A WHILE, WHENEVER GOD CHOOSES IT WILL GO THE PROPER CHILD,

HE SEES EVERYTHING THAT YOU DO, SO THAT EVERYTHING YOU DO TO ME COMES BACK TO YOU,

THERE ARE TWO THINGS GOD ORDERED EVERYONE NOT TO CURSE,

HIS HOLY LAMB, AND BECAUSE OF HIS SEED, AND OUR FAITHFUL FATHER ABRAHAM,

IF YOU DON'T WANT TO BE LIVING IN AN UNASSIGNED TIME, DON'T MESS WITH GOD'S FAMILY LINE,

GOD IS YOUR KEEPER AND YOU SHOULD NOT BOAST, HE IS THE HIGHER POWER OVER YOUR EVIL MASTERS HOST,

AS YOU CAN SEE LIFE IS SCALING DOWN TO NONE, VERY SOON, YOU WON'T BE ABLE TO COPY ONE,

WHAT WILL YOU DO, WHEN THERE IS NOTHING THERE, I GUESS YOU WILL START COPYING THE AIR,

THESE WORDS, WILL FIND YOU THEY WILL SURELY COME, TO GIVE YOU BACK THE THINGS YOU HAVE DONE,

FALSIFIED REALITY

DON'T GET YOUR HOPES UP TOO, HIGH BECAUSE THE DEVIL IS FULL OF LIES,

ONCE HE GETS INSIDE OF YOUR HEAD, HE MAKES YOU THINK AND SEE THINGS THAT ARE ALREADY DEAD,

HE WILL BEWITCH YOU AND CONJURE UP A FALSE REALITY, TO MAKE YOU THINK AND BELIEVE WHATEVER YOU SEE,

SO DON'T GET MIXED UP IN THE DEVILS FALSIFIED REALITY, HE CHANGES TIME PERIODS JUST TO FOOL YOU AND ME,

PEOPLE WHO LEFT THIS EARTH A LONG TIME AGO, THESE ARE THE PEOPLE HE IS USING FOR YOU TO KNOW,

THEY ARE PEOPLE UNDER HIS CONTROL AND DESTINED FOR HELL, HEAVEN COULDN'T USE THEM BECAUSE IT WAS JESUS THEY FAILED,

THE DEVIL HAS PROMISES TOO, HE WILL PROMISE YOU THAT IF YOU SWITCH, HE WILL CHANGE YOUR LIFE AND MAKE YOU FILITHY RICH

WHAT IS MONEY IF YOU LOSE YOUR SOUL, THE DEVIL IS NOT EQUIPPED OR DIVINE ENOUGH TO MAKE YOU WHOLE,

HE WILL BEWITCH YOU AND CONJURE UP A FALSE REALITY, TO MAKE THINK AND BELIEVE WHATEVER YOU SEE, GOD IS OUR ONLY TRUE AND DIVINE REALITY,

FOOTPRINTS OF A PRINCE

Natural people walk in worldly realms, they create and devise worldly films,

That has footage they want to remember, some films are cruel and criminal, and some are loving and tender,

You cannot weigh or measure the steps of a King, his footsteps are governed by more heavenly things,

Nor can you see with a spiritual sense, what God has planned for a Kingdom PRINCE,

In the hands of God walks the footprints of a PRINCE, his path is already laid out by God's providence,

I believe that we are in the last times, but for a Prince or a child of God's, we exist within his Divine Mind,

We don't worry nor do we fret, about what this world brings God has never failed us yet,

So when things look dim and far beyond our control, just remember who it is that made every surviving soul,

To walk in a physical plane is to have a physical life, Yet to walk in a spiritual mind your spiritual life paid for by Christ!

In the hands of God walks the footprints of a PRINCE, his path is already laid out by God's Providence,

It is not humanely possible for us to see, Infinity or a sacred God given Destiny,

We leave our footprints on Earth, clay and sand, Christ has left footprints within and carried every man,

FOR HIS GLORY

ALL THINGS WITHIN THIS PHYSICAL LAND, WAS GIVEN BY GOD TO MAN,

AND WAS HEAVEN SENT, TO BE CONTROLLED BY THE DESIGNATED PRESIDENT,

GOD LEFT WITH US ALL DIVINE INSPIRIATION, THROUGH THE HOLY SPIRIT AS A WAY OF CONNECTION,

GOD DESIGNED US ALL FOR HIS AND THE SON'S GLORY, FOR THE MANIFESTATION OF A SACRED STORY,

WE DON'T HAVE TO LOOK ANY FARTHER, THE STORY BEGINS AND ENDS, WITH CHRIST, AND NOT ANOTHER,

GOD DESIGNED US ALL FOR HIS AND THE SON'S GLORY, FOR THE MANIFESTATION OF A SACRED STORY,

SOME PEOPLE LOOK FOR FORTUNE AND FAME, WHAT HAS TO DO WITH GOD HAS ALREADY BEEN NAMED,

WHILE EVIL IS TRYING TO UNDO AND RESET, WHAT GOD HAS PURPOSED HAS BEEN PLACED AND ALREADY MET,

ON A PHYSICAL PLANE WHAT PEOPLE DON'T REALIZE, WITH GOD'S SUBSTANCE IN THEM, NOTHING REALLY EVER DIES,

FROM BODY TO BODY FROM PLACE TO PLACE, MY GOD IS THE GOD OF EVERY LIVING RACE,

YOU CANNOT RUN FROM GOD, NOR CAN YOU HIDE, HE IS YOUR GOD TOO, HE LIVES INSIDE OF YOU!

SO BE CAUTIOUS HOW YOU TREAT YOUR FELLOW MAN,
GOD IS WATCHING YOUR EVERY DEMAND,

BE GENTLE WITH GOD'S DELICATE CREATIONS, HE MADE
THEM FOR ENJOYMENT, AND NOT DEGRADATIONS,

BEHOLD! THE LAMB OF GOD...

WHO TAKES AWAY THE SINS OF THE WORLD?

FORGIVE US

SOMETIMES WORDS CANNOT EXPRESS, HOW WE TRULY FEEL AND WHAT WE WANT TO CONFESS,

CONSOLATION ISN'T ALWAYS ENOUGH, ESPECIALLY WHEN WE ARE DEALING WITH EMOTIONAL STUFF,

WE THEN HAVE TO RELY ON A HIGHER SOURCE, AND PRAY THAT GOD WILL PUT US BACK ON COURSE,

TO A LOVING RELATIONSHIP THAT WE ONCE TRUST,

WE ASK AND PRAY THAT YOU WILL FORGIVE US,

THERE IS NO DOUBT, WE ARE TRULY GOD'S OWN, YOU KNOW US BY THE SEEDS HE HAS SOWN,

WE ARE GODS HELPERS ONE TO ANOTHER, I MUST CONSIDER HELPING YOU AS MY BROTHER,

LET US REKINDLE A RELATIONSHIP, WE CAN TRUST, AS YOUR SISTER, BROTHER, AND FRIEND, I ASK THAT YOU FORGIVE US,

FREE YOUR PEOPLE

IN YOUR WORD LORD YOU HAVE PROMISED US,

THAT EVIL AND HATRED WILL NEVER DOMINATE THE JUST,

WE WILL ALWAYS BE UNDER YOUR PROTECTION,

THE SWORD OF YOUR WORD, WILL BE PUT INTO ACTION,

REMOVING ALL LIES AND FALSEHOODS, THAT ARE THERE
TO DECIEVE,

THEY ARE AGAINST EVERYTHING THAT TRUE
CHRISTIANS BELIEVE,

THERFORE LORD, WITH THESE WORDS I CRY OUT
AND PETITION,

THAT YOU REMEMBER, AND SECURE YOUR PEOPLE
FROM DERISION,

FROM MY HEART, SPIRIT AND SOUL, I DO BLEED,

EXPECTING YOU TO MEET YOUR FAMILY AND
PEOPLE'S NEEDS,

FREE YOUR PEOPLE LORD THIS IS MY BLOOD
SHED REQUEST,

YOU HAVE GIVEN THEM YOUR WORD YOU HAVE GIVEN
THEM YOUR BEST,

NONE WILL BE IN VAIN AND NONE WILL BE LOST,

THIS IS THE COMPLETE, FINISHED WORK UPON THE CROSS,

EACH WORD ON THIS PAGE IS WRITTEN IN RED,

TO REMIND OUR ENEMIES, THIS WAS YOUR BLOOD THAT WAS SHED,

THANK YOU LORD, FOR YOUR MERCY AND YOUR BLOOD SHED GRACE,

THAT HAS GIVEN EACH OF US A HERITAGE, AND A GOD SANCTIONED PLACE,

FREE YOUR PEOPLE LORD, THIS IS MY BLOOD SHED REQUEST,

YOU HAVE GIVEN THEM YOUR WORD, YOU HAVE GIVEN THEM YOUR BEST,

GIFT OF GOD!

IT IS YOUR RIGHT TO ENJOY YOUR OWN LABOR,

THIS IS THE GIFT OF GOD IT IS CALLED FAVOR,

EAT DRINK AND BE MERRY, WITH YOUR OWN LABOR, NO ONE ELSE ON THIS EARTH WILL SHOW YOU THIS FAVOR,

GOD HAS PUT WITHIN YOU YOUR OWN WEALTH, IT KEEPS YOU AND RESTORES, YOUR OWN HEALTH,

ALL WEALTH IS NOT MONETARY GAIN, WHAT GOD GIVETH IS WORTH MORE THAN FORTUNE AND FAME,

KEEP YOUR GIFT, KNOW YOUR RIGHTS, HONE YOUR SKILLS, PERFECT YOUR LIGHT,

JUST KNOW THAT YOUR WEALTH COMES FROM WITHIN, GOD HAS SUSTAINED ALL YOUR NEEDS, HE IS YOUR BEST FRIEND,

YOUR GIFT FROM GOD IS A TREASURE, WHEN IT IS A DIVINE GIFT, IT CANNOT BE MEASURED,

GOD HAS GIVEN YOU THE DIVINE RIGHTS, TO SHINE FORTH FROM YOUR OWN LIGHT,

SOME GIFTS ARE FOR THE HEALING OF THE NATION'S AND OTHERS,

WHEN IT IS A UNIVERSAL GIFT, YOU HEAL YOUR SISTERS AND BROTHERS,

JUST PRAY AND ASK GOD TO GUIDE YOU IN YOUR QUEST, TO DO HIS WILL AND BE HIS INSPIRED BEST,

MY COVENANT EYES

GOD MADE A COVENANT WITH MAN, THAT WE WILL ONE DAY UNDERSTAND,

WHAT IS INVESTED IN ME AND THEE, WITH COVENANT EYES, YOU WILL BE ABLE TO ONE DAY SEE,

THE COVENANT SURROUNDS GOD'S THRONE, SEVEN SPIRITS THAT NEVER LEAVE GOD ALONE,

SPIRITUAL STATUTES THAT CANNOT BE SEEN UNIVERSAL LAWS, WORKING FOR THE GOOD OF MAN REMOVING EVIL AND PHYSICAL FLAWS,

ALL POWER IS IN THIS COVENANT, IS FOR THE SON OF GOD THIS WAS MEANT,

GOD DESIGNED THIS POWER IN SEVEN SPHERES, IT HAS BEEN USED AND EXISTING FOR THOUSANDS AND MILLIONS OF YEARS,

WHAT WE MUST KNOW AND ONE DAY WILL SEE, A RAINBOW EXIST INSIDE OF YOU AND ME,

GOD PUT HIS COVENANT INSIDE OF MAN, PLANNING ONE DAY HE WOULD UNDERSTAND,

THAT HE IS THE CHARACTER OF GOD AND HAS THE KEY, TO THE COVENANT SPHERES AND REALMS OF HIS/HER DESTINY,

I KNOW WHY THE RAINBOW, GOD HAS SET WITH A LIMIT, IT IS NOT AN OBJECT FOR SALE NOR CAN A CHALLENGER WIN IT,

IT IS THE POWER OF GOD AND MAN SET IN A BOW, A REMEMBERED OATH AND COVENANT, FOR THE WHOLE WORLD TO KNOW,

GOD IS STILL, HERE AND YET ALIVE , YOU CAN SEE HIM IN THE RAINBOW, WITHIN HIS COVENANT EYES.

SACRED STONES

THE END PRODUCT OUR DIVINE PROCESSES, IS WE ARE GEMS, IN GOD'S CROWN. WE ARE EITHER NOBLES GASES, LIKE THE HELIUM ON THE SUN. OR A SACRED STONE LIKE A DIAMOND (FIRE), RUBY, EMERALD, OR SAPPHIRE. THE BIBLE IS RICH WITH JEWELS, AND PRECIOUS METALS, (e.g., GOLD, SILVER, PLATINUM).

THE ANSWER COMES WHEN THE SUBSTANCE HAS BEEN FIXED, AND APPROPRIATELY PLACED WITH AND WHERE ALL GOD'S JEWELS ARE AND SHOULD BE!

GOD'S TEMPLE ITSELF WAS COMPOSED OF PEARLY GATES AND HEAVENS STREETS OF GOLD.

I DON'T KNOW IF WE REALIZE THE IMPORTANCE OF STONES AND THEIR CHEMICAL PROCESSES THEY ARE VERY SIGNIFICANT TO GOD, THEY SHOULD BE TO US ALSO. WHY DO YOU THINK GOD ELECTED TO ASSOCIATE ALL 12 TRIBES OF ISRAEL TO A SPECIFIC SACRED STONE! DO YOU KNOW EACH STONE HAS A CHEMICAL PROCESS IT GOES THROUGH? DO YOU KNOW ALL BASE METALS ALLOYS, ARE RAISED ARE RAISED BY NOBLES, GOLD/SILVER.

IF THERE IS ANY GREATNESS IN US IT IS BECAUSE WE HAVE BEEN PROCESSED WITH SOMETHING GREATER THAN OURSELVES. ANCIENT TIMES CALLED IT THE PHILOSOPHER'S STONES, WE IN THE RELIGIOUS WORLD KNOW HIM AS "JESUS". HE RAISES ALL BASE THINGS TO A LEVEL OF UNDERSTANDING/WISDOM. HE COMPELS MAN TO TAKE A LOOK AT HIMSELF, HIS BRETHERN, HIS ONTOLOGICAL STATE, HIS GOD.

IN DEFENSE OF GOD'S WORD

Today there is a miscarriage of Justice, as well as a rape of Justice and misconceptions of Justice! All done under the disguise of Temporal control/Hell.

Those of us who are true believers, know what the word of God has said, and his word is the infallible and inerrant word of God!

How can we make laws that oppose the maker of laws? We must not be consulting God! How can you make a law for the man to take a woman's name in marriage when God has set forth the right of inheritance by the father's surname not the woman's?

Why would we even consider making a law God has told you in his word is vile! What makes them think, same sex marriage, will change with you instituting it as a law. What has happened when we you oppose God's laws and statutes, we subject involve our destinies, values, and spiritual inheritances to a devaluation situation. We are not directed toward the pathways, "God" has set forth for adhering Christians and righteous people.

Wearing the attire of "Jesus" that God recognizes. In sin they are changing Christ's coat of righteousness and heavenly light, to a coat of death and reprobates.

They are putting on the attire of Satan.

We are known that we are in and under God's control by the things that are first in our lives. God would not put something in your life that you cannot control. When you are in the proper place in God sex does not just mean physical, there is a spiritual intimacy. The whole earth fecundates (i.e., is intimate in producing in the Earth), according to its season, it is an intimate relationship of spring with it primary source, to bring forth life in a very intimate way. Spring brings forth life in its due season, it is just as valid as sexual union between man and woman. Symbolically, the earth is woman/feminine, and the sun/masculine is man, or vice versa. The two most powerful forces in the universe, is positive and negative, equated to male and feminine powers. Both, of these powers are under God's control. I believe when we have these forces in us under control, God will deem us worthy of carrying, sacred powers, we don't throw out the baby "Jesus", with the bath water for sex! We must keep "God" first.

That is why some of us cannot receive the power of God and some are worthy. Some FORGET who God is! Their flesh becomes their God!

So, when I see a tree blossoming, or a flower budding, I know, I am in the presence of God's mighty and powerful creative forces and processes in the earth! I feel and see the unseen processes, as well as the physical. I am a vital part of nature my birth, is also a part of me because God made me creative!

Even in death there is a process, God's word says you can sow a seed in hatred, but you can raise it a spirit. Meaning it can die naturally, it can be raised spiritually.

So, when it looks like it's over it can just be the beginning in another space!

I believe that is what happened to Jesus. The whole world hated him because they would be the vehicle by which he would be raised.

In Christ the power of hate was converted to love and life.

There are explicitly four types of flesh stated, in the Book of Corinthians: That is Men, Animals, Birds, Fish. It also mentions the two distinct bodies, in the physical and spiritual world, a celestial body and a terrestrial body. A body of Heaven and Earth, if you will. As far as glory, there is a glory of the sun moon and stars, they differ from each another!

Let us practice being good stewards of the word of God, and build the worthy Kingdom God should inhabit with us!

METAMORPHASIS

The Butterfly is known for its ability to ascend to a metamorphic species from a earthly crawling insect to a flying insect. I don't know of any other life form that changes it's form to this alternate extreme!

God would not provide death without providing LIFE! After all isn't that what God is, "Life". I believe that there are miraculous changes already here, we just haven't found them yet.

Since, God has already attributed his spirit, to all things that might be a good place to start. I don't know of any other instance

in life where a complete physical and elemental change takes place from terrestrial/crawling upon the Earth, to celestial/flying within the heavens! From crawling/walking to flying in the atmosphere.

Let's look at what God has already done. I believe they say that most of the earth we live on is formed by insects/fossils. Let' look at life from, a prehistoric stand-point in time. To see what "God" did!

What did the dinosaur live on, since it was the largest and most gargantuan animal? It had to live on vegetables/plants or bugs. Just like the killer whales today, they live on microscopic organism!

I often wonder, what was the purpose of gigantic life forms, then reduced to smaller ones. I believe consumption and space played a predominating part in making organisms of life smaller.

Everything "God" created was a chemistry. I just found out Bees, as well as ants, have association to Formic Acid, which is associated to Formaldehyde. I also found of out certain snake venom us used in medicine for cures of certain types. Could that mean we have other cures and secrets right in our midst that we have not ascertained yet? I believe that flesh cannot inhabit heaven because it is flesh, God has already prepared a place and organisms to consume flesh, like ants and other in dwelling insects in the earth.

I also believe that Earthly organisms cannot consume spiritual essence without consequence. Just like Nocturnal is not suppose to sit where Diurnal is designed to sit.

This would create a world of disease and sickness. Princes will be walking, while servants will be riding. The whole social scale would backwards. People would be given abnormalities, disease as well as, inversions/untruths abnormal, untimely births. Nothing would be in the correct order.

Rejection is not an answer! Christ was rejected and he still became the greatest benefit to mankind. He was an answer to all mankind's ills including rejection. You cannot deny the inevitable when it precedes all that you are and will ever be! It was named and done before this time ever happened. Read Ecclesiastes, the preacher tells us the past, present and future! Good or bad he lets us know about what has already happened. This time is not the only time, God knew the hearts and evils man would cause, thus time has three dimensions. Seconds, Minutes, and hours, each happening within the hour.

You cannot have a minute without a second, you cannot have an hour with each of them! There is existence on all three levels. So that man cannot find out the work of "God", divine providence takes over and secures all things out of man's control.

WITH GOD WE ARE WALKING IN GRACE, FAITH, EVERYDAY

Steps are ordered by God! So is the universe and all that is in it. We order meals and food, God orders life, destines, and futures. We utilize and pray for divine gifts, God distributes blessings, and gifts. We ask questions of and about life, God has incorporated answers to our questions in our quest for wisdom, knowledge, within what the has given us.

In all of God's handyworks we can find wisdom, knowledge, in some even life! Look at the human body, it is the perfect example of the organon! A vast body of organs that has varied potentials, and reveals great knowledge when investigated properly. All made with God's awesome divine providence and sacred rites of divinity.

We as humans are only images of God's greatness, power, and eternal being. However, he has granted to us his divine attributes, through the suffering of his son, the Jesus Christ.

If we adhere to the divine plan of our savior, Jesus Christ, as the compassionate giver of Soteriology (e.g., salvation) for the redemption our lives. We are then guaranteed, to be heirs of the Kingdom of God,

GOD'S SIGNATURE FOR YOU

HAVE YOU EVER THOUGHT ABOUT THE DIMPLES IN YOUR SMILE, HOW IT MAY BE A SIGNATURE FOR YOUR SMILE,

OR WHAT ABOUT THE DIMPLE IN YOUR CHIN, IT MIGHT SIGNIFY WHAT'S DEEPLY WITHIN,

WHAT ABOUT THE BEAUTY OF A WELL DEFINED HIGH CHEEK, BEAUTY MAY NOT HAVE A MOUTH BUT DEFINITIONS DO SPEAK,

JUST AS THERE IS A PEAK TO EVERY MOUNTAIN, WHERE ONCE THERE WAS A RIVER THERES NOW IS A FOUNTAIN,

I BELIEVE GOD'S SIGNATURES ARE ON US DEFINED IN SPECIFIC WAYS, THEY STAY WITH US FROM OUR BIRTH TO THE END OF OUR DAYS,

EVERYONE OF US HAVE DIFFERENT FINGER PRINTS, GOD KNOWS EACH ONE OF THEM LIKE ANGELS THAT ARE HEAVEN SENT,

HUMANS SIGN WITH PENCIL AND PEN, GOD'S SIGATURE IS DEEPER AND WRITTEN FROM WITHIN,

HACKED MIND

GOD GAVE ME A STRONG AND FRUITFUL MIND,

WITHIN IT HE PLACED A PORTION OF TIME,

HE MADE THE BRAIN/MIND AN ORGAN LIKE NO OTHER,

THE BRAIN/MIND WAS IN THE LIKENESS OF A MOTHER,

THE BRAIN IS THE EPITOME OF WHO WE ARE, IT CAN BE YOUR GUIDE AND TAKE YOU VERY FAR,

THE BRAIN IS LIKE A COMPUTER, IT CAN BE HACKED, BY A COMPUTER THIEF,

SOMEONE WELL VERSED IN AUTOMATED/ COMPUTERS, AND HAS NO BELIEFS,

COMPUTERS HAVE MANY TIMELINES,

I KNOW BECAUSE, I HAVE BEEN BREECHED, AND

THEY HACKED MY MIND,

THROUGH MY MIND THEY ALTERED, MY WAY,

THEY STOLE MY GRACE AND DEFILED MY DAY,

THEY SHARED MY LIFE AND ALTERED MY LINE,

THEY BREECHED MY BODY AND HACKED MY MIND,

I BELIEVE IN ALL THINGS WRONGED HAVING A SECOND CHANCE,

TO GIVE THEM THE OPPORTUNITY BE RESTORED AND TO ADVANCE,

I KNOW THEIR PURPOSE WAS TO MAIN AND DAM,

BUT I ALSO KNOW, THAT GOD HAS FOR ME
ANOTHER PROGRAM,

HERE FOR ME!

I MUST TAKE UP THE BANNER, AND BE HERE SOME PEOPLE WANT TO STEAL YOUR PLACE, SOME PEOPLE WANT TO USE YOUR GRACE,

SOME PEOPLE ARE MADE OF FLAWS, SOME PEOPLE BREAK ALL THE LAWS,

IT PAYS TO CONNECT TO WHAT IS GOOD, THEY ARE PROBABLY DOING THE THINGS YOU WOULD,

WHEN YOU FIND SOMEONE IS OBVERSE TO YOU, THERE'S ONLY ONE THING LEFT FOR YOU TO DO,

MAKE SURE YOU SEARCH YOURSELF AND YOUR LIFES WILL,

SOME PEOPLE HAVE NO CONSCIOUS, NO SPIRITUAL LIFE AND THEY CAN'T FEEL,

YOU MUST THEN SAY TO YOURSELF, I AM HERE FOR ME, NO-ONE ELSE HERE IS BETTER FOR ME THAN ME,

I SET THE BAR FOR MY MIND, FOR MY FAITH AND FOR MY TRUTH, I UTILISE MY ADOLESCENCE TO CONTROL MY YOUTH,

I HAVE TO TRUST GOD, ALWAY SEAL MY NEEDS, TO LET ME KNOW, TO CORRESPOND TO THE THINGS I NEED TO GROW,

MOST OF ALL I MUST PERCEIVE MY INTENTS, IN A WORLD MADE OF GOD'S STATUES AND PRESEDENTS,

NO MATTER HOW MANY PHYSICAL FLAWS, WE ARE STILL BOUND BY GOD'S SPIRITUAL LAWS,

WHEN NO-ONE ELSE HERE CARES IN THE WORLD CARED, FOR ME,

FOR ME,

HYPNOTIC CUES

I WAS TOO YOUNG TO REALIZE, WHAT IT WAS YOU DID WITH YOUR EYES,

I AM OLDER NOW AND I UNDERSTAND, WHAT YOU CAN DO WITH THE SNAP OF YOUR HANDS,

I WAS TOO GULLIBLE TO KNOW THE TECHNIQUE, YOU USE, WAS ALL ASSOCIATED WITH HYPNOTIC CUES,

I WONDERED WHY EVERY TIME YOU CAME NEAR, I WOULD HEAR FINGERS SNAP IN MY EARS,

I WAS UNDER YOUR SPELL BY YOUR CONTROLLING WORDS,

THAT YOU PROGRAMMED AND MADE SURE I HEARD,

I WAS TOO GULLIBLE TO KNOW THE TECHNIQUE YOU USE, WAS ALL ASSOCIATED WITH HYPONOTIC CUES,

I REALIZED I HAD BEEN HEXED, THE MANY TIMES WE HAD ILLICIT SEX,

I AM REALLY NOT SURPRISED, WHAT YOU CAN DO WITH THOSE HYPNOTIC EYES,

I BELIEVE I REALLY UNDERSTAND, WHAT YOU CONTROL WITH THOSE MARVELOUS HANDS,

WITH THE STUFF YOU USE, YOU COULD NOT LOSE,

I WAS A HOPLESS PUPPET TO DO WHATEVER YOU CHOOSE,

I AM A BELIVER

IN LIFE WE CHOOSE MANY DIFFERENT PATHWAYS, GOD GAVE THE CHOICES WHEN HE GAVE US A DAY,

HE GAVE US THIS DAY WITH HOPES THAT WE ONE DAY, WOULD UNDERSTAND THAT IN THIS LIFE HE HOLDS OUR FUTURE PLANS,

MANY EXPERIENCES HELPS US TO SEE, THE DIFFERENCE BETWEEN EVIL AND DIVINITY,

GOD WANTS US TO KNOW AND CHOOSE THE GOOD,

HIS DIVINE PLANS ARE FOR ALL HUMANITY'S BROTHERHOODS,

EVERY LAST ONE OF US HAS A FUTURE FATE, FULL OF LOVE WITH THE FATHER OR WITH SATAN FULL OF HATE,

I MADE MY CHOICE, I AM A BELIEVER, I AM NOT A HATER, KILLER OR DECEIVER,

WHEN I CONSIDER ALL THE SUFFERING CHRIST HAS DONE, I CAN'T HELP BUT SURRENDER MY LIFE TO THE HOLY ONE,

GOD CHOSE ME, KNOWS ME, AND EVEN MARRIED ME, WHEN I WAS LOST IN THIS EVIL WORLD HE CAME AND CARRIED ME,

HE CARRIED ME AWAY FROM SIN AND DEATH, AND GAVE ME A NEW LIFE WITH LOVE AND HIS BREATH,

CHOOSE YE THIS DAY WHOM YOU WILL SERVE AND OBEY, WILL IT BE GOD'S GOODNESS OR SATAN'S EVIL WAYS,

THESE WORDS ARE REAL AND SPEAKS TO YOUR SOULS,

TO DIRECT GUIDE AND HELP YOU REALIZE WHAT YOU DON'T KNOW,

TO BE A TRUE BELIEVER IT'S NOT HARD TO DO OR BE, YOU MUST BELIEVE THAT GOD IS DIRECTING YOUR DESTINY,

YOU MUST READ YOUR BIBLE SO THAT YOU CAN SEE, WHAT GOD SAID IN JEREMIAH 29:23 FOR YOU AND FOR ME,

REMEMBER GOD WILL NOT, DOES NOT, AND CANNOT LIE, HE WILL BE WITH US TIL THE END EVEN WHEN WE DIE,

DON'T BE AFRAID, GO AHEAD AND GIVE GOD A TRY, HE HAS NEVER FALLEN NOR HIS ANGELS FALLEN FROM THE SKY,

THAT'S ENOUGH FOR ME TO KNOW,

I'M BELIEVER IN MY GOD THAT'S THE WAY I GO,

JESUS'S PREPARED BODY (ANATOMY)

GOD PREPARED ME A BODY, A VERY SIGNIFICANT ANATOMY,

MADE AND SOWN WITH SPECIAL SEED, CONSTRUCTED WITH EVERYTHING THAT I WOULD NEED,

IT WAS ONE OF THE REASONS FOR MY BIRTH, A PLACE OF GOD'S TO SOW THE WHOLE EARTH,

I HAD TO BE NUMERICALLY FIRST, IN ME EXISTED THE WHOLE UNIVERSE,

GOD PREPARED EVERYTHING RIGHT DOWN TO THE DAVIDIC LINE, IN JESUS GOD PLACED ALL HERITAGES DOWN TO THE LAST IOTA OF WORDS/TIME,

THE FOUNDATION IS SURE MADE WITH GOD'S BEST TO ENDURE,

GOD FILLED IT WITH FAITH, TRUTH, FOR THIS FAITH IN HIS PRECIOUS LAMB,

GOD FOR THIS FAITH GOD CHOSE THE WHOLE SEED OF FAITHFUL ABRAHAM,

FOR YOUR SERVITUDE, YOU HAVE PREPARED ME A SPECIAL BODY,

WHERE EVIL WILL NOT DWELL, HEAVEN CAN NEVER SERVICE HELL,

DAY AND NIGHT CANNOT SIT IN THE SAME SEAT, DAYLIGHT IS OVER DARKNESS, BECAUSE OF DEFEAT,

GOODNESS OVER-POWERED EVIL, AND CAST IT TO HELL, RIGHT WHERE ITS MASTER WAS WHEN HE FELL,

HEAVEN IS CULTIVATED RIGHT IN JESUS'S PREPARED BODY AND DIVINE ANATOMY,

AN ETERNAL PLACE FOR THE WHOLE DIVINE TRINITY,

JUDGEMENT

GOD HAS GIVEN TO US SEVERAL SENSES, PHYSICAL SENSES, DIVINE SENSES, TO JUDGE MOST ANY RECOMPENSES,

SOME ACTIONS MUST BE TAKEN TO A HIGHER LEVEL, ESPECIALLY WHERE THERE ARE SPIRITUAL DEVILS,

WICKNESS IT IS SAID IS IN HIGH PLACES, IT IS GOVERNING AND TRYING TO RULE ALL, NATIONS,

HOWEVER GOD'S RULE SET PRESEDENCE, IS STILL IN FORCE AND ENACTING JUDGEMENT,

JUDGEMENT FOR ME AND JUDGEMENT FOR YOU,

NO SPIRITUAL LIMITS FOR JUDGEMENT TO ASCEND TOO,

IN YOUR LIFE YOU WILL FIND JUDGEMENT FOR A BOY AND JUDGEMENT FOR A GIRL,

IS MUCH DIFFERENT THAN JUDGEMENT FOR AN ENTIRE WORLD,

I KNOW OF A JUDGEMENT OF AN ENTIRE UNIVERSE, THEY WERE JUDGED BECAUSE OF WHAT THEY DID TO CHRIST BIRTH,

THEY ALL BENEFITTED FROM THE USE OF HIS DIVINE SEED, INSTEAD OF RECOGNIZING THE UNIVERSAL NEED, THEY CHOOSE, THEIR GREED,

CHRIST LIFE WAS TO BENEFIT ALL, NOT TO DEGRADE AND DEMEAN MAN AND REINSTITUTE MAN'S FALL,

I KNOW THAT GOD'S WORDS ARE LIFE AND FOR WHAT THEY ARE MEANT,

THEY WILL ALWAYS BE IN FORCE AND PRODUCING ISSUING SOME FORM OF JUDGEMENT,

EVEN WHEN WE DON'T SEE THE WORKING AND ACTIONS OF GOD'S WORDS,

THEY ARE STILL TRANSCENDING AND PERFECTING A TRUTH FOR THOSE WHO HAS HEARD THE WORD,

LAUGHING DEVILS

I STILL DON'T SEE THE HUMOR OR WHY, DEVILS LAUGH, WHEN THEY SHOULD CRY,

GOD PLACED A MARK ON THEM NOT TO EMBRACE, THE THINGS OF HEAVEN, OR TO EVEN TASTE,

IN GOD'S BOOK THEY WILL ALWAYS BE LAST, THE PLACE MEANT FOR THE HATERS, SOULESS, EVIL AND BAD,

THE DEVIL CANNOT IMITATE DIVINITY, GOD IS ALL HEAVENLY FIRE,

THE DEVIL HAS FLAMES AND HEAT BUT GODS FIRE IS HIGHER,

SO WHEN WICKEDNESS BACKS YOU AGAINST THE WALL,

KEEP IN YOUR MIND IT WAS FROM HEAVEN SATANS FALL,

WHEN DEVILS TRY TO INTIMIDATE YOU AND TAUNT AND LAUGH,

JUST LOOK AT THEM AND REMEMBER, GOD MADE YOU FIRST, IN EXISTENCE GOD MADE THEM LAST,

THEIR LAUGHTER IS FOR EVIL PURPOSES AND TO DESTROY,

YOUR LAUGHTER IS FOR PURPOSES OF LOVE, LIFE AND TO BRING JOY,

IF YOU ONE DAY FIND YOURSELF IN THEIR MIDST, JUST REMEMBER WHAT GOD TOLD YOU AND HOW TO RESIST,

LEFT FOR DEAD

YOU ONLY MEANT ME HARM AND TROUBLE, EVERY BAD SITUATION WITH YOU SEEMED TO DOUBLE,

I DIDN'T SUSPECT YOU WOULD CONSIDER OR EVEN FEEL, THAT ONE DAY MY LIFE YOU WOULD WANT TO KILL,

YOU PLOTTED AND PLANNED WHAT YOU WOULD DO, WITH THOSE WHO WANTED ME DEAD TOO,

I WAS JUST A MEEK AND HUMBLE CHILD, FULL OF GOD'S JOYS AND SMILES,

WHAT I FOUND OUT WAS YOU WANTED ME LEFT FOR DEAD, BECAUSE EVERYONE WANTED MY PLACE, MY LIFE AND MY BED,

I MYSELF HAVE NEVER EVEN THOUGHT, OF COMMITTING MURDER AND THE EVILS THEY WROUGHT,

I GET JOY OUT OF SEEING MY FRIENDS AND FAMILY BE BLESSED, WATCHING GOD MOVE THEM FROM THEIR WORRIES AND THEIR STRESS,

I ALWAYS BELIEVED THAT WHEN YOU HAD A FRIEND THAT THEY WOULD SHARE, IN YOUR PROSPERTITY AND SHOW THEY CARE,

A FRIEND SHOULD NOT BE SOMETHING TO DREAD, AND WONDER IF THEY ARE TRYING TO LEAVE YOU FOR DEAD,

NOW I KNOW IT IS TRUE, STORIES THAT HAVE BEEN UNTOLD,

A REAL FRIEND IS TRULY WORTH THEIR WEIGHT IN GOLD,

LOOSE THE BAND'S

LIFE IS FULL OF STRINGS, AND FULL OF HOPE, IT IS ALSO FULL OF CONSEQUENCES, OF SOME WE CAN'T COPE,

WE ARE CONNECTED IN THIS UNIVERSE EVERYWHERE, FROM PLACE TO PLACE,

WE ARE ALL PART OF THE MAIN, RACE TO RACE,

EVEN IN HEAVENS WE ARE LINKED TO SPECIFIC THINGS, SOMETIMES WE DON'T KNOW WHAT AN ATTACHMENT WILL BRING,

ORIONS BAND'S ARE AN INTRICATE PART OF US, MOTIVATING, MOVING, PENETRATING THROUGH US,

I BELIEVE THAT ORION HAS A DIRECT TIE, TO WHAT WE DON'T REALIZE,

I BELIEVE THAT ORION'S BAND'S, ARE TELEVISED THROUGH EVERY MAN,

ORION IS THE LINK AND CHAIN, TO ALL FREQUENCIES ALREADY NAMED,

PEOPLE ARE ASSOCIATED BY BAND'S OF COLOR AND LIGHT, ORION IS HOLDING THEM IN PLACE IN THE NIGHT,

RIGEL AND BETALGEUSE, ARE FOR ORIONS SECRET USE,

A STAR IS IN PLACE FOR PARTICULAR REASONS, NOT JUST FOR LIGHT, BEAUTY, OR SEASONS,

WHEN ORIONS BAND'S ARE LOSSED, IT RELINQUISHES THE HOLD, ON EVERY MAN, WOMAN, CHILD USED,

LOOSING ORIONS BAND IS A SACRED RITE, ENACTED BY GOD, SET TO WORK IN THE NIGHT,

MAN SHALL NOT LIVE BY BREAD ALONE

HOW DOES MANKIND EXPECT TO FLOURISH, IF IT IS GOD THEY NEGLECT TO NOURISH,

WITH PRAYERS AND TIME IN EACH DAY, SO THAT GOD CAN INTERVENE AND SHOW US THE WAY,

TO THE DIVINE AND WHAT IS MEANT, TO GIVE US THE BLESSINGS THAT IS GOD'S HOLY INTENT,

HE GAVE US NATURAL FOOD TO NOURISH OUR FLESH, HE ALSO GAVE US SPIRITUAL LAWS FOR OUR SPIRITS TWO DIGEST THE BEST,

MAN SHALL NOT LIVE BY BREAD ALONE, BUT BY EVERY WORD OUT OF THE MOUTH OF GOD FROM HIS THRONE,

WHEATHER THE WORD IS WRITTEN SPOKEN OR SENT, THE POWER WITHIN THEM ARE EVIDENT,

THEY ARE SENT TO BLESS, HEAL, OR ADORN, WHATEVER THE PURPOSE GODS WORD WILL PERFORM,

ONE THING GOD'S WORDS WON'T DO OR TRY, IT IS IMPOSSIBLE FOR GOD'S WORDS TO LIE,

I WANT TO DO LIKE, DAVID, THE PSALMST SAY, THE WORD OF GOD IS IN MY MOUTH EVERYDAY,

IN A SPIRITUAL WORLD YOU NEED SPIRITUAL THOUGHTS, DON'T HESITAT TO USE WHAT JESUS CHRIST'S BLOOD BOUGHT,

THE HOLY GHOST PROTECTS YOU, AS WELL AS THE FATHER AND THE SON,

YOUR GETTING EVERLASTING SECURITY FROM THE TRINITY, THE GODHEAD ALL THREE MANIFESTED INTO ONE,

MAN SHALL NOT LIVE BY BREAD ALONE, BUT BY EVERY WORD OUT OF THE MOUTH OF GOD, SPOKEN FROM HIS THRONE,

WE KNOW FOR SURE THAT GOD IS ALL EMPYREAN AND HEAVENLY FIRE, HE DOES NOT WELCOME MURDERS, EVIL, HATRED OR LIARS,

MAN SHALL NOT LIVE BY BREAD ALONE, BUT BY EVERY WORD OF GOD'S SPOKEN FROM HIS THRONE,

MY WORTH

FOR TOO LONG I COULD NOT UNDERSTAND, WHY I WAS SO MISUNDERSTOOD ALMOST BY EVERY MAN,

UNTIL I FOUND OUT MY WORTH, WAS GIVEN TO ME AT BIRTH,

EVERYONE IN MY LIFE WAS VERY VERY BRIEF, BECAUSE I WAS SURROUNDED COUNTLESS THIEVES,

THEY NEVER WOULD TELL ME THE TRUTH ABOUT ANYTHING, SO AFRAID THAT IT MIGHT WAKE UP SOMETHING,

AND CAUSE THEM TO LOSE A BENEFIT, THEY DIDN'T TO AWAKEN OR TO FORFEIT,

I REALLY DIDN'T PLACE A VALUE ON MYSELF, UNTIL I FOUND OUT I CREATED MY OWN WEALTH,

I FOUND OUT MY WORTH, WAS GIVEN TO ME AT BIRTH,

HOW DO YOU LET A DIAMOND KNOW HOW MANY FACETS ARE ENOUGH, I WAS TOLD I WAS A DIAMOND IN THE ROUGH,

GOLD NEVER TARNISHES AND GROWS OLD, THE BLOOD THAT RUNS THROUGH MY FATHER'S VEINS COULD BE SOLD,

IT IS LIKE HAVING THE FOUNTAIN OF TRUTH, FLOWING IN THE VESSEL OF MY FATHER'S YOUTH,

YES I AM IN THE IMAGE OF GOD ALMIGHTY, AN EXPRESS REPLICA OF HIM AS THEY CAN SEE,

SOMETIMES I MAKE THE DECISION, TO BE OUTSIDE OF HUMAN VISION,

IT MAKES PEOPLE MISERABLE, WHEN I AM INVISIBLE,

I FOUND OUT MY WORTH, WAS GIVEN TO ME AT MY BIRTH,

MY DESCENDENTS

GOD HAS GIVEN TO ME AND TO YOU, EVERLASTING LINEAGE ATTACHED TO YOU,

FAMILY IS LIKE ATTENDENTS, WHEN THEY PRECEDE YOU THEY ARE CALLED DESCENDENTS,

MUCH OF YOUR FAMILES HISTORY, IS BOUND UP IN JESUS CHRIST MYSTERY,

CHRIST IS ONLY ONE LINE CHRIST, IS ONLY IN ONLY ONE MIND,

CHRIST IS NOT OF HUMAN OR GENETIC SEED, HE WAS BORN OUT OF A SPIRITUAL NEED,

A NEED MANKIND COULD NOT PAVE, AN ACTION THAT ONLY SALVATION AND REDEMPTION GAVE,

THAT IS WHY HE IS CALLED JESUS CHRIST, HE WAS THE ONLY ONE WORTHY ENOUGH TO SAVE ALL MANKIND'S LIFE,

WHETHER THEY ARE DESCENDENTS OR ASCENDENTS ALIKE,

THEY MUST ALL PASS BY JESUS CHRIST,

GOD HAS A PLACE FOR THE LIVING AS WELL AS THE DEAD, EACH PLACE HE IS THE LIVING SPIRITUAL HEAD,

GOD IS THE GOD OF THE RICH AS WELL AS THE POOR, HE IS THEIR FATHER, EVEN WHEN THEY ARE SPOKEN FOR,

THE BEST THING ABOUT BEING SPIRITUAL, IS YOU CAN ALWAYS SUMMON UP A MIRACLE,

IF YOU EVER FEEL ALONE AND NEED AN ATTENDENT,
JUST REMEMBER YOU HAVE MULTITUDES OF FAMILY AND
DESCENDENTS,

PAVED PATHWAY

GOD HAS A WAY FOR US TO GO, GOD HAS KNOWLEDGE AND WISDOM FOR US TO OBTAIN AND KNOW,

THESE PATHWAYS HAVE BEEN PAVED OF OLD, FOR THE RIGHTEOUS AND CHOSEN WHO HAS DEDICATED THEIR SOULS,

TO GOD FOR THE PURPOSE OF ALL GOOD, TO UNITE AND PERFECT A UNIVERSAL BROTHERHOOD,

GOD HAS A PAVED PATHWAY, FOR CHRISTIANS AND SAINTS TO TRAVEL THAT WAY,

HIS WORDS ARE FIRST AND HIS WORDS ARE LAST, HIS WORDS ARE THE LIGHTS FOR YOUR FEET AS A PATH,

MORE THAN JUST WORDS THEY ARE BEYOND THE NORM, HIS WORDS ARE EVERYTHING YOU NEED HIS WORDS PROTECT AND TRANSFORM,

HE HAS PROMISED HIS WORDS ARE LIGHTS, THEY ARE THE GUIDES THAT PIERECE THROUGHT THE NIGHTS,

WHEN YOUR VISION IS DIM AND YOU CAN'T SEE, IN GOD'S WORD IS WHERE YOU WANT TO BE,

IN OBSERVING HIS WORDS YOU WILL FIND, HIS WORDS DOES GIVE SIGHT TO THE BLIND,

WHEN IN DOUBT AND IN DERISION, REMEMBER GOD HAS GIVEN YOU THIS VISION,

A VISION OF HOPE FOR THE WHOLE WORLD TO SEE, FROM HIS WORDS DESIGNED AND DIRECTED DESTINIES,

WHO WOULD HAVE THOUGHT, FROM ONE VERSE YOU MIGHT CREATE A UNIVERSE,

SOME WORDS WE CANNOT UTTER AND WE CANNOT SAY, WE JUST HAVE TO CONTINUE TO WALK FOLLOWING THEIR PATHWAYS,

PROMISED SEED

LORD YOU PLACED MY SEED WITHIN ME, AND TOLD ME I COULD BE ANYTHING I COULD DREAM OR WANTED TO BE,

FOR MY OWN HEALTH, YOU PLACED MY OWN SEED WITHIN MYSELF,

YOU KNEW THAT ONE DAY I WOULD NEED, TO MANIFEST MY PROMISED SEED,

GOING BEYOND MY PRESENT STATE, TO ASTONISH MY ENEMIES AND DEFY THEIR FATE,

MANY STARTED OUT WITH ME, NOW I AM DOWN TO YOU MY CELL ME, THAT MAKES THREE,

I CARRIED MANY BURDENS AND A MULTITUDE OF JOY, IN MY LIFETIME IT WAS SPREAD TO MOST EVERY GIRL AND GOD BORNE BOY,

YOUR FIRST IS ALWAYS THE BEST, SO MUCH BETTER THAN ALL THE REST,

YOU KNEW THAT ONE DAY I WOULD NEED, TO MANIFEST MY PROMISED SEED,

THE PROMISE IS IN ABRAHAM'S SEED, I KNOW THAT TIME IS AN EMBRACER OF THIS NEED,

I BELIEVE THIS WAS AN ORDERED TIME, GIVEN BY GOD TO PERFECT A GIVEN LINE,

YOU KNEW THAT ONE SAY I WOULD NEED, TO MANIFEST MY PROMISED SEED,

PURIFIED

SOMETHING'S IN LIFE ARE SO IMPURE, WE MUST LEARN TO ABSTAIN AND ENDURE,

WE MUST TRY TO KEEP OUR HANDS CLEAN, THERE ARE SO MANY THINGS THAT CAN DEFILE THAT ARE UNSEEN,

FOR THOSE OF US WHO BELIEVE, WE WILL ALWAYS BE ABLE TO RECEIVE,

ON GOD'S GRACE ALONE WE RELIED, HE PROTECTED US FROM ALL DISEASE, GERMS, BACTERIA, AND KEPT US PURIFIED,

GOD HAS ALL THE ANSWERS, AND GOD HAS ALL THE KEYS, HE IS THE CURE FOR ALL AILMENTS, THAT NO HUMAN SEES,

WE MUST OBEY AND BE TRUE TO GOD'S WORD, THAT IS THE ULTIMATE GRACE, WE HAVE HEARD,

ADULTURATED BY THE IMPURITIES, IN A SIN SICK PLACE,

"JESUS CHRIST", RECLAIMED US ALL EVERY HUMAN RACE,

BY THE SALVATION AND SOVEREIGNITY OF HIS GRACE,

THROUGH HIS GRACE AND HIS GRACE ALONE,

WE ALL HAVE ACCESS TO A HOLY CITY AND A GOD SANCTIONED HOME,

IT TOOK TIME FOR ME TO REALIZE, THROUGH CHRIST I WAS ALREADY PURIFIED,

PRAYED UP

SOMETIMES PROBLEMS IN LIFE, CAN SEEM PRETTY BIG, THEY CAN BE SO DEEP YOU NEED A SHOVEL TO DIG,

DON'T EVER LET YOUR PROBLEMS COVER YOU UP, KEEP YOUR HEAD UP AND STAY PRAYED UP,

THE WORD OF GOD WAS DESIGNED TO BRING YOU THROUGH, ANY SITUATION THAT WAS TOO HARD FOR YOU,

THE WORD OF GOD WAS ALSO TO MAKE YOU PURE, TO CLEAN YOU UP AND HELP YOU TO ENDURE,

LIKE WATER IS TO OUR BODY ESSENTIAL TO OUR CELLS, INSIDE OF US WE HAVE OUR OWN CISTERNS AND OUR OWN WELLS,

DON'T LET YOUR PROBLEMS COVER YOU UP, KEEP YOUR HEAD UP AND STAY PRAYED UP,

BEING PRAYED UP IS LJKE HAVING MONEY IN THE BANK, WHEN YOU CALL FOR GOD'S PROTECTION CASH IN YOUR PRAYER, DON'T FORGET GOD IT IS YOU THANK,

WHEN YOU NEED A LITTLE MONEY CASH IN YOUR PRAYER, GOD WILL MAKE SURE YOUR FINANCES ARE THERE,

WHEN YOU NEED A LITTLE LOVE HE HAS THAT TOO, CASH IN YOUR PRAYER, NO HUMAN CAN LOVE YOU THE WAY GOD DO,

PRAYER IS THE ANSWER AND THE KEY TO EVERY DOOR, GOD WILL OPEN THEM IF WE PRAY A LITTLE MORE,

JESUS DIED TOO BRING SALVATION, FOR EVERY HUMAN AND BLOOD BOUGHT NATION,

DON'T EVER LET YOUR PROBLEMS COVER YOU

UP, KEEP YOUR HEAD UP, AND STAY PRAYED UP,

REST HOME

GOD SUPPLIES MY EVERY NEED, GOD CREATED MY COUNTLESS SEEDS,

HE MADE MY BODY A POWERHOUSE AND A LIVING WELL,

HE CONSTRUCTED MY BODY TO NEVER TO FAIL,

WHY THEN DO PEOPLE WANT ME IN A REST HOME, WHEN GOD WANTS ME FERVENT, FERTILE AND STRONG,

JUST BECAUSE I LIVE ALONE, THAT DOESN'T MEAN I BELONG IN A REST HOME,

I AM STILL FULL OF LIFE AND GOD'S VESTMENTS, HE IS THE ONLY ONE SHOULD BE MAKING ANY ADJUSTMENTS,

DON'T TRY TO PUT ME IN A REST HOME, WHEN YOU KNOW THAT IS NOT WHERE I BELONG,

FOR PURPOSES OF HEALTH AND WEALTH, YOU WANTED ME PUT AWAY,

SO YOU COULD CLAIM EVERYTHING AND HAVE YOUR OWN WAY WITH MY DAY,

THE ONLY PLACE I WANT TO BE, IS WHEN JESUS COMES FOR ME,

THEN I WON'T BE IN A REST HOME, I WILL BE IN MY BEST HOME,

RESTING WITH THE KING, I WON'T HAVE TO WORRY ABOUT PEOPLE OR ANYTHING,

IT IS IN MY FATHERS WILL, THAT IN THIS LIFE HE GIVES ME TO BE FULFILLED,

ROYAL BLUE

ROYALTY COMMANDS ATTENTION AND RESPECT, IT IS NOT A GAME TO PLAY WITH OR SOME FARFETCHED PROJECT,

SOME THINGS CAN BE REPRESENTED IN COLOR AND STYLE, SOME THINGS WE ONLY REMEMBER AS A CHILD,

I BELIEVE SOME ANSWERS HARBOR UNSEEN INTENTS, WE MUST FIND FOR WHOM THEY ARE SENT AND MEANT,

I KNOW JESUS IS ROYAL, I ASSOCIATE HIM WITH ROYAL BLUE, IF I NEED AN ANSWER, I SAY TO MY SELF, WHAT WOULD JESUS DO,

JESUS HAS BEEN MY INSPIRATION FOR ALL MY DAYS, ON THIS EARTH, HE IS MY EVERYTHING FROM MY GOD GIVEN SEED TO MY BIRTH,

WE ALL KNOW ALL CHRIST'S WORDS ARE WRITTEN IN RED, THAT'S TO SIGNIFY HIS BLOOD AND HIS ROYAL POSITION AS GODHEAD,

IN TODAY'S CHANGING TIMES, WE FIND INSURMMOUNTABLE ODDS AND UNHOLY LINES,

WITH PASSION AND GRACE, I SEEK TO RUN IN THIS HUMAN RACE OF MINE,

JUST WHEN I THOUGHT THINGS COULD GET NO BETTER, THEY COME UP WITH A BIBLE WITH BLUE LETTERS,

I KNOW JESUS IS ROYAL, I ASSOCIATE HIM WITH ROYAL BLUE, WHEN I NEED SOME ANSWERS I SAY WHAT WOULD JESUS DO,

THE LETTERS ARE NOW IN BLOOD RED AND ROYAL BLUE, WE CAN ALL READ WHAT WOULD JESUS DO,

SATAN CANNOT HAVE YOU!

FOR EVERY BLOOD WASHED AND SPIRIT FILLED, CHILD OF GOD'S,

SATAN ALREADY KNOWS THE TASK IS, ETERNALLY HARD,

GOD NEVER GAVE SATAN CHARGE OVER A SAINT, HIS SON'S, AND DAUGHTERS, NOT EVEN THOSE THAT FAINT,

SATAN KNOWS HE MUST GET PERMISSION, HE IS NOT THE PROGENITOR OF GOD'S MISSION,

HE IS JUST USED AS A THORN IN THE SIDES, OF THOSE THAT GOD HAS PURPOSED TO ABIDE,

GOD HAS SET YOU ASIDE, NO NEED FOR YOU TO EVEN DECIDE,

GOD HAS NEVER FAILED YOU YET, HE USES SATAN WHEN YOU NEED TO BE BUFFETED,

SATAN CANNOT HAVE YOU, SATAN CAN NEVER DO WHAT GOD CAN DO,

THE PLAN WAS FOR A HOLY GOD TO REDEEM YOU, NOT SOME IGNOBLE ENTITY TO DECEIVE YOU AND SUE YOU,

SATAN KNOWS HE CANNOT HAVE YOU, HE CAN NEVER DO WHAT GOD CAN DO,

GOD HAS CREATED A PURE AND HOLY LINE, FOR HIS PEOPLE TO BECOME ONE OF A KIND,

GOD KNEW EVERYTING WE NEEDED, WITH THIS HOLY LINE WE HAD TO BE RESEEDED,

WITH GOD IS WHERE WE WILL BE, HIS BLOOD HAS GIVEN US IMMORTALITY,

WE ARE HEIR'S OF GOD'S IMMORTAL BLOOD LINE, IN HIM WE EXIST, LIVE AND ARE GENUINE,

SHUTTING OUT

GOD HAS SET WATCHES AT EVERY GATE, HE HAS SOLDIERS AND WARRIORS THAT ARE GREAT,

IN GOD'S HOUSE IT IS THE HOUSE OF PRAYER, NOTHING EVIL SHOULD WANT TO BE THERE,

IF WE FIND EVIL THERE TRYING TO MAKE US DOUBT, IMMEDIATELY WE START THE PROCESS TO SHUT EVIL AND HATRED OUT,

GOD HAS WARNED US OF THE TATICS OF THE EVIL ONES, THEY STEAL YOUR MIND AND DARKEN YOUR SUN,

HATRED HINDERS GOD'S PLANS FOR HIS KINGDOM AND THIS UNIVERSE,

THE BIBLE TELLS YOU ABOUT GOD'S LOVE IN EVERY VERSE,

IF WE FIND EVIL IN OUR MIDST TRYING TO MAKE US DOUBT, IMMEDIATELY WE START THE PROCESS TO SHUT EVIL AND HATRED OUT,

GOD SAID MY HOUSE WILL BE CALLED THE HOUSE OF PRAYER, EVERY BLOOD WASHED CHRISTIAN SHOULD BE THERE,

DON'T LET THE OPPOSERS MAKE YOU DOUBT, KEEP YOUR PLACE IN GOD, HE WON'T SHUT YOU OUT,

STAR CROSSED

WHEN YOUR LIFE HAS BEEN TURNED UPSIDE DOWN, AND YOU DON'T KNOW WHY, THE ANSWER MAY BE TO LOOK TO THE SKY,

IT IS IMPORTANT THE DAY YOU WERE BORN, THERE ARE SOME THINGS TRYING TO KEEP YOU FROM WHAT IS NOT THE NORM,

WE CAN LOOK AT OUR LIVES AND SEE WHAT IS EVIDENT, DON'T BE SURPRISED IF YOU SEE OTHERS EVIL INTENTS,

IN YOUR LIFE YOU WERE MEANT TO BE BOSS, EVILNESS WANTED YOU TO BE STAR CROSSED,

WHEN GOD BLESSES US BEYOND MEASURE, THERE IS ALWAYS EVIL SEEKING YOU OUT FOR YOUR TREASURE,

SOME PEOPLE ARE RESTLESS, WHAT THEY STEAL, THEY KEEP, THAT IS THE ONLY WAY THEY FIND ANY SLEEP,

IN DAY LIGHT HOURS ,THEY STILL WALK IN THE DARK, THEY AIM AT THE SIMPLE AND INNOCENT, AND LEAVE THEIR MARK,

THEY ENTER YOUR HOUSE AFTER DARK SEEKING TO STEAL, ROB, REMOVE, DESTROY AND EVEN KILL,

THAT IS WHO THEY ARE, NOT A SUBSTANCE FOR GOOD, THEY ARE HERE TO DESTROY ,LIFE AND MARK YOUR BROTHERHOOD,

IN YOUR LIFE GOD MADE YOU THE BOSS, EVIL WAS, JEALOUS, HATEFUL, AND ENVYIOUS AND WANTED YOU STAR CROSSED,

SUBCONSCIOUS EVILS
AND LIMBIC LIES

DIMENSIONS EXIST WITHIN US ALL, RECORDING FROM THE VERY FIRST MAN, TO MAN VERY FIRST FALL,

WHERE YOU HAVE BEEN IN YOUR LIFE WILL SHOW, GO FAR ENOUGH AND WHO YOU ARE YOU WILL KNOW,

SOMETHINGS HIDE IN YOUR LIFE AND MIND, SOMETHINGS ARE BENEATH YOUR THRESHOLD CONTAINED IN IN YOUR LIMBIC TIME/MIND,

THE SUBCONSCIOUS MIND IS YOUR LIMBIC SOURCE, MAKES UNCONSCIOUS IMPRESSIONS,

THAT FILTER THROUGH YOUR BODY AS ANATOMICAL LESSONS

YOUR BODY AND SENSES TO FOLLOW YOUR MIND AS IT GIVES DIRECTIONS,

OUR MIND GIVES US ANATOMICAL LESSONS,

YOU MUST KNOW WHO IS CONTROLLING YOUR MOODS, AND IF EVIL IS THE REASON FOR ALL YOUR HATEFULNESS AND ATTITUDES,

BEYOND YOUR NATRUAL MIND IS YOUR, SUBCONSCIOUS MINDS EYE,

WE ARE SUSCEPRRABLE TO HYPNOTIC CUES AND LIMBIC LIES,

THAT HAS INFILTRATED YOUR MENTAL STATE, SEEKING TO CAUSE YOU A DISASTERIOUS FATE,

GOD GAVE YOU THESE MENTAL TOOLS, TO USE AND NOT TO BE ANY BODIES FOOL,

TO LIFT ENHANCE AND GROW YOUR STATE, AND IN HIS IMAGE BECOME SOMETHING OR SOMEONE GREAT,

SO DON'T LISTEN TO EVIL, HATRED OR LIMBIC LIES, THAT PENETRATRATE THROUGH YOUR CONSCIOUS MIND,

REPLACE EVIL AND HATEFUL THOUGHTS WITH EASE, AND KNOW THAT GOD HAS GIVEN YOU THE POWER TO CHANGE THESE,

JESUS SAID, ...SUFFER NOT THE LITTLE CHILDREN TO COME UNTO ME

SUNDIAL

LIFE LIKE ROADS HAVE DIRECTIONS, SOME TIMES YOU MAY NEED A RIDE AND A LITTLE PROTECTION,

MOST MAPS ARE DIRECT AND ACCURATE GUIDES, WHICH WAY TO GO YOU WILL HAVE TO DECIDE,

GOD GAVE US WISDOM TO USE THE SUN DIAL, IT IS AN ASTRONOMICAL DEVICE THAT CAN CAST SHADOWS FOR MILES,

IN THE MATHEMATICAL WORLD THEY USE GNOMIC PROJECTIONS, SOMETIME THIS HELPS THEM TO MAKE AND CAST GEOMETRICAL PERFECTIONS,

A SUNDIAL IS AS OLD AS YOU AND ME, IT TELLS TIME BY THE SHADOWS YOU SEE,

WE THINK WE LIVE OUT VERY LONG LIFE TIMES, TO GOD IT IS ONLY A SHADOW OF TIME,

THE UNIVERSE IS FULL OF WINDOWS AND DOORS, WE LIVE LIFE SOMETIME IT'S JUST LIKE A VAPOUR,

WHAT I REMEMBER ABOUT SUNDIALS, ARE THAT THEY ARE POINTERS, THAT POINT THE WAY TO SUNDOWN,

NO MATTER WHERE IT IS YOU GO, JUST REMEMBER THAT THE SHADOW ALWAYS KNOWS,

A SUNDIAL IS USED TO POINT THE WAY, NOT VERY MANY PEOPLE USE SUNDIALS TODAY,

THE ONLY TIME YOU COME AROUND ME

YOU MADE ME THINK YOU CARED FOR ME, I FOUND OUT YOU ONLY WANTED TO STEAL MY KEYS,

EVERY TIME YOU CAME AROUND, THERE WAS SOMETHING YOU TOOK OR YOU SAID YOU FOUND,

THE ONLY TIME YOU COME AROUND ME, IS WHEN YOU NEED SOMETHING NEW OR WANTED A NEW KEY,

WHEN YOUR ANATOMY, MONEY OR FUNDS GOT LOW, I AM THE BANK WHERE YOU GOT YOUR CASH FLOW,

IT DIDN'T MATTER TO YOU WHAT THE GRADE, YOU JUST WANTED SOMETHING VALUABLE, EVEN IF IT WAS TAKEN OUT AS TRADE,

NOW THAT I AM LOOKING AT THE REAL YOU, I MUST BE TRUE TO MYSELF, I BELIEVE WE ARE DEFINITELY THROUGH,

WHEN YOU CAN FIND IT IN YOUR HEART, THAT WE CAN MAKE A BETTER START,

SOME THINGS TO A REAL FRIEND YOU SHOULD NOT DO, DON'T JEOPARDIZE LIES IN PLACE OF THE TRUTH,

YOU HAD SO MUCH MORE UNDERSTANDING ON HOW TO APPREHEND, HOW TO GET WHAT YOU NEEDED FROM AN UNSUSPECTING FRIEND,

RIGHT NOW I HAVE YOU TO THANK, I FOUND OUT I AM RICHER THAN I KNEW, I HAVE A PHYSICAL AND A SPIRITUAL BANK,

THAT GOD SUPPLIED ME WITH FOR MY USE, NOT FOR GREEDY THIEVES TO USE AND ABUSE,

THE ONLY TIME YOU COME AROUND ME, IS WHEN

YOU NEED SOMETHING NEW, OR YOU NEEDED A NEW KEY,

YOU NEVER CHECK TO SEE IF I WAS ALRIGHT, YOUR ONLY CONCERN WAS IF MY MONEY OR SUPPLIES WERE RIGHT,

STOP USING MY SUBSTANCE AND MY GRADE, FOR YOU NONE OF MY PARTS WERE MADE,

I KNOW YOUR EVERY PLACE AND YOUR EVERY MOVE, SO HOW CAN YOU AVOID HAVING TO LOSE,

THE ONLY TIME YOU CAME AROUND ME, WAS WHEN YOU NEEDED A SOMETHING NEW OR YOU WANTED A NEW KEY,

TEARS FOR NOTRE DAME

I CAN NOT EXPRESS MY DEEP SEATED GRIEF, WHEN BEAUTY HAS BEEN DESTROYED THERE IS NO RELIEF,

I MUST LEARN TO STAND FIRM AND BEAR IT, I KNOW IN THE END MY GOD WILL BE THE ONE TO DECLARE IT,

IT IS HIS FOUNDATIONS THAT ARE AT STAKE, NO MAN OR ANGEL OTHERS SHOULD TRY TO REMAKE,

EVERYTHING BELONGS TO HIM, HE CREATED EVERY SINGLE WAY,

HE IS GOD OF ALL LIFE, AND CREATOR OF EVERY SUN RISEN DAY,

MY PETITION TO GOD TODAY IS FOR NOTRE DAME, A BEAUTIFUL CREATION BUILT TO EXEMPLIFY WHY JESUS CAME,

A HOUSE OF WORSHIP FOR ALL THOSE WHO BELIEVE, A PLACE WHERE THE SPIRITUAL COULD GO RECEIVE,

PROTECTED BY THE SAINTS AND WARRIORS OF OLD, EACH ONE OF THEM A HAGIOGRAPHIC STORY HAS BEEN TOLD,

SAINTS AND ANGELS NEW AND OLD WE CAN FIND IN THEIR STORY UNFOLDS,

THE GREATEST ONE OF ALL IS JESUS CHRIST, HIS HISTORY INCLUDES ALL SAINTS AND ANGELS LIFES,

MY PETITION TO GOD TODAY IS FOR NOTRE DAME,

A BEAUTIFUL CREATION TO EXEMPLIFY WHY JESUS CAME,

THIS FORM I AM

God wrought me and made me his child, I was pure, clean, and undefiled,

God put inside of me in his Holy Word, and his divinity, So that Angels, could visit and enter into me,

One day I was accosted by hoards of demons, and people, with evil intents, who they were I cannot tell,

They forced me to succumb and took away my veil,

They stole God's Holy Word, and tore me and my son's heart apart into several pieces, They did not stop it seems their evil never ceases,

They forced us to do, wickedness that is against our grain, for all their evils we were the ones Godly ashamed,

This form I am I loath and detest, How do you love what is no longer God's best,

I cannot say and I cannot tell, what now has replaced my veil, I do know what was once Godly adorned, Is now a very different form,

Oh father, father, this form I am, couldn't be anything less than demonically dammed,

What was once your greatest, has now become their least, they were preparing me to be a wife for a hideous beast,

Lord I am fighting to keep my one scintilla of the great I am,
Praying that one day it will lead me and back home as God's
blessed LAMB,

THREE ASPECTS OF ME

I AM WONDEROUSLY MADE, I AM NOT JUST AN
ORDINARY GRADE,

THE MATERIAL GOD GAVE ME, WAS DIVINLY

INCORPORATED INTO THREE,

THE FIRST PART IS CALLED THE EGO, IT IS A FORCE WE ALL
NEED TO KNLOW,

SECOND IS THE ALTER EGO, IT IS IN OPPSITION, TO THE
FIRST EGO,

THE THIRD IS THE LIBIDO, THE ULTIMATE MOST
PLEASURABLE FORCE OF ALL THREE, THIS COMPLETES THE
THREE ASPECTS OF ME,

EACH PART IS DIMENSJONAL INSIDE, IT IS A
RECOGNIZABLE ASPECT WE CAN'T HIDE,

IT IS THE EXPRESSION OF YOU AND ME, EACH PART
DEVELOPES INTO A WHOLE PERSONALITY,

I KNOW I AM IN THE IMAGE OF GOD, AND HIS
SOVEREGINITY,

HE HAS GIVEN TO YOU AND ME SACRED ABILITY, IN A
DIVINE FORM CALLED TRINITY,

THERE ARE THREE ASPECTS OF ME, EACH ONE A WEALTH
OF INFORNATION, ABOUT MY INSPIRED TRINITY,

YOU MUST FIRST KNOW WHO YOU ARE, THEN YOU CAN ADDRESS AND MEASURE EACH DIMENSION ACCORDING TO YOUR PERSONALITY BAR,

GOD DESIGNED VIRTUES, FAITH, HOPE, AND CHARITY,

EGO, ALTER EGO, LIBIDO, HE DESIGNED AS THREE ASPECTS OF ME

TODAY

WE ARE LIVING IN TIMES AND PLACES, WHERE THE ONLY PEACE YOU WILL FIND IS WHAT GOD GRACES,

PEOPLE ARE VERY INDIFFERENT TO GOD'S RULES,

THEY MURDER AND KILL HUMAN LIFE TO USE AS HUMAN TOOLS,

DON'T PUT IT OFF YOU NEED GOD TODAY, UNLESS YOU WANT TO BE PART OF AN EVIL DAY,

GOD NEVER INTENDED FOR HIS CHILDREN TO BE LEAST, HE CREATED THAT SPACE FOR ALL OF SATANS BEAST,

GOD'S CHILDREN ARE THE HEAD NOT THE TAIL, CREATED TO PERFECT A SYSTEM, THAT SHALL NOT FAIL,

ONE GLIMSP OF OUR LIGHT AND YOU CAN TELL, WE ARE NOT SATANS PROPERTY, WE ARE NOT PRODUCTS OF HELL,

DON'T PUT IT OFF YOU NEED GOD TODAY, UNLESS YOU WANT TO BE PART OF AN EVIL DAY,

WE BELONG TO GOD, AND WE ARE VERY PROUD, WE CAN STAND ON ANY MOUNTAIN AND SING IT ALOUD,

WE KNOW THE TRUTH AND GOD'S INTENT, WE KNOW WHY THE HOLY SPIRIT WAS SENT,

WE ARE THE REDEEMED, THE RESURRECTED HOLY SEED,

HERE TO MAKE SURE GOD'S HOLINESS IS WHAT WE BREED,

GODLY CHARACTERS AND ATTRIBUTES FROM GOD WE INHERIT AND ENGENDER,

FROM THE BOTTOM OF OUR FEET, TO THE TOP OF OUR HEADS WE SUPPLY EVERY MEMBER,

DON'T PUT IT OFF YOU NEED GOD TODAY, UNLESS YOU WANT TO BE PART OF AN EVIL DAY,

TOMMORROW

THERE IS NO TIME LIMIT TO WHAT GOD WILL DO, HE IS THE MEASURE OF TIME THAT WE ALL MUST USE,

WITHOUT GOD WE WOULD NOT HAVE OUR BEING, ROYALTY WOULD HAVE NO QUEEN OR KING,

NO MATTER WHO YOU ARE, GOD MUST BE KNOWN, HE IS THE CREATER OF EVERY SINGLE TIME ZONE,

GOD REQUIRES ALL OUR PAST, TO CREATE FOR US A FUTURE THAT WILL LAST,

LIFE IS A GIFT FROM GOD CALLED THE PRESENT, WE MUST LIVE IT WITH TRUTH AND GODLY INTENT,

THE FUTURE IS WHAT IS GOING TO BE, GOD HAS TAKEN THE PAST AND PRESENT AND IS CONSTRUCTING MY DESTINY,

GIVE GOD YOUR HEART MIND BODY AND SOUL, HE DESERVES IT HE KEEPS YOUR ANATOMY WHOLE,

DON'T SAY I WILL SERVE HIM TOMORROW, YOU WON'T HAVE ONE IF HIM YOU DON'T FOLLOW,

DON'T LIVE YOUR LIFE LIKE A YESTERDAY, WHEN THE DAY IS OVER THEY THROW IT AWAY,

I HAVE SEEN MANY PEOPLE LIVING IN SORROW, THEY THREW AWAY WHAT THEY SHOULD HAVE KEPT FOR THEIR TOMMOROW,

VICTORY IN ME

LORD LET ME NEVER FORGET, HOW YOU SAVED ME AND THAT YOU PAID FOR ME,

YOU SHED YOUR PRECIOUS BLOOD FOR ME, SO I COULD HAVE A VICTORY,

WHATEVER MY DECISION IN LIFE OR WHATEVER MY GRADE, MY RIGHT TO THE TREE OF LIFE HAS BEEN PAID,

I PAY NO ATTENTION, TO WHAT EVIL HAS MADE, THEY WILL NEVER MAKE A BETTER GRADE,

THEY MOLDED AND CRAFTED DECEITFUL LIES, THEY STILL ARE NOT ENDURING, AND THEY HAVE TO EVENTULLY DIE,

THE DIVINE TRUTH I HAVE TO FIND AND SEE, IS THAT VICTORY CAME IN WHEN YOU DIED FOR ME,

I SHOULD BE LIVING A BETTER LIFE, ONE THAT IS NOT FILLED WITH EVIL AND WITH STRIFE,

YOUR DEATH MADE THE DIFFERENCE, IT CONNECTED ME TO THE EVERLASTING COVENANT,

I SHOULD BE TELLING THIS WHOLE WORLD THE VICTORY IS IN ME, CHRIST PAID THE PRICE THAT I MIGHT BE FREED,

JUST REMEMBER WHEN, YOUR LIFE SEEMS INVERTED, THAT THROUGH CHRIST BLOOD YOU ARE CONVERTED,

THAT YOU HAVE BEEN SET FREE, YOUR NEW PLACE IN CHRIST IS NOW CALLED VICTORY,

WAR

WAR IS AN EXPRESSION OF MAN'S INHUMANITY TO MAN,

THAT DESTRUCTIVE EXPRESSION WAS NEVER IN GOD'S PLAN,

GOD GAVE US LIFE AS A PRECIOUS PRIZE, WE CONTINUED TO DESTROY, ENSLAVE, AND VICTIMIZE,

LIFE HAS BECOME COMMON PLACE TO US AND HAS NO DIVINE VALUE,

WE HAVE ALLOWED GOD'S PRECIOUS GIFT OF LIFE TO DEVALUE,

WE ARE THE LOSERS IN THIS WAR, GOD HAS NOTING TO LOSE IN HUMAN WARS

WHEN WILL WE LEARN THAT NO-ONE WINS, WHEN WE OUR DEFIE GOD,

HE MADE US IN HIS IMAGE, HE WILL ALWAYS BE LORD,

WHAT HAPPENED TO THE LOVE GOD PLACED IN SIDE OF YOU,

IT'S THE SAME LOVE INSIDE OF HIM, HE ENGENDERED TO CREATE YOU ANEW,

WITH HIS LOVE IN YOU SHOULD BE HELPING YOUR BROTHERS, YOUR SISTERS, YOUR MOTHERS AND OTHERS,

LOVE IS THE ULTIMATE UNIVERSAL POSITIVE EXPRESSION, REAL LOVE CAN MAKE WAR A PASSING IMPRESSION,

BEFORE MY LIFE IS OVER, BEFORE HUMANITY IS THROUGH,

I WILL STAND AND TELL THE WORLD, HOW MUCH MY GOD AND I LOVED YOU,

WEARING MY
OWN CLOTHES

EVERYDAY GOD DRESSES AND FEEDS THE FOWLS IN THE AIR,

JUST SHOW THEM AND THE WORLD IT IS HE THAT IS THE KEEPER AND REALLY CARES,

HE DOES THE SAME THING FOR ME AND FOR YOU, HE DRESSES US AND FEEDS US TOO,

OUR LIFE AND TIME IT IS A MEASURED REWARD, GOD BLESSED US WITH THAT NO MONEY COULD AFFORD,

EVERY ORGAN IN YOUR BLOOD FED SYSTEM, HAS BEEN GOD DESIGNED AND ORDERED BY HIM,

WHEN GOD DRESSES YOU EVERYBODY KNOWS, HE IS THE ONLY ONE THAT CAN PUT YOU INTO HEAVENLY CLOTHES,

YOU CAN HAVE A BIT OF HEAVEN RIGHT HERE ON EARTH, WHEN GOD DRESSES YOU FOR A HEAVENLY BIRTH,

EVERYDAY I AM WEARING MY CLOTHES, WITH A STAMP OF APPROVAL FROM HEAVEN, THEY WERE GODLY SOWN,

NOW I KNOW WHY BIRDS GATHER EVERY TIME I AM NEAR, THEY WERE SEEDED BY THE SAME GOD, AND HAVE THE SAME GODLY FEAR,

EVERYDAY I AM WEARING MY CLOTHES, WITH A STAMP OF APPROVAL FROM HEAVEN, THEY WERE GODLY SOWN,

EVERY ORGAN HAS BEEN METICULOUSLY GROWN, GOD ORDAINED AND HEAVENLY SOWN,

THIS PHYSICAL BODY WAS REARRANGED TO MAKE ROOM FOR WHATEVER GOD WOULD CHANGED,

BUILT WITH A LOVE THAT WILL NEVER TIRE, ENDLESS JOY AND FULL OF DIVINE FIRE,

GIVE GOD YOUR LIFE AND LET HIM DRESS YOU UP, HE CAN SATISFY YOU DESIRES AND FILL YOUR CUP,

WHERE YOU WILL NEVER AGAIN THIRST, HE IS YOUR LAST AND HE IS YOUR FIRST,

FOR ALL THINGS TO MANIFEST THEMSELVES HE PERSISTED,

TO COME INTO THE WORLD WHERE HE EXISTED,

HE HAS PLANTED AND WATERED EVERY ROOT,

TO BEAR AND BRING HIM FORTH GODLY FRUIT,

I KNOW THAT I AM GOD'S CHILD, MY BODY WAS NEVER MEANT TO BE DEFILED,

IT WAS DESIGNED TO ONE FULFILL ITS REST, AND TO GATHER WITH ALL THOSE WHO ARE ETERNALLY BLESSED,

WHY!

I DON'T HAVE ANSWERS TO ALL OF THE LIFE'S QUESTIONS, NOR HAVE I LEARNED THE CONSEQUENCES OF ALL OF LIFE'S LESSONS,

I HAVE A FEW PERSONAL HEARTFELT EXPERIENCES, THAT WILL ALWAYS COME TO MY MIND AS REMINSCES,

I FIND MYSELF ASKING THE QUESTION, LORD WHY, DO THEY MURDER AND KILL PEOPLE THAT DON'T HAVE TO DIE,

YOU GAVE TO US ALL A MEASURE OF LIFE, YOU PUT INSIDE OF US SEED THAT COULD PERFECT YOUR LIGHT,

A LIGHT THAT ONLY YOU COULD DISTINGUISH, THAT HATE, EVILNESS AND JEASLOUSY WANTED TO EXTINGUISH,

I FIND MYSELF ASKING THE QUESTION, LORD WHY,

DO THEY KILL AND MURDER PEOPLE, THAT SHOULDN'T HAVE TO DIE,

I THEN REMEMBER THAT THIS WHOLE WORLD IS NOT LIKE YOU, SOME PEOPLE CHOOSE TO LET SATAN COME THROUGH,

THERE ARE THOSE THAT CHOOSE DEATH, IN MY OBSERVATIONS LIFE AND DEATH, THESE TWO ENTITIES HAVE NEVER MET,

IF AND WHEN THEY EVER DO LET'S GET THIS STRAIGHT,

THERE IS ONLY ONE OF THEM THAT IS TRULY GREAT,

DARKNESS DOES NOT EXTINGUISH LIGHT, A LITTLE BIT OF LIGHT CAN PASS THROUGH THE NIGHT,

LIGHT EXTINGUISHES DARKNESS, AND PASSES RIGHT ON THROUGH,

GOD MADE EVERYTHING THAT IS WHAT LIGHT WAS CREATED TO DO,

TO REVEL THE REAL AND HIDDEN PURPOSES, THAT EVIL WANTS TO HIDE,

IF IT WAS LEFT TO SATAN, THE WHOLE WORLD WOULD BE DENIED,

ALL OF THE INNOCENT LIVES AND STOLEN HISTORIES THAT WAS MADE,

THEY USED THEIR HOUSES, THEIR SOULS EVEN THEIR GRAVES,

SATAN MAY NOT ADMIT IT ONE THING THAT I KNOW IS TRUE,

HE WAS AND IS STILL, A SERVANT OF MY GOD TOO,

YOU DON'T HAVE TO MOVE

IN LIFE YOU WILL FIND SOME THINGS TRYING TO TAKE YOUR PLACE,

THOSE THINGS ARE OUTSIDE OF GOD'S LOVE AND AMAZING GRACE,

THEY WERE NOT CREATED LIKE YOU AND LIKE AND ME,

STRAIGHT FROM THE PITS OF HELL, AN EVIL SEED,

GOD PLACED YOU IN A CONFORTING SPACE,

HELL WANTED YOU TO BE ERASED,

THEY WANTED TO STEAL AND SLEEP IN YOUR BED,

THEY WANTED TO CHANGED YOUR VERY ESSENCE, FROM YOUR FEET TO YOUR HEAD,

IN SPITE OF IT ALL, JUST KNOW, YOU DON'T HAVE TO MOVE, WITHIN THERE OWN TRANSGRESSIONS THEY WILL HAVE TO LOSE,

IN THE HANDS OF THE CHOSEN GRACE ABOUNDS, BUT IN THE HANDS OF EVIL GRACE WILL FROWN,

IN THE SPHERE OF THE RIGHTEOUS GRACE SMELLS LIKE A ROSE,

IN THE ENVIRONMENT OF EVIL THE SMELL IS REPUGNANT TO THE NOSE,

TO THE LIPS OF THE JUST GOD'S WORDS ARE SWEET AS HONEY,

BUT TO THE EVIL GOD'S WORDS ARE FOR SALE AND EQUATED WITH MONEY,

IN SPITE OF IT ALL JUST KNOW YOU DON'T HAVE TO MOVE, THROUGH THERE EVIL TRANSGRESSIONS THEY WILL HAVE TO LOSE,

YOU WANTED MY WOMB

GOD DID NOT DESIGN ME FOR YOUR USE, FOR YOUR MONSTROSITIES TO BE SPAWNED, OR YOUR SATANIC ABUSE,

GOD MADE ME FOR THE GOOD OF MANKIND, TO LIFT TO PUSH THE RIGHTEOUSNESS OF CHRIST LIKE MIND,

GOD USED MY WOMB TO SEED THE WORLD, THAT WAS SOWN IN ME AS A LITTLE GIRL,

EVIL WANTS TO POSSES AND USE MY WOMB, AS A PRISON AND AS A SATANIC TOMB,

GOD WANTS TO USE MY WOMB TO BLESS OTHERS, COVER NOURISH AND HIDE MY SISTER'S AND BROTHERS,

I KNOW FOR A FACT YOU WANTED MY WOMB, TO SPAWN YOUR DEVILS AND EVILS AND CAUSE EARTHLY DOOM,

I PRAY THAT GOD WILL ALWAYS INTERCEDE, WHERE I AM CONCERNED, TO GIVE ME WHAT I NEED,

I PRAY THAT YOUR EVILS, GO AWAY AND THAT GOODNESS, DISSIPATES ALL THE EVIL DAYS, GOD IS MY KEEPER AND YOU CANNOT MY WOMB, IT IS RESERVED FOR EVERY ANGEL TO ONE DAY BE RESUMED,

SATAN YOU CANNOT HAVE MY WOMB, IT IS RESERVED AS A SACRED PLACE HIS SON'S SPIRITUAL ROOM

MY SHIELD

MANY TIMES IN LIFE I DID NOT TRUST YOU LORD, I HAD TO FIND OUT FOR MYSELF TRUSTING AND LOVING YOU IS NOT HARD,

NOW THAT I KNOW ITS REALLY NOT THAT HARD, I'M LEARNING TO TRUST, LOVE, AND DEPEND ONLY ON YOU MY LORD,

I DON'T NEED TO WEAR A MASK OR BUILD A FAÇADE, I JUST NEED TO LET GO, AND LET GOD BE GOD,

I FEEL SAFE NOW MORE THAN I EVER, I WILL KEEP MY FAITH AND PRAYERS, AND LEAVE YOU NEVER,

I FOUND OUT WITHOUT YOU LORD, I HAVE NO SHIELD, I HAVE NO SWORD, I HAVE NO WORD AND I HAVE NO WILL,

YOU HAVE BEEN AND WILL ALWAYS BE MY GUIDING LIGHT, YOU ARE THE SACRED AND HOLY VISION IN MY DIVINE SIGHT,

I AM SEEKING TO REACH THAT BLESSED PLACE CULTIVATED WITHIN,

A PLACE WHERE ONLY GOD AND HEAVEN DWELLS AND CAST OUT ALL EVIL AND SIN,

KEEP ME LORD IN YOUR PERFECT PEACE, AND WRAP ME IN YOUR HOLY LOVE, LET ME ALWAYS REMEMBER TO THINK OF HOLY THAT ARE THINGS UP ABOVE,

I FOUND OUT WITHOUT YOU LORD, I HAVE NO SHIELD, I HAVE NO SWORD, I HAVE NO WORD AND I HAVE NO WILL,

WHAT WOULD THE UNIVERSE BE WITHOUT JUST ONE WORD, IT COULD NOT EXIST, IT WOULD BE LIKE FABLES UNTOLD, OR A UNMANIFIESTED MYTH,

WORDS ARE OUR DISCIPLINED AND SPOKEN WILL, THE UNMANIFEST COMING FROM INSIDE TO BECOME WHATS REAL,

LORD HELP US TO REALIZE YOUR TRUTHS AND YOUR MAJESTY, HOW WHAT WE SAY OUT OF MOUTHS IN THE ATMOSPHERE IS A KEY,

THOSE SAME WORDS WILL ONE DAY BE JUDGED ONLY BY YOU,

ONLY YOUR WORDS WILL BE WHAT WILL LAST, AND GET US THROUGH,

I FOUND OUT WITHOUT YOU LORD, I HAVE NO SHIELD, I HAVE NO SWORD, I HAVE NO WORD AND I HAVE NO WILL,

SEPARATED FROM SIN

GOD MADE A PROMISE TO ALL HIS SAINTS, HE EVEN MADE A STATEMENT TO ALL THOSE WHO FAINT,

THOSE NOT KNOWING THE WORD OR THE PATH, IN CHRIST YOU DON'T HAVE TO BE LAST,

KEEP CHRIST ON YOUR HEART AND MIND, FORGET ABOUT THE EVILS INTERRUPTING YOU TIMES,

ALWAYS REMEMBER GOD SEPERATED YOU FROM SIN, SO THAT OVER ALL EVIL YOU COULD WIN,

EVIL MAY BE IN A VERY HIGH PLACE, BUT THAT SHOULD NEVER STOP YOU FROM RUNNING GOD'S RACE,

GOD IS DOING WHAT HE DOES BEST, PUTTING ALL SATANS TRICKS AND MIND CONTROLS TO THE TEST,

SATAN HAS A HOLD ON A KINGDOM OF PEOPLE THROUGH FLESHLY LUST,

GOD HAS A REALM OF SPIRIT FILLED ANGELS WHO ARE HOLY AND JUST,

KEEP CHRIST ON YOUR HEART AND MIND, FORGET ABOUT THE EVILS INTERRUPTING YOU TIMES,

ALWAYS REMEMBER GOD SEPERATED YOU FROM SIN, SO THAT OVER ALL EVIL YOU COULD WIN,

EVEN THE PERSON, IN HEAVEN THAT IS LAST MAY BE LEAST, THEY WILL STILL BE A PART OF GOD'S HEAVENLY FEAST,

GOD THE FATHER IS EVERYTHING ABOVE, ONE ATTRIBUTE THE DEVIL CANNOT IMITATE OF HIS IS AGAPE LOVE,

A BOOK FOR EVERY YEAR

THANK YOU, LORD, FOR YOUR FAVOR AND GRACE, THANK YOU, LORD, FOR KEEPING MY PLACE,

WE ARE ALL UNDER YOUR SOVERIGNE CONTROL, WE ARE ALL MADE FROM THE DUST AS ONE CAST AND ONE MOLD,

I HAVE BEEN GRATEFULLY UNDER YOUR CARE, WHEN UNWARRENTED EVILS CAME YOU WERE ALWAYS THERE,

I AM MUCH OLDER NOW, I CAN CARRY ALL YOUR BOOKS WITHOUT FEAR, YOU GAVE ME EXTENDED TIME IN LIFE, NOW I CAN ENCOMPASS 66 BOOKS, FOR EVERY SINGLE YEAR,

NO MATTER WHAT THIS WORLD SAYS AND DOES, THEY WILL NOT COMPLETELY CHANGE ALL THE PAST AS IT WAS,

THERE ARE ATTRIBUTES ABOUT WHAT YOU CREATE, THAT ARE FAR BEYOND WHAT HUMANS CAN ANTICIPATE,

MAN WAS NOT CREATED TO ALTER OR CHANGE, DIVINITY'S CREATIONS, FORMATIONS, OR TO REARRANGE,

BUT IF THEY DO JUST KNOW FOR A FACT, THEY BRING UPON THEMSELVES, FAMINE, DISEASE, AND SPIRITUALS ATTACKS,

LITTLE DO THEY KNOW THAT EACH AND EVERY HOUR, IS PACKED WITH YOUR SPIRITUAL POWER,

IT PAYS TO KNOW WHO YOU ARE WITH, GOD CAUSES AND DIRECTS ALL YOUR BENEFITS,

ONE THING I KNOW FOR SURE AND THAT IS THIS, WITHOUT YOUR SPIRIT I NEVER WOULD HAVE MADE SIXTYSIX,

I AM MUCH OLDER NOW, I CAN CARRY ALL YOUR BOOKS WITHOUT FEAR, YOU GAVE ME EXTENDED TIME IN LIFE, NOW I CAN ENCOMPASS 66 BOOKS, FOR EVERY SINGLE YEAR,

ALL LAND IS GOD'S LANDS

WE LIVE AND BREATHE AND SIN WITHOUT A THOUGHT, OF THE TRUTH, THE FREEDOM, SALVATION, THROUGH SUFFERING THAT CHRIST BOUGHT,

HE DID SOMETHING HE DID NOT HAVE TO DO, THIS LAND IS HIS CREATION, JUST LIKE ME, JUST LIKE YOU,

HOW DO YOU PAY FOR SOMETHING YOU ALREADY OWN, TO A HOLY GOD IT IS A HOLY RITE TO ATONE,

ALL LAND IS GOD'S LANDS, FROM THE BOTTOM OF THE EARTH, TO THE HEAVENLY EXPANSE OF ALL SUPERNAL BIRTHS,

ANGELS ARE NOT BORN LIKE PEOPLE OF THE EARTH, THEY ARE CONSTRUCTED OF ETERNAL SUBSTANCE MORE THAN MATERIAL WORTH,

ANGELS DO NOT ABIDE BY PHYSICAL LAWS, THEY JUST APPEAR IN SPIRIT WITHOUT FLESH WITHOUT FLAWS,

ANGELS TRANSFORM, ASCEND AND UNITE, KEEPING GOD LAWS, OF WHAT IS GOOD, DIVINE AND RIGHT,

THE EARTH, THE SUN, SKY AND THE MOON, ARE ALL KEPT IN A SACRED FREQUENCY AND ATTUNED,

THE EARTH WAS GOD'S TO DEDICATE, BUT IT IS THE ANGELS WHO FECUNDATES,

EVERY SEASON IS A SPECIFIC TIME THAT THE ANGELS, PERFORM WHAT IS GODLY WHAT IS DIVINE,

THERE IS A TIME FOR EVERYTHING UNDER THE SUN, THERE WAS A TIME WHEN ALL LANDS WERE ONE,

GOD DECIDED TO SEPERATE THE LAND, AND CREATE DIFFERENCES IN THE DIALOG OF EVERY MAN,

SO WHEN WE BUY REAL ESTATE IT IS ONLY A TEMPORARY LOAN, FROM A HOLY GOD WHO SITS ON A HOLY THRONE,

SO ABOVE SO BELOW, WHAT IS YOURS IN HEAVEN, HOW WILL YOU KNOW, IF YOU DON'T GO,

DON'T BE FOOLED BY THE DEVILS TRICKS OF HIS TRADE, HE IS ALWAYS LOOKING FOR SOMEONE THAT WILL SELL OUT HE CAN UP-BRAID,

THROUGHT FORNICATION AND LUST HE WILL MOVE YOU TO ANOTHER SIDE, AND NEVER TELL YOU ALL HIS LIES,

WHILE SATAN IS TRANSFERRING CONVERTING THE REAL FORCE, THAT HAS NOTHING TO DO WITH HIM, HE IS NOT THE REAL SOURCE,

SATAN HAS FOOLED MANY PEOPLE USING AND STEALING GOD'S POWERS, THAT GOD INSTITUED TO BE DISSEMINATED EVERY TWELVE HOURS,

ALL LAND IS GOD'S LANDS, FROM THE BOTTOM OF THE EARTH, TO THE HEAVENLY EXPANSE OF ALL SUPERNAL BIRTHS,

ALL GOD'S PROPHETS

REMEMBERING THE MIGHTY DAYS, YOU INSTALLED GODLY MEN, TO LEAD, TO WARN, TO ADMONISH US OF OUR SINS,

EVERY ONE OF YOUR PROPHETS, CAME WITH VEHEMENT MESSAGES, THEY ALL WERE GODLY MESSENGERS, WALKING US AND LEADING US THROUGH BIBLICAL PASSAGES,

SOME CAME WITH GIFTS, AND THEY ALL HAD A CALLING, THEIR MAIN PURPOSE WAS TO KEEP ISRAEL FROM FALLING,

IN EACH PROPHETS BOOK, GOD IS UNLEASHING HIS MIGHTY POWERS, TO CORRECT, WARN, OR RESTORE, HIS PEOPLE EVERYDAY AND EVERY HOUR,

GOD IS BRINGING HIS PEOPLE TO A RIGHT STANDING WITH HIS LAWS, ESPECIALLY HIS COMMANDMENTS SO THAT THERE WILL BE NO FLAWS,

THAT IS WHY HE GAVE US PROPHETS, WHO COULD LEAD THE WAY, THERE ARE 12 MINOR PROPHETS, THERE ARE 12 HOURS IN A DAY,

LORD I THANK YOU, FOR YOUR GOVERNANCE IN THIS MATERIAL WORLD, WHERE THEIR PROFITS ARE FOR PHYSICAL GAIN, BUT YOUR PROPHETS EXHALT YOUR HOLY NAME,

THANK YOU FATHER FOR ALL YOUR PROPHETS, THAT UP HELD THE CROSS, IN TIMES YOUR PEOPLE, ISRAEL, WOULD HAVE BEEN LOST,

LORD IN TIMES LIKE THESE WE DEPEND ON YOUR AWESOME STRENGTH, TO MAKE IT THROUGH THE BATTLES OF THE DAY AND NIGHT YOU ARE OUR DEFENCE,

I REMEMBER LORD, YOUR GREATEST ARMY, IS NO LONGER HERE BUT ARE GONE, BUT WHEN EVER YOU NEED THEM YOU JUST RAISE THE ARE OF ISRAEL, IN THE VALLEY OF DRY BONES,

THESE BONES WILL LIVE AND DO YOUR INFINITE WILL, THE GREATEST ARMY KNOWN TO MAN, IS BURIED BENEATH THE LAND,

THANK YOU LORD FOR ALL YOUR PROPHETS, THAT UP HELD THE CROSS, IN TIMES YOUR PEOPLE ISRAEL, WOULD HAVE BEEN LOST,

BE YE PERFECT AND HOLY

HOW CAN A PERSON BECOME PERFECT WITHOUT ANY MAN MADE FLAWS, IN A WORLD LADEN WITH TEMPORAL LAWS,

HOW CAN A PERSON BECOME HOLY AND PURE, AND HOLD UP THE BANNER OF CHRIST AS HIS FAITH ENDURES,

YOU MUST BELIEVE AND BE WHO GOD MADE YOU, GOD HAS THE EVIDENCE THAT CHRIST WAS FORMED IN YOU,

WHATEVER IT IS YOU WILL NEED, WAS PLANTED IN YOU WITH YOUR GENERTIC SEED,

WHEN CHRIST FILLS YOUR SPIRIT, MIND, BODY AND SOUL, YOU ARE NO LONGER ORDINARY YOU HAVE BECOME SPIRITUALLY WHOLE,

SO WHEN YOU READ THE WORD AND IT SAYS BE YE PERFECT AND HOLY, YOU MUST UNDERSTAND GOD IS LETTING YOU KNOW YOU ARE NOT ORDINARY,

YOU HAVE ALL THE POTENTIALS OF A HOLY GOD'S POWER, HE MADE YOU IN HIS IMAGE AND GAVE YOU AUTHORITY AS HE EMPOWERED,

WE MUST UNDERSTAND WITH GOD ALL THINGS, ARE PERFECTLY MADE, A FLOWER, A TREE, A ROCK, NO MATTER WHAT THE GRADE,

WE MUST BE EXAMPLES FOR THE WORLD TO SEE, THEY MUST UNDERSAND IT IS NO LONGER I, BUT THAT CHRIST LIVES INSIDE OF ME,

SO, WHEN YOU READ THE WORD AND IT SAYS BE YE PERFECT AND HOLY, YOU MUST UNDERSTAND GOD IS LETTING YOU KNOW YOU ARE FAR BEYOND ORDINARY,

EMERGENCY PRAYER

WE MUST ALWAYS PRAY FOR THE EVIL THINGS WE MAY HAVE DONE, IN THIS WORLD THEY CALL FOR 911,

CHRISTIANS MUST CALL ON A HIGHER SOURCE, THAT PERPETUATES EVERYTHING AND IS OUR UNIVERSAL LIFE FORCE,

IT IS DIVINE TO REVERENCE GOD AND PRAY, WHO KNOWS THE LITTLE SINS ONE MIGHT COMMITT IN A DAY,

CHRISTIANS SHOULD ALWAYS HAVE AN EMERGENCY PRAYER, WHENEVER YOU PRAY GOD WILL MEET YOU THERE,

PRAYER IS YOUR KEY TO A SACRED DOOR, TO THE FAITHFUL AND UNSEEN THINGS YOU ARE PRAYING FOR,

JUST KEEP IN MIND WE MUST ALWAYS PRAY, THAT IS THE EPITOME OF EACH AND EVERYDAY,

WHY DO YOU THINK FOR PRAYER GOD HAS SPECIAL HOURS, PRAYER IS GOVERNED BY DIVINE POWERS,

CHRISTIANS SHOULD ALWAYS HAVE AN EMERGENCY PRAYER, WHENEVER YOU PRAY GOD WILL MEET YOU THERE,

NEVER DOUBT WHAT GOD CAN DO, HE IS THE PROVIDER AND PROTECTOR OVER YOU,

WHEN YOU THINK YOU ARE LOST AND THERE IS ONLY DOUBT, PRAYER BECOMES YOUR DOORWAY OUT,

CHRISTIANS SHOULD ALWAYS HAVE AN EMERGENCY PRAYER, WHENEVER YOU PRAY GOD'S FAITH, MIRACLES AND POWERS WILL MEET YOU THERE,

HOLY THINGS ARE NOT MEANT FOR THE DEVILS

IT IS APPARENT WHAT IS GOOD AND WHAT IS BAD, HOLINESS IS SOMETHING THE DEVIL HAS NEVER HAD,

WHEN HE WAS IN HEAVEN HE WAS NOT PURE, THROUGH HIS JEALOUSY, OF GOD'S MAJESTY HE COULD NOT ENDURE,

HIS SCHEMES TO BECOME THE REIGNING AUTHORITY, REMOVED HIM FROM HEAVEN'S LIGHT AND HEAVEN'S IMMORTALITY,

HE WAS CAST INTO A NEGATIVE LIGHT, HE WILL ALWAYS BE KNOWN AS THE ANTICHRIST,

HE IS THE FATHER OF ALL FILTH PIGS AND HOGS, HE HAS AN UNHOLY ARMY OF HELL HOUNDS AND DOGS,

SATAN'S THOUGHTS ARE THE WORST, GOD SENTENCED HIM WITH AN ETERNAL CURSE,

ALL HE WILL EVER DO IS STEAL KILL AND DESTROY, BE DETESTIBLE, NEGATIVE, HATEFUL AND HE WILL ALWAYS ANNOY,

HE WILL NEVER LOVE YOU AND WILL ALWAYS HATE YOU, EVERYTHING ABOUT YOU HE JUST WANTS TO DAM YOU,

HE CANNOT LOVE WITH THE ESSENCE OF GOD'S DIVINE SOURCE, THAT IS THE ULTIMATE ESSENCE OF GOD'S DIVINE FORCE,

AS YOU SEE HOLY THINGS IS NOT MEANT FOR THE DEVIL, HE CAN NEVER AGAIN REACH GOD'S HOLY LEVEL,

GOD'S THOUGHTS ARE SPIRITUAL, PURE, RIGHT, LIGHT AND SUBLIME, WE SHOULD EXPECT NOTHING BUT THE BEST FROM THE DIVINE,

AS REPRESENTATIVES OF GOD'S DIVINE LIGHT, WE MUST BE ABLE TO UPHOLD WHAT IS DIVINE AND RIGHT,

WE CANNOT IGNORE WHAT IS HATEFUL, VENGEFUL AND UNJUST, BECAUSE OF THIS WORLDS EVILNESS, PROMISCURITY AND LUST,

AS YOU SEE HOLY THINGS ARE NOT MEANT FOR THE DEVIL, HE CAN NEVER AGAIN REACH GOD'S HOLY LEVEL,

YOU CANNOT FEED TWO OPPOSING FORCES, WITHOUT CATERING TO ONE AS A PRIMARY SOURCE,

YOU MUST LOVE ONE AND HATE THE OTHER, BECAUSE LOVE AND HATE OPPOSE EACH OTHER,

THE DEVILS PRIMARY SOURCE IS HATE, HE CANNOT LOVE WHAT GOD HAS MADE GREAT,

THOSE OF US WHO HAS CHOSEN TO LIVE FOR CHRIST, LIVE IN THE IMAGE OF HIS DIVINE LIFE AND LIGHT,

I AM NOT AN ATTENDANT OF HELL

LOOK DEEPLY INTO MY EYES CAN'T YOU SEE, THERE IS A GOD LIVING INSIDE OF ME,

I WAS MADE BY AND FOR GOD ALONE, TO BE BY HIS SIDE IN JUDGEMENT WHEN HE RULES FROM HIS THRONE,

I KNOW I AM PART OF HEAVEN'S BEST, I AM STRONG, FAITHFUL, AND ETERNALLY BLEST,

SO, I CAN NEVER BE AN ATTENDANT OF HELL, I HAVE TOO MUCH HEAVEN INSIDE IF YOU REALLY LOOK AT ME YOU CAN TELL,

GOD LET ME KNOW I AM A CHOSEN ONE, HE GAVE ME A KINGLY NAME, AFTER KING SOLOMON,

HE SAID IF MY PEOPLE, CALLED BY MY NAME WILL HUMBLE THEMSELVES AND PRAY, I WILL HEAL THEIR LAND AND REINSTITUTE THEIR DAY,

I HAVE NO DOUBT HEAVEN IS MY HOME, IT IS WHERE MY GOD RULE AND SITS ON HIS THRONE,

I DON'T HAVE TO THINK ABOUT IT TWICE, GOD DESIGNED MY LIFE TO BE AN ATTENDANT TO AND FOR JESUS CHRIST,

SO, I CAN NEVER BE AN ATTENDANT OF HELL, I HAVE TOO MUCH HEAVEN INSIDE IF YOU REALLY LOOK AT ME YOU CAN TELL,

YOU MUST FIRST EXCEPT ME FOR WHO I AM, AND STOP TRYING TO CURSE ME, AND MAKE ME DAMMED,

WHEN YOU EXCEPT ME FOR WHO GOD MADE ME, ONLY THEN WILL YOU BE ABLE TO SEE THE HIDDEN SIDE OF MY DESTINY,

I AM VERY GLAD THAT IT WAS GOD'S WILL, TO KEEP PART OF MY LIFE CONCEALED,

I WAS TOO MEEK AND HUMBLE FOR THIS WICKED WORLD OF OURS, TOO MANY THIEVES, HATRED, RUMORS AND WARS,

I AM MEEK AS GOD'S LAMB, BUT I CAN BECOME LIKE STEEL AND IRON,

GOD'S SECOND RETURN WILL BE AS A FEROCIOUS AND RAVENOUS LION,

I PREFER TO SEE GOD'S GENTLE SIDE, WHEN HE COMES AS THE LAMB I DON'T HAVE TO RUN AND HIDE,

IN MY HEART SOUL AND SPIRIT, I KNOW THAT IT'S RIGHT, TO ALWAYS BE AN ATTENDANT TO JESUS CHRIST,

ILLUMINATED SUN

I KNOW THE REAL LIGHT OF THE SUN, IT IS NOT A MAGNIFIED LIGHT THAT THEY CALL THE SUN,

THE DIFFERENCE BETWEEN THE TWO, IS THAT WITH PROPER INSTRUMENTS ANYONE CAN BE ILLUMINATED EVEN YOU,

HOW IT IS DIFFERENT FROM THE SUN, IT'S POWER NEVER TIRERS, IT IS NOT JUST LIGHT IT IS COMPOSED OF PURE FIRE,

THEY CALL IT THE EMPYREAM, A PLACE OF PURE FIRE, WHERE THE ANGELS AND GOD HIMSELF RELAX AND REPOSE IN THE FIRE,

I HAVE SEEN ILLUMINATION, THAT WAS BRIGHTER THAN THE SUN, THAT STILL DID NOT POSSESS THE HEAT AND FIRE THAT SHOULD GENERATE FROM A SUN,

THIS ANIMATED TIME IN WHICH WE LIVE, IS ALL DIGITALLY CONSTRUCTED, BY A MACHINES WILL,

IT TAKES FIRE TO GENERATE LIFE AND GENERATIONS, NOT A MAGNIFYING GLASS FOR ILLUMINATION,

THE SUN WILL PRODUCE FIRE NO MATTER WHERE IT IS, THE SUN'S NATURE IS UNCHANGING AND ITS ALL HIS,

THE SUN REPRESENTS THE DAY AND IS CALLED DIURNAL TIME, THE MOON REPRESENTS THE NIGHT AND IS CALLED NOCTURNAL TIME,

NO REPROBATE SHALL BE GREAT

GOD MADE EVERYTHING FOR HIMSELF, HE IS THE EPITOME OF ALL OUR WEALTH,

WHEN WE OPPOSE GOD AND LIVE IN SIN, THE GATES ARE CLOSE FOR US ALL TO ENTER IN,

IF GOD GIVES US OVER TO BE REPROBATE, GOD HAS DEEMED THAT NO REPROBATE SHALL BE GREAT,

WITH A REPROBATE THE MIND HAS BEEN TAINTED, THE TRUTH, THE SPIRIT, AND THE ETHNIC COLORS HAS BEEN EVILLY PAINTED,

A REPROBATE HAS BEEN DEFILED IN THE WORST WAYS, HE OR SHE HAS NOTHING BENEFICIAL AT NIGHT NOR FOR THE DAYS,

WITH A REPROBATE WHAT GOD MADE MALE, THEY TRY TO SWITCH TO BECOME FEMALE,

WHAT GOD HAS DEEMED RELIGIOUS LAWS, A REPROBATE CONSIDERS RELIGIOUS FLAWS,

WITH GOD NO REPROBATE SHALL BE GREAT, THEY HAVE BEEN CONSUMMED BY EVIL AND IS FULL OF HATE,

WHEN ONE HAS A REPROBATED MIND, IT NO LONGER BELIEVES IN OR RESPECTS WHAT IS DIVINE,

THE CREATIVE AND INSPIRED ESSENCE OF GOD CANNOT ABIDE IN A REPROBATE, GOD WILL NOT LIVE WHERE THERE IS ONLY HATE,

ON AMERICA I STAND

THE PROMISE LAND IS WHAT GOD PROMISED US, IF WE WOULD BELIEVE, SEEK AND TRUST,

WE MUST KNOW GOD IS ABLE TO BRING US THROUGH, HE IS ABLE TO DELIVER ME AND DELIVER YOU,

IT IS NOT ABOUT GOLD, SILVER, OR NOT EVEN MONEY, GOD IS PLACING US IN A LAND OF RICHNESS, A LAND FLOWING WITH MILK AND HONEY,

THROUGH ALL GENERATIONS GOD HAS DEVISED A PLAN, THAT FOR HIS CHILDRED WE MUST DWELL IN THE PROMISED LAND,

WHEN GOD DECIDED TO WIPE AWAY ALL OF OUR TEARS, HE RAISED UP SOMEONE TO HELP ERASE ALL OF OUR FEARS,

IT WAS NOT AN ACCIDENT WHAT THE PRESIDENT HAD DONE, GOD WAS DIRECTING PRESIDENT ABRAHAM LINCOLN,

TO BRING HIS PEOPLE OUT OF BEING A SLAVE, HE MADE A PRESIDENT THAT WAS DARING BOLD AND BRAVE,

GOD MADE SURE THE PRESIDENT WOULD ADHERE TO GRACE, SO HE PICKED A PRESIDENT NAMED AFTER THE FATHER OF FAITH,

A LAND THAT SETS THE PRECIDENT FOR ALL OTHERS, A PLACE OF RESPECT FOR ALL CHILDREN, SISTERS AND BROTHERS,

IN THIS PLACE OF BLOOD, SWEAT AND TEARS, PEOPLE HAVE TOILED FOR TOO MANY YEARS,

NOW IT IS TIME FOR THE DOWN TRODEN, TO
VEHEMENTLY DEMAND,

WE TOO ARE HEIRS AND ON AMERICAN WE STAND,

AS CONSTITUTENTS TODAY WE DEPEND ON OUR
DEMOCRACY,

THE TRUTH IS WE HAVE A HIDDEN HIEROCRACY,

THE GOVERNMENT WAS DESIGNED AND MADE FOR
JESUS CHRIST,

TO RULE AS OUR KING, PRIEST, GOVENOR AND PRESIDENT
TO GIVE US BETTER LIVES,

AMERICA WAS DESINGED AND MADE BY GOD, A LAND
FILLED WITH HIS BEST,

A LAND WHERE ALL INHABITANTS AND CHILDREN COULD
BE BLESSED,

JESUS SAID. MY PEACE I LEAVE WITH YOU...

WE SHALL LIVE AND SHALL NOT DIE

GOD'S COVENANT WITH HIS PROPHETS, HIS PEOPLE AND ALL LIFE HE CREATED, WAS A COVENANT, AND A PROMISE THAT COULD NOT BE NEGATED,

THE COVENANT OF LIFE WAS ON THE RIGHT, A CURSE AND PATHWAY OF DEATH WAS ON THE LEFT,

GOD GAVE US SURE MERCIES AND BENEFITS EVERYDAY, OUR PROMISE OF LIFE HAS ITS OWN PATHWAY,

THAT LEADS US TO CHRIST AND ETERNITY, SALVATION, AND BLESSEDNESS FOR YOU AND ME,

GOD MADE US SPECIAL, DON'T STOP, DO NOT HALT, GOD ALSO GAVE YOU A COVENANT OF SALT,

YOU ARE SPECIAL IN THIS EARTH, SALT GIVES LIFE AND PURIFIES IMPURE BIRTHS,

ALWAYS REMEMBER GOD'S PURPOSE, AND REMEMBER HE TOLD US WHY, WE SHOULD LIVE AND WE SHALL NOT DIE,

HE MADE A SACRIFICE JUST FOR YOU AND ME, HE SENT HIS SON JESUS FOR THE WHOLE WORLD TO SEE,

OUR SIN DEBT HAS BEEN PAID CHRIST BLOOD HAS BEEN SHED, CHRIST SUFFERED AND DIED FOR US AND PAINFULLY BLED,

I HAVE MANY MANY REASONS TO JOYFULLY PROCLAIM, I BELONG TO JESUS CHRIST HE DIED IN MY NAME,

YES, I AM ONE OF HIS OWN I AM HIS HEIR, JESUS CHRIST IS MY SAVIOUR, HE HAS PROVEN TO ME HOW MUCH HE CARES,

ALWAYS REMEMBER GOD'S PURPOSE, AND REMEMBER HE TOLD US WHY, WE SHOULD LIVE AND WE SHALL NOT DIE,

HE'S SO MAJESTIC TO ME!

THERE ARE NO WORDS TO DESCRIBE THE UNDESCRIBILE, THERE ARE SOME THINGS WE WILL NEVER KNOW,

I CAN SAY THAT ONE DAY I WILL SEE, THE ONE WHO IS SO SPIRITUALLY MAJESTIC TO ME,

HE PAINTS AND IMBUES CREATION WITH COLORS WE DON'T EVEN KNOW, SOME OF THESE COLORS ARE FAR BEYOND OUR RAINBOW,

ALL OF CREATION ARE HIS HANDY WORKS, HE BREATHED INTO THIS UNIVERSE, EVERY SPOKEN WORD HAS BECOME A BIBLICAL VERSE,

FOR US TO KNOW AND READ WHAT OUR GOD HAS DONE, HE PUT THEM INTO 66 BOOKS INTO A HOLY BIBLE AS ONE,

HE HAS INSPIRED MEN TO WRITE ALL THE COMMANDMENTS AND ALL THE LAWS, HE ENTERED INTO A PERFECT COVENANT WITH MANKIND WITHOUT FLAWS,

THROUGH THIS COVENANT WE WOULD HAVE SALVATION, THROUGH HIS SON JESUS CHRIST BORN TO SAVE EVERY NATION,

I CAN SAY THAT ONE DAY I WILL SEE, THE ONE WHO IS SO SPIRITUALLY MAJESTIC TO ME,

NO ONE BUT GOD CAN TRULY SAY WHO, WHAT OR HOW, THE LORD WILL SAVE IN THE END, BUT WE DO KNOW WE ARE ALL HIS CHOSEN CHILDREN,

I THANK GOD FOR THE IMMACULATE GIFT OF LIFE, WE NOW KNOW AS JESUS CHRIST,

WITHOUT HIM I WOULD HAVE BEEN LOST, WITH NO-ONE TO PAY MY SIN DEBT COST,

YOU ARE OMNIPOTENT, OMNIPRESENT AND ENTERNALLY PLACED WITHIN THE HEAVENLY SPHERES, TIME HAS NO FACTOR IN YOUR EXISTENCE YOU ARE CREATOR OF ALL YEARS,

YOU CAN NEVER LEAVE YOURSELF NOR CAN YOU LEAVE YOUR HEALTH, BECAUSE YOU ARE EVERYTHING YOU ARE THE ENTIRE EARTH'S WEALTH,

WHEN I HERE EVIL DEMONS LIE AND SAY, JESUS CHRIST IS NOT HERE, I KNOW THAT THEY ARE LYING, BECAUSE THEY ONLY EXIST BECAUSE OF FEAR,

I KNOW THAT WHEN CHRIST IS NO LONGER HERE, EVERY EVIL ENTITIY WILL BE CAST INTO THE LAKE OF FIRE TO BURN FOR ETERNAL YEARS,

I CAN SAY THAT ONE DAY I WILL SEE, THE ONE WHO IS SO SPIRITUALLY MAJESTIC TO ME,

EXPOSING EVIL

WE ARE MEANT TO SHINE A LIGHT, TO EXPOSE THE EVIL THAT INHABITS THE NIGHT,

TO LET THE PEOPLE TRULY SEE, THAT EVIL IS NOT WHERE THEY WANT TO BE,

TO WIN SOULS FOR CHRIST AND THE KINGDOM OF THE JUST, REMOVING THEM FROM SATAN'S ARMIES OF HATRED AND LUST,

WE MUST NOT TURN OUR HEADS, WHEN WE SEE SOMEONE DOING A WRONG, WE SHOULD INFORM OUR BRETHERN, SO THEY CAN SEE WE ARE STRONG,

WE MUST NOT PARTICIPATE IN EVIL DEEDS, WE ARE COMMITTED AND DEDICATED TO HELP PEOPLES IN NEED,

THAT IS WHAT TRUE CHRISTIANS DO, WE BRING PEACE AND HARMONY TO THE WORLD THROUGH GOD'S TRUTH,

WE KNOW THAT RIGHT WORDS SPOKEN INTO A SITUATION, BRINGS ABOUT A CHANGE, FROM EVIL TO GOOD IT CAN BE REARRANGED,

JUST LIKE OUR CREATOR SPOKE THIS UNIVERSE INTO EXISTENCE, WE BELIEVE THAT WE CAN SPEAK PEACE AND LOVE INTO ANY INSTANCE,

WE CAN ESCHEW AND REBUKE THE DEVIL AND ANY OF HOARDS, BY CALLING ON OUR MASTER AND CONQUEROR, JESUS CHRIST OUR LORD,

SATAN HAS ALREADY BEEN DEFEATED, HE IS ONLY AND IMAGE IN OUR MINDS, IF WE LET HIS HE WILL BECOME MORE POWERFUL AND USURP OUR TIME,

DO NOT PLAY WITH THE DEVIL NOR ANY OF HIS HOST, HIS JOB IS TO SEDUCE YOU AND PLACE YOU IN ONE OF HIS POST,

SO, TAKE YOUR STAND AND EXPOSE ALL EVIL, WHEN WE DO, WE ARE DEFEATING THE DEVIL,

HOLY THINGS ARE NOT MEANT FOR THE DEVILS

IT IS APPARENT WHAT IS GOOD AND WHAT IS BAD, HOLINESS IS SOMETHING THE DEVIL HAS NEVER HAD,

WHEN HE WAS IN HEAVEN HE WAS NOT PURE, THROUGH HIS JEALOUSY, OF GOD'S MAJESTY HE COULD NOT ENDURE,

HIS SCHEMES TO BECOME THE REIGNING AUTHORITY, REMOVED HIM FROM HEAVEN'S LIGHT AND HEAVEN'S IMMORTALITY,

HE WAS CAST INTO A NEGATIVE LIGHT, HE WILL ALWAYS BE KNOWN AS THE ANTICHRIST,

HE IS THE FATHER OF ALL FILTH PIGS AND HOGS, HE HAS AN UNHOLY ARMY OF HELL HOUNDS AND DOGS,

SATAN'S THOUGHTS ARE THE WORST, GOD SENTENCED HIM WITH AN ETERNAL CURSE,

ALL HE WILL EVER DO IS STEAL KILL AND DESTROY, BE DETESTIBLE, NEGATIVE, HATEFUL AND HE WILL ALWAYS ANNOY,

HE WILL NEVER LOVE YOU AND WILL ALWAYS HATE YOU, EVERYTHING ABOUT YOU HE JUST WANTS TO DAM YOU,

HE CANNOT LOVE WITH THE ESSENCE OF GOD'S DIVINE SOURCE, THAT IS THE ULTIMATE ESSENCE OF GOD'S DIVINE FORCE,

AS YOU SEE HOLY THINGS IS NOT MEANT FOR THE DEVIL, HE CAN NEVER AGAIN REACH GOD'S HOLY LEVEL,

GOD'S THOUGHTS ARE SPIRITUAL, PURE, RIGHT, LIGHT AND SUBLIME, WE SHOULD EXPECT NOTHING BUT THE BEST FROM THE DIVINE,

AS REPRESENTATIVES OF GOD'S DIVINE LIGHT, WE MUST BE ABLE TO UPHOLD WHAT IS DIVINE AND RIGHT,

WE CANNOT IGNORE WHAT IS HATEFUL, VENGEFUL AND UNJUST, BECAUSE OF THIS WORLDS EVILNESS, PROMISCURITY AND LUST,

AS YOU SEE HOLY THINGS ARE NOT MEANT FOR THE DEVIL, HE CAN NEVER AGAIN REACH GOD'S HOLY LEVEL,

YOU CANNOT FEED TWO OPPOSING FORCES, WITHOUT CATERING TO ONE AS A PRIMARY SOURCE,

YOU MUST LOVE ONE AND HATE THE OTHER, BECAUSE LOVE AND HATE OPPOSE EACH OTHER,

THE DEVILS PRIMARY SOURCE IS HATE, HE CANNOT LOVE WHAT GOD HAS MADE GREAT,

THOSE OF US WHO HAS CHOSEN TO LIVE FOR CHRIST, LIVE IN THE IMAGE OF HIS DIVINE LIFE AND LIGHT,

JESUS I WILL NEVER GIVE YOU UP!

NO MATTER WHAT THE WORLD SAYS ABOUT YOU, I WILL NEVER LEAVE YOU,

THERE'S NOTHING THEY CAN DO, TO PERUADE AND SEPARATE ME FROM YOU,

I WAS TAUGHT TO NEVER GIVE UP, ON WHAT YOU KNOW IS RIGHT, ALWAYS BELIEVE IN THE TRUTH KEEP IT IN YOUR SIGHT,

THE OLD SAYING SAYS, KEEP YOUR EYES ON THE PRIZE, THEREFORE I DO SO AND KEEP MY MIND POSITIVE PRAYERFUL AND SPIRITUALLY REALIZE,

JESUS I WILL NEVER GIVE YOU UP, YOU HOLD THE REINS TO MY LIFE, AND SUPPLY MY SPIRITUAL STUFF,

I ESTEEM YOU AS THE ONLY TRUE SOURCE THAT CAN HEAL EVERYTHING, GOD VESTED IN YOU THIS RIGHT WHERE YOU CAN HEAL EVERY HUMAN BEING,

YOU MY LORD HAVE THE WORDS OF LIFE LIGHT AND LOVE, IF MANKIND WOULD FOLLOW YOU WE WOULD HAVE EVERYTHING WE COULD THINK OF,

ALL DISEASES WON'T AND DON'T HAVE A CURE, THEY ARE THE PERFECTIONS OF THE WORK OF GOD'S, TO SHOW HIS HOLY WORDS ARE PURE AND ARE THE CURE,

THAT IS WHY, JESUS I WILL NEVER GIVE YOU UP, YOU HOLD THE REINS TO MY LIFE, AND SUPPLY MY SPIRITUAL STUFF,

JESUS WILL NEVER DIE

OH! HOW THEY WANT ME TO BELIEVE, JESUS DIED LIKE A MORTAL MAN,

THEN THE MIRACLE OF SALAVATION AND HIS RESURRECTION COULD NOT STAND,

THAT WOULD MEAN THE WHOLE WORLD WOULD BE LOST, IF THEY COLD MAKE US BELIEVE CHRIST DID NOT PAY REDEMPTIONS COST,

I SPEAK FOR ME, MYSELF, AND I, I KNOW THAT CHRIST PAID FOR ME, AND THAT ON THE THIRD DAY HE ROSE, WITH ALL POWER, AND ALL THE SPIRITS HE CHOSE,

LET ME BE THE FIRST TO SAY, JESUS CHRIST CAN NEVER DIE A MORTAL DEATH,

HE IS THE EPITOME OF ALL LIFE , IT IS ALL IN HIS BREATH,

HIS VERY ESSENCE IS TOO POWERFUL FOR ANY GRAVE, EARTH WOULD PROBABLY LIFT HIM UP FROM THE GROUND,

OBEYING DIVINE ORDER, KNOWING HIS SPIRIT IS TOO SPIRITUALLY SOUND, TO BE IN ANY GROUND,

EVERYTHING IN EXISTENCE KNOWS WHO JESUS CHRIST IS, THEY MUST OBEY THIS WHY AND HOW THEY LIVE,

EVERYTHING IN EXISTENCE KNOWS WHERE JESUS CHRIST BELONGS, CREATION KNOWS HEAVEN IS HIS HOME,

JESUS WILL NEVER DIED LET ME TELL YOU THE REASON WHY, THERE WOULD BE NO ONTOLOGICAL EXISTENCE OF ANY LIFE EVERY SINGLE THING STARTS WITH CHRIST,

WE ALL KNOW THAT HE WAS HEAVEN SENT, HE UNDERSTOOD AND CONTROLLED ALL THE ELEMENTS,

GOD KNEW THAT MANKIND WAS CAPABLE OF BEING UNSOUND, THAT IS HOW THE BEGGARLY ELEMENTS KEPT MAN BOUND,

JESUS CHRIST CAN NEVER DIE SO LET ME TELL YOU WHY, HIS FATHER GAVE HIM ALL THE WORLD SEES, HE REMOVED SATAN AND SNATCHED AWAY HIS KEYS,

JESUS IS NOW KEEPER OF DEATH, HELL, AND THE GRAVE, HE HAS THE KEYS AND IT IS HIS CHOICE TO WHO HE SAVES,

JESUS CHRIST LOVE IS STONGER THAN DEATH, HE IS THE COMPOSITIONS OF ALL ETERNITY IN ONE ENDLESS BREADTH,

NO AUTHORITY OVER ME

I MAY LOOK DOCILE TIMID AND WEAK, BUT I KNOW THE TRUTH MY FATHER SPEAKS,

HE PROMISED TO TAKE GOOD CARE OF ME, WHERE I AM NO DEVIL SHOULD BE,

GOD NEVER GAVE EVIL AUTHORITY OVER ME, BECAUSE HIS SPIRIT RESIDES IN ME,

MY BODY IS THE TEMPLE OF THE HOLY GHOST, NOT THE DWELLING OF SATAN OR HIS EVIL HOST,

SATAN YOU HAVE NO AUTHORITY OVER ME, GOD MADE ME SUBLIME, WHEN HE FILLED ME WITH HIS SPIRIT, HE DESTINED MY TIME,

SATAN YOU HAVE NO AUTHORITY OVER ME, THIS BODY GOD CONTROLS, HE CAST OUT DISEASE AND KEEPS ME PURE AND WHOLE,

CHRIST GAVE ME THIS AUTHORITY, TO KEEP SATAN UNDER SUBMISSION, SATAN CAN NEVER BE OVER A SAINT IN HIS POSITION,

BE WARNED SATAN, I AM ARMED WITH THE HOLY GHOST, IT IS THE POWER THAT DEFEATED YOU AND YOUR SATANIC HOST,

YOU WILL NEVER HAVE AUTHORITY OVER ME, I HAVE THE POWER OF JESUS CHRIST LIVING INSIDE OF ME,

THE SAME POWER THAT CONQUERED DEATH, HELL AND THE GRAVE, TOOK ALL SATANS KEYS, FOR THIS PURPOSE, JESUS SAVES,

BE WARNED SATAN OF THIS ELECTION, I AM PART OF JESUS CHRIST'S HOLY RESSURECTION,

HE REMOVED YOU AND TOOK YOUR KEYS, MADE YOU SUBMIT AND FALL DOWN TO YOUR KNEES,

SATAN, JESUS TOLD YOU IT IS WRITTEN, YOU ARE A SERVANT TOO, WITHOUT GOD THERE IS NOTHING EVEN YOU CAN DO,

WE MUST LOVE
ONE ANOTHER

GOD LEFT US AN EXAMPLE OF HIS GIFT OF LOVE WE MUST FOLLOW, IF YOU ARE A TRUE CHILD OF HIS CHRIST YOU MUST KNOW,

IT WAS THE SACRIFICE OF HIS SON, THAT MADE A PATHWAY FOR YOU AND ME, HIS BLOOD PAVED THE FOUNDATION THAT SET US ALL FREE,

GOD JUST ASKED US TO LOVE ONE ANOTHER, LIKE THEY ARE YOUR HEAVENLY SISTERS AND BROTHERS,

GOD DID NOT GIVE US A HEART OF STONE, ALLOWING US TO TREAT OUR SISTERS AND BROTHERS WRONG,

WE ARE SUPPOSE TO BE THE TRUE ESSENCE OF GOD'S SPIRIT, IF WE CAN'T SHOW HIS LOVE WISDOM SAYS THEN WE SHOULD SURLY FEAR IT,

THE SAGES HAVE WRITTEN, IT IS THE BEGINNING OF WISDOM TO FEAR THE LORD, TO KICK AGAINST HIS PRICKS, WOULD BE PHYSICALLY, AND SPIRITUALLY HARD,

WE ARE THE EXAMPLES OF HEAVEN'S BEST, SURLY WE CAN LOVE EACH OTHER AS WE SHOULD, THEN THE WORLD WE CAN BLESS,

WE CAN SHARE GOD'S LOVE NATION WIDE, PUTTING HATRED ON THE RUN WITH NO WHERE TO HIDE,

I APPEAL TO YOUR HEART AND SPIRIT, MY SISTER, MY BROTHER, LET'S LET THE WORLD SEE AND KNOW WE ARE GOD'S CHILDREN LET'S LOVE ONE ANOTHER,

WE SHALL LIVE AND SHALL NOT DIE

GOD'S COVENANT WITH HIS PROPHETS, HIS PEOPLE AND ALL LIFE HE CREATED, WAS A COVENANT, AND A PROMISE THAT COULD NOT BE NEGATED,

THE COVENANT OF LIFE WAS ON THE RIGHT, A CURSE AND PATHWAY OF DEATH WAS ON THE LEFT,

GOD GAVE US SURE MERCIES AND BENEFITS EVERYDAY, OUR PROMISE OF LIFE HAS ITS OWN PATHWAY,

THAT LEADS US TO CHRIST AND ETERNITY, SALVATION, AND BLESSEDNESS FOR YOU AND ME,

GOD MADE US SPECIAL, DON'T STOP, DO NOT HALT, GOD ALSO GAVE YOU A COVENANT OF SALT,

YOU ARE SPECIAL IN THIS EARTH, SALT GIVES LIFE AND PURIFIES IMPURE BIRTHS,

ALWAYS REMEMBER GOD'S PURPOSE, AND REMEMBER HE TOLD US WHY, WE SHOULD LIVE AND WE SHALL NOT DIE,

HE MADE A SACRIFICE JUST FOR YOU AND ME, HE SENT HIS SON JESUS FOR THE WHOLE WORLD TO SEE,

OUR SIN DEBT HAS BEEN PAID CHRIST BLOOD HAS BEEN SHED, CHRIST SUFFERED AND DIED FOR US AND PAINFULLY BLED,

I HAVE MANY MANY REASONS TO JOYFULLY PROCLAIM, I BELONG TO JESUS CHRIST HE DIED IN MY NAME,

YES, I AM ONE OF HIS OWN I AM HIS HEIR, JESUS CHRIST IS MY SAVIOUR, HE HAS PROVEN TO ME HOW MUCH HE CARES,

ALWAYS REMEMBER GOD'S PURPOSE, AND REMEMBER HE TOLD US WHY, WE SHOULD LIVE AND WE SHALL NOT DIE,

WHEN I FALTER

LORD YOU KNOW EVERYTHING THERE IS TO KNOW ABOUT ME, YOU CREATED ME WITH YOUR IDENTITY,

YOU DESTINED MAN TO BE CREATED IN YOUR IMAGE, ALL MANKIND IS CREATED FROM YOUR DIVINE LINEAGE,

KNOWING HOW I WAS MADE, MADE ME EXCEPT MYSELF CREATED WITH YOUR DIVINE GRADE,

YET I SEEM SOMETIMES TO FALL SHORT, OF YOUR GRACE, MERCY, AND PEACE, I AM WIDE AWAKE AND SOMETIMES MY SPIRIT SEEMS TO BE IS ASLEEP,

LORD FORGIVE ME IF AND WHENEVER I FALTER, REMIND ME TO ALWAYS TAKE IT TO YOUR ALTER,

WHERE MERCY AND GRACE KNOWS MY NAME, THEY WILL ONLY SEE JESUS, WHERE THERE IS NO BLAME,

HIS REDEMPTION PAID FOR ME AND HIS BLOOD COVERS ME, HIS BLOOD HAS SET ME FREE, HALLELUJAH!

HIS BLOOD HAS RESSURECTION POWER, I NEED IT EVERY HOUR,

I WILL NEVER THINK OF GIVING IN, TO ANY OF SATAN'S MORTAL SINS,

LORD I AM ONLY PERFECT THROUGH JESUS CHRIST, ONLY WHEN HE EXIST IN MY LIFE,

THEN THI

I NEVER GAVE UP

LORD YOU ARE THE ANSWER TO MY EVERY PRAYER, YOU PROMISED TO MEET ME WHEN I PRAYED YOU WOULD BE THERE,

YOU GAVE ME THE ASSURANCE I COULD STAND ON YOUR WORDS, IF I KEPT YOUR COMMANDMENTS THAT I HAVE HEARD,

YOU CARRIED ME THROUGHT THE TROUBLE AND VISSITUDES OF LIFE, YOU GAVE ME PROMISES IN YOUR SON JESUS CHRIST,

I WENT THROUGH SO MUCH PERSONAL LOSS, BUT IT IS NOT ABOUT ME, IT IS ABOUT THE CROSS,

I REALIZED WHAT JESUS WENT THROUGH, I DREW IN HIS SPIRIT IN ME, I SAID I CAN GO THROUGH TO,

FATHER, FATHER, YOU KNOW I NEVER GAVE UP, EVEN WHEN THE TIMES WERE HARD AND FINANCIALLY TOUGH,

I DON'T HAVE ALL THE ANSWERS RIGHT NOW, BUT I KNOW THEY ARE COMING TO ME SOME HOW,

IT SEEMS THAT EVERYTHING THAT WAS MEANT FOR ME, THAT'S WHERE EVERYONE ELSE IN THE WORLD WANTED TO BE,

THEY WANTED MY LIFE MY FINANCES, MY HUSBAND, AND EVEN MY CHILD AND MY GOD, THEY SUFFERED ME ENDLESSLY AND MADE MY LIFE EXTREMELY HARD,

FATHER, FATHER, YOU KNOW I NEVER GAVE UP, EVEN WHEN TIMES WERE SPIRITUALLY TOUGH,

YOU TOLD ME NO MATTER WHAT, JUST NEVER GIVE IN AND NEVER GIVE UP,

MONEY IS NOT THE ANSWER NOR MONETARY PROFIT, JUST REMEMBER IT IS JESUS CHRIST WHO LOVES AND BLESSES YOU NEVER QUIT,

MY VISION BECAME DERISION, I WAS CONFUSED DESTITUTE AND LOST, DEMONIC VOICES INSIDE AND OUTSIDE OF MY MIND RIDICULED THE CROSS,

NEVERTHELESS I SAID, YOUR WILL FATHER LET IT BE, WHATEVER YOUR WILL LET IT BE CHRIST THEY WILL SEE IN ME,

I AM A TRUE CHILD OF GOD'S I CAN NEVER, EVER, GIVE UP, NO MATTER HOW BAD IT GETS NO MATTER WHAT,

TAKE A DOLLAR FOR EVERY WORD

I BELIEVE IN SELF WORTH, GOD HAS GIVEN US ALL AT OUR BIRTH,

WHAT EVER YOU CREATE BECOMES YOUR PERSONAL PROPERTY, A PART OF YOU THE WORLD CAN SEE,

CREATION COMES FROM WITHIN OR FROM THE INSIDE, A PART NONTHE LESS,

WHATEVER YOU CREATE IS ALREADY BLESSED,

GOD'S WORD HAS SAID, WHATEVER YOU PUT YOUR HANDS TO, HE HAS ALREADY BLESSED WHATEVER YOU DO,

I HAVE WRITTEN MANY LITERARY BOOKS OF MY OWN, EACH ONE WAS PERSONALLY AND SPIRITUALLY SOWN,

THEREFORE I WILL TAKE A DOLLAR FOR EVERY ONE OF MY INTELLECTUAL WORDS,

THAT OTHERS ARE USING I HAVE HEARD,

THEY TAKE CREDIT FOR EVERYTHING THAT I DO, THEY PLAGIARIZE MY CREATIONS AND STEAL MY HERITAGE TOO,

IN CASE THEY WANT TO KNOW, WRITING IS PART OF MY DAY,

I CAME HERE WRITING, I CAN WRITE MY WAY,

I AM TRULY FULLY VESTED IN SPRITUAL CONTENT,

LOOK AT MY WORKS, IT IS ALL EVIDENT, SINCE EVERYBODY WANTS TO USURP MY DAY, I THINK THEY ALL SHOULD CONSIDER THEIR FAULT AND THEY SHOULD PAY,

AT LEAST A DOLLAR FOR EVERY SINGLE WORD, I HAVE EVER PUT ON PAPER AND WROTE,

I HAVE WRITTEN AND DESIGNED ENOUGH WORDS, TO FASHION AND DESIGN A BIBLICAL COAT,

BURNING A CANDLE
AGAINST THE MIDDLE

ISN'T IT AMAZING HOW SOME PEOPLE WILL PRETEND TO BE YOUR FRIEND, WHEN THE TRUTH IS THEY ARE BURNING A CANDLE ON BOTH ENDS,

THEY SAY THEY LOVE YOU EVERYTHING THEY TELL YOU IS UNTRUE, WHEN YOU FIND OUT FOR YOURSELF YOU WILL FIND THEY REALLY HATE,

THEY KEEP YOU IN THE MIDDLE SO THEY CAN PLAY BOTH SIDES, AGAINST THE MIDDLE THEY WILL TELL YOU LIES HOPING YOU NEVER REALIZE,

THEY KEEP YOUR ENEMY CLOSE THEY KEEP YOU EVEN CLOSER, SO THAT IN THE END THEY HAVE CREATED A HATRED YOU CAN'T SEEM TO GET OVER,

THESE KINDS OF RELATIONSHIPS USUALLY STEM FROM INSECURITIES, YOU HAVE EVERYTHING THAT THEY WANT AND WHO THEY WANT TO BE,

IF EVER THEY LEAVE AND YOUR RELATIONSHIP ENDS TOO ABRUPT, IT PROBABLY BECASUSE THEY HAVE STOLEN WHAT THEY WANT AND MOST EVERYTHING IS USED UP,

FOR PEOPLE LIKE THAT YOU CAN'T LET THEM MAKE YOU LAST, YOU MUST KEEP BACK YOUR BEST QUALITIES AND KEEP A PERSONAL EMERGENCY STASH,

NEVER LET THEM SEE AND KNOW IT ALL, THEY ARE ALWAYS TRYING TO MAKE YOU LATE OR TO MAKE YOU FALL,

THE BIBLE SAYS WICKEDNESS AND EVIL, DOES NOT SLEEP UNLESS THEY MAKE SOMEONE FALL,

THEIRE CAPACITY FOR LOVE IS VERY LITTLE, THAT IS WHY WHEN THEY BURN CANDLES, THEY BURN BOTH ENDS AGAINST THE MIDDLE,

GOD COVERS
ALL POSITIONS

NO MATTER WHO YOU ARE OR WHAT YOU DO,

YOU HOLD A POSITION, IN WHICH YOU FUNCTION THROUGH,

AS A MATTER OF FACT IT IS NOT ABOUT YOU, ITS ABOUT ALL
THE THINGS GOD HAS MADE FOR THE EARTH AND UNIVERSE
TO REVOLVE THROUGH,

GOD HAS SET CONSTRUCTED 32 POSITIONS, THAT DAY AND
NIGHT WORKS THROUGH,

EACH POSITTION GOD HAS PLACED A GUARD WHO
KNOWS WHAT TO DO,

32 POSITIONS IN THE DAY AND 32 POSITIONS FOR NIGHT,
EACH ORB HAS LUMINARY PORTALS THAT HOLD THEIR LIGHT,

GOD HAS THE TIME CLOCKS FOR EVERY HUMAN BEING, HE
HAS MAGNIFICANTLY SET THESE CLOCKS BIOLOGICALLY,

SOME OF US WALK IN THE DIURNAL, THE DAY WE USE THE
CONSCIOUSNESS TO SEE OUR WAY,

SOME OF US WALK IN THE NOCTURNAL, THE NIGHT, THEY
USE THE SUBCONSCIOUSNESS WHERE THINGS ARE NOT
SO BRIGHT,

WHATEVER THE CASE WE ARE ALL SITTING ON POSITIONS,
SOME COME WITH A HEAVENLY MISSION,

THERE IS NO POSITION OR DIRECTION THAT GOD
HAS NOT SEEN,

THAT IS WHY HE HAS BEEN CROWNED AS A KING, HE SEES AND KNOWS MOST EVERYTHING,

GOD HAS METED OUT EVERY TRACT OF LAND, YOU CANNOT WALK OR TRAVEL ANY WHERE WITHOUT BEING IN HIS HAND,

GOD COVERS ALL POSITIONS, HE DESIGNATES AND SENDS ALL HIS SAINTS ON THEIR MISSIONS,

CHANGING MINDS

IN TODAYS WORLD OF AFFAIRS, YOU WILL FIND MANY ARE INCOMPASSIONATE AND DO NOT CARE,

FOR THE THINGS GOD HAS PLACE IN THE UNIVERSE, FOR US TO ENJOY WITHOUT A CURSE,

PEOPLE CHANGE THEIR CLOTHES, THEIR HEARTS AND THEIR MINDS, ONE THING PEOPLE WILL NOT AND CAN NOT CHANGE IS THEIR TIME,

GOD IS THE MAKER AND KEEPER OF ALL TIME, PAST, PRESENT, AND FUTURE, IS HIS TO DESIGN,

CHANGE IS GOOD, CHANGE IS SOMETHING INSIDE, CHANGE IS SOMETHING GOD PLANTED IN YOU THAT WON'T BE DENIED,

NO MATTER WHAT THEY TAKE FROM YOU, THEY STILL CAN NEVER BE YOU, THEY ONLY HAVE A FORM AND SHADOW OF THE THINGS YOU CAN DO,

THEY HAVE THE FORMS, HOPES, AND DREAMS FROM YOUR IMAGINATION, THEY STILL ARE NOT THE CORE OF YOU THEY ARE IMITATIONS,

WHAT DO WE REALLY KNOW ABOUT CHANGE, IT CAN BE THE UTOPIAN WISH OF A BROKEN HEARTS PAIN,

CHANGE COULD BE THE OPPOSITE SIDE OF THE SPECTRUM, WHEN YOU ARE CREATING AN INVERSION,

CHANGE CAN ALSO MEAN A GENDER CHANGE, IT IS WHEN A MALE AND A FEMALE REARRANGE,

ALL THAT MEANS IS YOU ARE CHANGING LEFT TO RIGHT, BOTH SIDE WILL BE SEEN IN A DIFFERENT LIGHT,

IF WE COULD SEE INTO THE MIND WE WOULD SEE FRAME FOR FRAME, YOU WOULD SEE THE MIND CHANGING PLANE TO PLANE,

THE MIND I BELIEVE WAS BUILD WITH A CONSTRUCTED AND BIOLOGICAL TIME, FOR THE BRAIN TO ORDER THE ENTIRE BODY FROM THE MIND,

WE ARE UNIQUE AND IT WAS GOD'S INTENT, TO LET US KNOW HIS SPIRITUAL CONTENT,

OUR MINDS ARE SPIRITUAL PARTS BY THE ESSENCE GOD ORDAINED, NO OTHER CREATION HAS WHAT WE HAVE IN US SPIRITUALLY CONTAINED,

GOD MADE US SO MUCH IN HIS GODLY IMAGE, WHEN WE UNDERSTAND THIS OUR LIFE HAS NO LIMITS,

A CHANGE OF MIND OR A CHANGE OF FAITH, BOTH ARE CHANGES THAT CAN BE GREAT,

CHRIST COULD HAVE CHANGED HIS MIND ON THE CROSS, BUT HE REFUSED TO SEE OUR SOULS LOST,

IF YOU LOVE CHRIST JESUS STAY THE SAME, DON'T LET EVIL SUGGEST TO YOUR MIND TO MAKE A CHANGE,

WHEN THE DEVIL IS ARROUND THINGS START REARRANGING, BUT HOLD YOUR GROUND AND KEEP YOUR MIND FROM CHANGING,

CLOSE MY THE DOOR

GOD MADE THE HUMAN ANATOMY WITH GATES AND DOORS, WE DON'T HAVE TO WONDER WHAT THEY WERE MADE FOR,

THE ANSWER IS VERY SIMPLE, WE ARE THE DWELLING PLACE OF A HOLY GOD, WE ARE HIS TEMPLE,

DON'T JUST LET ANY ONE IN UNTIL YOU KNOW, THEY DESERVE TO ENTER YOUR GODLY DOOR,

EVIL IS WAITING AND LURKING TO KILL, STEAL, DESTROY A LIFE, THAT IS BUILT UP AND HONORED BY CHRIST,

WHEN YOU COME IN DON'T FORGET TO, JUST CLOSE MY DOOR, I REFUSE TO LET EVIL ENTER INTO MY DOOR ANYMORE,

YOU ARE THE WATCHER AT ALL OF YOUR GATES, YOU MUST REFUSE JEALOUSY, TROUBLE AND HATE,

YOU HAVE THE TIME CLEARLY SEE, WHO IS ENTERING YOUR GATES YOU HAVE ALL THE KEYS,

DON'T ALLOW SATAN TO TRICK YOU AGAIN, BY TELLING YOU HE IS YOUR ONLY FRIEND,

FIGHT BACK REBUKE HIM AND REFUSE ALL HIS ADVANCE, DON'T GIVE HIM AN INCH, DON'T GIVE HIM A CHANCE,

EVERYTHING SATAN HAS PROBABLY BELONGS TO YOU, HE IS AN EXPERT AT STEALING FROM YOU,

YOU ARE NOT THE ONLY ONE, HE HAS STOLEN FROM SO MANY OF GOD'S PEOPLE, HE HAS BUILT HIM A KINGDOM,

YOU MAKE SURE YOU CLOSE YOUR DOORS AND GATES, KEEP OUT MURDERS, KEEP OUT HATE,

TRAIN YOU HEART MIND AND SOUL UNTIL THEY REALIZE, SATAN AND HIS DEMONS WILL ALWAYS BE AT YOUR DOOR WITH TEMPTARIONS AND LIES,

WHEN YOU COME IN DON'T FORGET TO JUST CLOSE MY DOOR, I REFUSE TO LET EVIL ENTER INTO MY DOOR ANYMORE,

CURING CORONA VIRUS

LORD YOU ARE THE ONLY ANSWER TO OUR DILEMMAS TODAY, THEY ARE MOSTLY BECAUSE WE HAVE NOT FOLLOWED YOUR WAYS,

ANYTIME MANKIND FINDS HIMSELF FACED WITH DISEASES, STRIFES AND FAMINE,

WE NEED TO LOOK AT OURSELVES CLOSELY, TO SEE IF THIS IS SOMETHING GOD HAS TO END,

I AM NOT REALLY SURE HOW WE GOT THIS DISEASE, I KNOW GOD IS THE ONE WHO WILL STOP ITS INCREASE,

I CAN SPEAK FOR MYSELF, I AM NOT KNOWINGLY TRYING TO OPPRESS ANYONE'S CHILD, ESPECIALLY GOD'S CHILD,

I WANT TO AND AM TRYING TO LOVE MY SISTERS AND BROTHERS AS YOU HAVE COMMANDED, WHAT CAN I DO WHEN I AM CONSTANTLY REPREAMANDED,

NOTHELESS, I WANT TO DO YOUR WILL INSPITE OF HOW THE WORLDS FEELS,

TRUE CHRISTIANS MUST PERSEVERE, BECAUSE IT IS OUR OBLIGATION TO PUSH PAST WICKEDNESS,

IN SINFUL AND EVIL TIMES, MANIFEST GOD'S SOVERIGNITY AND HOLINESS,

ON EARTH YOUR SAINTS AND TRUE BELIEVERS ARE VICARS OF CHRIST HOLY SPIRIT, UNTIL YOU COME AND RULE, WE SHOULD ALL TRY TO GET NEAR IT,

MY HUMBLE REQUEST FATHER IS THAT YOU INSTILL IN THOSE YOU HAVE ALREADY CHOSE, THE BENEVOLENCE AND HOLYNESS, OF YOUR SACRED ROSE,

TO PERFECT THE CURES NECESSARY FOR MANKINDS HEALTH, PURITY AND SECURITY, FULFILLING THE PROMISED PROTECTION UNDER YOUR DIVINE ELECTION,

I KNOW PERSONALLY YOUR WORDS AND SPIRIT ARE FULL OF FAITH, HOPE, AND LIFE,

THEY ARE THE MANIFESTATIONS AND VOLUMES IN THE BOOKS THAT DESCRIBE AND PORTRAY CHRIST,

SO, FATHER SEND YOUR WORDS ONCE AGAIN, TO A WORLD SEEMINGLY WITHOUT JESUS AS A FRIEND,

TO KNOW YOUR TRUE LOVE FOR US, WE PRAY YOU DISPELL AND GET RID OF AND CURE OR CRONA VIRUS,

DIRT AND THE GRAVE WON'T HOLD HIM DOWN

A MISTAKE WAS MADE AT CALVARY, WHEN THEY THOUGHT THEY CRUCIFIED MY LORD FOR ME,

LITTLE DID THEY KNOW, HE WOULD RISE AGAIN, WITH ALL POWER AND CONQUERING ALL SIN,

YES, THEY PUT HIM IN A GRAVE, THEY DIDN'T KNOW HIS POWER TO SAVE, HE TOOK THE KEYS OF HELL AND DEATH, GOT UP WITH ALL POWER IN HIS HANDS AND LEFT,

DIRT AND THE GRAVE WON'T HOLD HIM DOWN, HIS POWER AND SPIRIT OPENS AND CONTROLS EARTH AND ALL GROUNDS,

YOU CANNOT BURY THE CREATOR OF EARTH, THIS IS WHERE EARTH HAD ITS BIRTH, GOD SEES AND KNOWS EVERY SPECK OF DUST, OF WHICH MAN IS MADE OF GOD DESIGNED US TO SEEK AND TRUST,

GOD IS OVER EVERYTHING ON EARTH BELOW, HE IS THE DESIGNER OF ALL HEAVENS WE WILL EVER KNOW,

REMEMBER CHRIST WAS THE IMMACULATE BIRTH, HIS CONCEPTION WAS NOT OF THIS EARTH,

CHRIST ONLY PUT ON ABRAHAMS SEED, TO FULFILL THE AND BE LIKE THE BROTHERS IN NEED,

HE IS TRULY NO MAN'S BLOOD OR SEED, THAT IS HOW HE CONQUERED, SATAN THROUGH PERFORMING SPIRITUAL AND GODLY DEEDS,

HE SURPASSES EVERYTHING WE CAN THINK AND CAN EVER KNOW, HE UPHOLDS YESTERDAY, TODAY, AND ALL TOMORROWS,

DIRT AND THE GRAVE WON'T HOLD HIM DOWN, HIS POWER AND SPIRIT OPENS AND CONTROLS EARTH AND ALL GROUNDS,

DON'T OPEN MY LIFE, DEVILS!

IT IS CLEAR TO ME WHY DEVILS HIDE, ESPECIALLY WHEN THEY HAVE BREACHED A LIFE AND ARE INSIDE,

THEY HAVE NO HOME AND PLACE OF THEIR OWM, SO THEY POSSESS, THOSE WHO THEY THINK ARE ALONE,

THEY BRAKE IN AND STEAL EVERYTHING OF WORTH, WHAT THEY REALLY WANT IS TO STEAL YOUR SOUL AND BIRTH,

THE INNOCENT THEY POLLUTE, DEFILE, AND MAIM, FOR THIS EVIL IS WHY JESUS CAME,

TO SET FREE THE SOUL BOUND, AND BREAK THE CHAINS OF HELL, WHEN JESUS TOOK THE KEYS OF HELL, THE DEVILS WHOLE KINGDOM FELL,

SO, DEVILS, DON'T COME HERE TRYING TO OPEN MY LIFE, I HAVE BEEN REDEEMED AND I BELONG TO CHRIST,

THEY ARE FULL OF THE POISON OF ASP AND SNAKES, THEY ARE CHILDREN SPAWN FROM HELL THAT THE DEVIL MAKES,

BE VERY CAREFUL AROUND THEM DO NOT SLEEP OR REST, THEY ARE JUST WAITING TO FEAST AND EAT YOUR FLESH,

STOLEN WATERS ARE IN THEIR POSSESSIONS, TRYING TO SECURE ALL THE WATER IN THE LAND IS THEIR OBSESSION,

TO THEM NEVER EVER GIVE IN AND NEVER TRUST, THE PRIMARY SECDUCER IS THEY CAPTURE YOU WITH THEIR LUST,

THEY USE LUST AND SEX AND TELL YOU IT IS GRACE, GOD WILL NEVER BE LUSTFULLY AND CARNALLY ABASED,

SO, DEVILS, DON'T COME HERE TRYING TO OPEN MY LIFE, I HAVE BEEN REDEEMED AND I BELONG TO CHRIST,

EMERGENCY PRAYER

WE MUST ALWAYS PRAY FOR THE EVIL THINGS WE MAY HAVE DONE, IN THIS WORLD THEY CALL FOR 911,

CHRISTIANS MUST CALL ON A HIGHER SOURCE, THAT PERPETUATES EVERYTHING AND IS OUR UNIVERSAL LIFE FORCE,

IT IS DIVINE TO REVERENCE GOD AND PRAY, WHO KNOWS THE LITTLE SINS ONE MIGHT COMMITT IN A DAY,

CHRISTIANS SHOULD ALWAYS HAVE AN EMERGENCY PRAYER, WHENEVER YOU PRAY GOD WILL MEET YOU THERE,

PRAYER IS YOUR KEY TO A SACRED DOOR, TO THE FAITHFUL AND UNSEEN THINGS YOU ARE PRAYING FOR,

JUST KEEP IN MIND WE MUST ALWAYS PRAY, THAT IS THE EPITOME OF EACH AND EVERYDAY,

WHY DO YOU THINK FOR PRAYER GOD HAS SPECIAL HOURS, PRAYER IS GOVERNED BY DIVINE POWERS,

CHRISTIANS SHOULD ALWAYS HAVE AN EMERGENCY PRAYER, WHENEVER YOU PRAY GOD WILL MEET YOU THERE,

NEVER DOUBT WHAT GOD CAN DO, HE IS THE PROVIDER AND PROTECTOR OVER YOU,

WHEN YOU THINK YOU ARE LOST AND THERE IS ONLY DOUBT, PRAYER BECOMES YOUR DOORWAY OUT,

CHRISTIANS SHOULD ALWAYS HAVE AN EMERGENCY PRAYER, WHENEVER YOU PRAY GOD'S FAITH, MIRACLES AND POWERS WILL MEET YOU THERE,

EXPANDING GRACE

THANK YOU, FATHER, FOR YOUR MERCY AND ENDLESS GRACE,
WHEN YOU SAW I WAS BEHIND IN MY SPIRITUAL RACE,

YOU LIFTED ME WITH YOUR WINGS OF LOVE AND STRENGTH,
NOW I AM ABLE TO PRAY AND WIN,

NO LONGER AM I JUST ONE IN THE CROWD, NOW I CAN
HOLD MY HEAD UP AND I CAN BE PROUD,

MY FATHER EXPANDED HIS GRACE, SO I COULD WIN MY
SPIRITUAL RACE,

I KNOW THAT YOU ARE ALWAYS AROUND, YOU HELP ME
KEEP MY FEET ON THE GROUND,

THANK YOU, LORD, FOR WATCHING OVER ME, AND GIVING
MOTHER EARTH HER GRAVITY,

WE NEED TO ALWAYS STAY CONNECTED WITH THE MOTHER
EARTH, THAT'S THE PLACE YOU PEOPLED, FOR US TO HAVE
OUR BIRTHS,

YOU DESIGNATED SPECIFIC PLACES AS HOLY AND
SANCTIFIED TO YOU, PLACES LIKE MOUNT SINAI AND
MOUNT MORIAH TOO,

FOR MOSES AND ABRAHAM, YOU EXTENDED AND EXPANDED
YOUR GRACE, ARE EXAMPLES TO THE WHOLE HUMAN RACE,

I SAVED THE BEST TO RECITE AS LAST JESUS CHRIST, THE
ACCOMPLISHMENT OF THE TWO PATRIARCHS LIFE,

THE HEART AND SOUL OF THE EPITOME OF THE MENTIONED TWO, JESUS CHRIST IS THE EXPANDING GRACE, FOR ME AND FOR YOU,

WHEN THEY EXTENDED CHRIST ARMS WHILE ON THE CROSS, THEY WERE EXPANDING HIS GRACE SO NO ONE WOULD BE LOST,

FROM YOUR HOLY NAME I GET MY HOLY GRAIN

IF YOU DON'T KNOW YOU JUST DON'T KNOW, HOW THE SPIRIT WORKS AND HELPS YOU TO GROW,

WE ARE BOUGHT AND PAID FOR WITH A PRICE, BY OUR SAVIOUR AND KING JESUS CHRIST,

THERE ARE MANY THINGS THE DEVIL CANNOT DO, HE MAY STEAL YOU BUT HE CANNOT CREATE YOU,

SATAN DOES NOT HAVE CREATIVE POWERS TO CREATE, WHAT HE STEALS HE MAKES FROM THE DEAD AND LIVES ON NEGATIVITY AND HATE,

SATAN WILL NEVER HAVE ANY SPIRITUAL ACCLAIM, HE WAS GIVEN AN UNHOLY, IGNOBLE, EVIL NAME,

IN HEAVEN AND EARTH SATAN'S EVIL EARNED HIM THE NAME ANTICHRIST, IN THIS WORLD AND FOR THE REST OF HIS EVIL LIFE,

I AM PROUD BECAUSE IT IS FROM YOUR HOLY NAME, IS WHERE I GET MY RIGHTEOUSNESS AND MY HOLY GRAIN,

LORD YOUR EVERY SINGLE WORD IS A WORD OF LIFE, THE VERY ESSENCE OF THE RESURRECTION POWERS THAT RAISED JESUS CHRIST,

I FOUND THE SECRET TO A LIVING AND LIFE-GIVING WELL, IN THE TRUTH OF YOUR WORDS THAT COMES FROM YOUR GOSPEL,

YOU CHANGED MY LIFE AND WRAPPED ME IN YOUR WORDS, AND GAVE MY LIFE NEW MEANING ONCE I ACCEPTED CHRIST AND REALLY HEARD YOUR WORD,

I AM OVER-JOYED AND ETERNALLY PROUD, BECAUSE FROM YOUR HOLY NAME, I GET MY RIGHTEOUNESS AND MY HOLY GRAIN,

GIANTS BIGGER THAN ME, LORD

WHEN THE TIDE WATERS ARE OVER MY HEAD, I REMEMBER EVERYTHING MY GOD HAS SAID,

WHEN LIFE SEEMS TO BIG AND THERE ARE GIANTS TOO, HE WILL REDUCE EVERYTHING BIGGER THAN YOU,

LORD WHEN I AM FACED WITH MY TUMULTOUS PAST, YOU REMIND ME WHERE IT WAS CAST,

YOU THREW IT INTO THE SEA OF FORGETFULNESS, SO MY FUTURE YOU COULD BLESS,

MY PAST WAS HOLDING ME BACK, TRYING NOT TO LET ME GO, YOU PUT A BIBLE IN MY HAND AND SAID NOT SO,

YOU LET ME SEE I HAD SO MUCH MORE IN FRONT OF ME, THAT MY PAST, WAS DECEIVING ME AND DID'NT WANT ME TO BE FREE,

YOU SHOWED ME THE GIANTS THAT WERE BIGGER THAN ME IN MY PAST, YOU REDUCED THEM ALL SO THAT I WOULD NOT BE LAST,

I KNOW LORD, I HAVE NOT BEEN MY BEST, FOR A VERY LONG TIME, MANY THINGS SEEM TO HAVE INTERRUPTED MY MIND,

BUT YOU LORD WILL PUT AN END TO ALL THESE MENTAL INFILTRATIONS, AND FILL ME WITH YOUR PEACEFUL MEDITATIONS,

CASTING OUT LIES AND EVIL HOST, PUTTING FAITH WHERE IT IS NEEDED MOST,

BEAT DOWN THE GIANTS AND THE DEVILS THAT STEAL, BEND THEM ALL LORD TO YOUR INFINITE WILL,

SEND YOUR WORDS LORD TO BATTLE ON THE EVIL DAY, TAKING BACK YOUR HERITAGE PUTTING THEM BACK IN GODS WAYS,

THERE IS NO GIANT, DEVIL IN HELL OR ON EARTH, CAN HAVE WHAT BELONGS TO JESUS CHRIST BIRTH,

WE PRAY THE PRAYER FOR DISSOLUTIONS OVER ALL THE ENEMIES HOST, THAT THEY MAY DISSOLVE FROM ALL OF THEIR POST,

THESE COUNTLESS ENEMIES HAS CAUSE ME UNTOLD PAIN AND ANGUISH, CAUSING ME TO HALT MY ACTIVITIES AND LANGUISH,

BUT YOU LORD HAVE DEFEATED EVERY GIANT IN THIS WORLD, AND THE WORLD TO COME THERE IS NO VICTORY YOU HAVE NOT WON,

I DO NOT FRET NOW WHEN I SEE THEM I SAY, GIANTS BIGGER THAN ME, I HAVE SOMEONE BIGGER THAN THEE,

GOD'S WORD ARMY

THE BATTLE IS ALWAYS WAGED FOR THE TRUTH TO GET THROUGH, GOD IS ALWAYS FIGHTING FOR ME AND FOR YOU,

ALL SOULS ARE PRECIOUS TO OUR LORD, HE IS EACH SAINTS SPIRITUAL BODYGUARD,

HE HAS AN ARMY OF TRILLIONS OF WORDS, EACH WORD IS COMMANDED BY OUR GOD AND IS HEARD,

HOW DO YOU DESTROY SOMETHING THAT HAS A SPECIAL LIFE, THAT CANNOT BE DESTROYED BY A GUN, SPEAR OR A KNIFE,

GOD'S ARMY OF SPIRITUAL WORDS, OF LIFE AND TRUTH, WILL ALWAYS STAND FIRM TALL AND FULL OF YOUTH,

THEY ARE DESIGNED AND CRAFTED FOR ETERNAL WARS, THEY HAVE NO PROBLEM WITH WOUNDS OR SCARS,

THEY HAVE BEEN FIGHTING WARS WITHIN YOUR MIND, FROM THE INCEPTION OF YOUR BEING AND THE BEGINNING OF YOUR TIME,

DON'T THINK IT'S OVER WHEN THERE ARE ONLY A FEW, THAT'S THE TIME WORDS MULTIPLY AND FORM ANOTHER CREW,

MY GOD HAS THE GREATER ARMY FOR ALL HIS INHERITANCE, GOD IS THEIR PROTECTOR, GOD IS THEIR DEFENCE,

WE FIGHT WITH SPIRITUAL WORDS THAT CAN NEVER DIE, YOU MIGHT WOUND THEM BUT YOU CAN NEVER CONSUME THEM,

IF IT HAPPENS THAT ONE THOUSAND DID FALL, TEN TIMES, (TEN THOUSAND), THAT WILL BE MULTIPLIED AND RAISED UP AT GOD'S CALL,

IN THE HANDS OF GOD EVERY SINGLE WORD OF THE LORD, IS TRANSFORMED FROM A MAN OR WOMAN TO A DIVINELY COMMANDED SWORD,

DO NOT CROSS SWORDS WITH THE MASTER, HE WEILDS HIS WORDS AND HIS SWORDS THROUGH HIS CREATIONS, THE BIBLE AND HIS PASTORS,

THE HOLY BIBLE IS A WEAPON, WHY DO YOU THINK IT IS CALLED GOD'S WORD, HIS PEOPLE TRANSFORM INTO SWORDS WHEN THEY HEAR THE WORD,

THEIR NUMBERS ARE GREAT, THEY ARE AS ENDLESS AS ETERNITY, THEY ARE GOD'S OWN SPIRITUAL WORD ARMY,

THY WORD OH LORD,

IS A LAMP UNTO MY FEET

GOD IS WRITING MY STORY

WHEN YOU SEE TROUBLES IN YOUR LIFE EVERYDAY, JUST KNOW THAT GOD IS THERE MAKING YOU A WAY,

YOU MUST BE VIRTUOUSLY AND OVERTLY PATIENT, FOR YOU TO RECEIVE OF GOD'S DIVINE INTENT,

YOU WILL HEAR MANY OPPOSING VOICES, DON'T LISTEN TO THEM, THEY ARE THE NEGATIVE CHOICES,

THEY WILL TRY TO KEEP YOUR MIND UNBALANCED, YOU MUST ALWAYS BE READY FOR THEIR EVIL CHALLENGES,

MANY OF THEIR FORCES WILL TRY TO ALTER AND CHANGE, WHAT GOD IS HERE TO REARRANGE,

I WAS OUT OF MIND AND OUT OF TOUCH, GOD RECONCILED ME BECAUSE HE LOVED ME THAT MUCH,

WHEN I THOUGHT THERE WAS NO-ONE THERE FOR ME, GOD WAS THERE WRITING, MY LIFE'S HISTORY, TO CREATE A STORY AND LIFE FOR ME TO BE ME,

TRIALS AND TRIBULATIONS ARE COMMON PLACE IN A CHRISTIAN'S LIFE, THAT IS WHY WE SERVE JESUS CHRIST,

WE ARE THE TESTIMONIES OF JESUS CHRIST, WE SUFFER SOMETHINGS AS HE DID IN THIS LIFE,

WHEN I THOUGHT NO-ONE WAS THERE FOR ME, GOD WAS THERE WRITING MY LIFE'S STORY, SO I COULD LIVE AND BE ME,

GOD REIGNS
OVER MY SOUL

NO MATTER WHAT THIS WORLD MAY DO TO ME, OF THIS I AM SURE, GOD IS THE ONLY SOURCE OF MY LIFE THAT WILL ENDURE,

HE IS THE EPITOME OF MY VERY BEING, GOD IS MY ENTIRE LIFE, HE IS MY SOURCE, GOD IS MY EVERY THING,

BE WARNED IF YOU HAPPEN TO DESTROY, KILL OR STEAL, JUST KNOW THAT EACH ORGAN IN ME WAS CREATED BY GOD'S WILL,

FROM THE BOTTOM OF MY FEET, TO THE TOP OF MY HEAD, GOD HAS PRONOUNCE HIS BLESSINGS OVER ME, WORDS OF LIFE IS WHAT HE SAID,

GOD SAID YOU SHALL LIVE, AND YOU SHALL NOT DIE, I AM YOUR RESURRECTION OF LIFE, THROUGH ME YOU WILL LIVE I CANNOT LIE,

I AM ELATED TO KNOW THAT GOD REIGNS OVER MY SOUL, EVERY SINGLE PART OF ME HE KEEPS IT WHOLE,

HE IS THE VEIL OVER MY LIFE THAT COVERS ME EVERYDAY, HE DIRECTS MY COURSES, HE PLANS MY WAYS,

THERE IS NOT ONE PART OF ME THAT GOD DID NOT FILL, HE DESIGNED THEM, HE BLESSED THEM, AND INCORPORATED THEM INTO HIS WILL,

AS LONG AS I HAVE ANY PART OF ME MY GOD REIGNS, HE IS MY MAKER AND MY CREATOR HE IS MY EVERYTHING, HE IS MY KING,

I AM ELATED TO KNOW THAT GOD REIGNS OVER MY SOUL, EVERY SINGLE PART OF ME HE KEEPS THEM WHOLE,

GOD'S SEVEN WONDERS
OF THE WORLD

WHY DO WE EQUATE THE MAJESTIC EARTHLY THINGS, WITH THE SUPERIOR OR PHYSICAL BEINGS,

WE DON'T EVEN ASSOCIATE THAT THESE THINGS ARE GREAT, ONLY BECAUSE GOD ALLOWED THEM TO BE GREAT,

WHEN YOU HAVE TIME TAKE A LOOK, YOU WILL FIND THESE SEVEN WONDERS IN GOD'S HOLY BOOK,

THE WONDERS I DID FIND WAS IN THE NEW TESTAMENT, WAS ALL PURPOSED WITH GOD'S INTENT,

FOR MAN TO FIND THE TRUTH'S THAT HAS EXISTED, FROM ALL OUR YOUTH,

WHEN COUPLED WITH GOD'S PROPHESY, HAS THE ABILITY TO SET ANYONE FREE, THROUGH GOD'S DIVINITY,

ONE OF THE WONDERS THAT HAD THEIR DAY, IS IN THE BOOK OF COLOSSAE, A GREAT WORK DONE IN THE CITY TO LET HISTORY STAND AS A MASTER PIECE IN THE LAND,

ANOTHER WONDER IS THE GREAT TEMPLE AT EPHESUS, JESUS REDEFINED EVERYTHING TO CREATE A PEOPLE WHO ARE JUST,

THE ALEXANDRIAN LIGHTHOUSE WAS HIGHLY RECOGNIZED BY MOST, ESPECIALLY THOSE TRAVELLING WITHIN IT'S COAST,

DON'T NEGLECT TO RECALL THE HANGING GARDENS OF BABYLON, FOR WONDER THEY HAD DONE,

WE ALSO MENTION MT. OLYMPUS, WHERE THE ANCIENT GOD'S RESIDED,

I MAY NOT MENTION ALL SEVEN, THE GREATEST WONDER WAS IN HEAVEN, JESUS CHRIST, MAKER AND GREATEST WONDER OF ALL, HIS CREATIONS WAS BEYOND AND AFTER MAN'S FALL,

HE IS SEVEN WONDERS ALL WRAPPED IN TO ONE, IS THE SUBSTANCE AND BEGINNING OF WHY THEY BEGUN,

THE REAL AND TRUE WONDER TO EVVERYONE'S LIFE, THE NAME IS EXALTED IT IS JESUS CHRIST,

GOD'S DRIVING FORCE

SOME OF US ARE DRIVEN BY THE WRONG ATTITUDES AND POWERS, SOME OF US ARE USED FOR SHORT PERIODS OF TIME SOME FOR EXTENDED HOURS,

WHATEVER THE USE YOU CAN BE ASSURED, ONLY THROUGH GOD ARE WE ALL ABLE TO ENDURE IT,

MAN AND WOMAN WAS CREATED WITH SPECIFIC APPETITES, LIKE COMPUTERS DRIVES WE MUST BE FULFILLED TO EVEN FEEL RIGHT,

BELIEVE IT OR NOT THOSE SUPERIOR INSTINCTS AND DRIVES, ARE HOW WE LIVE AND HOW WE HUMANISTICALLY THRIVE,

WE ARE SO MUCH MORE THAN COMPUTERIZED CONNECTIONS AND WIRES, THE REAL ESSENCE OF US REACHES SO MUCH HIGHER,

FAR BEYOND BASE METAL, DIODES, URETHANE AND PLASTIC, ANGELS ARE COMPOSED OF AN ETHERIAL SUBSTANCES, AND THE HOLY SPIRIT,

THERE IS ONE THING THAT CAN'T BE DENIED WITHIN EVERY FOUNDATION AND COURSE, GOD IS SOLE SPIRITUAL DRIVING FORCE,

JUST TO LET HUMANITY KNOW WE ARE NOT IT, WE ARE NOT EVEN A ALITTLE BIT, IT IS ALL GOD ALL THE WAY THROUGH, HE IS SPIRITUALLY EMANATING FROM ME AND YOU,

SO JUST KNOW WHENEVER YOU DO SOMETHING WRONG, YOU ARE DOING IT IN THE PRESENCE OF GOD, YOU ARE NOT ALONE,

WHEATHER IT IS GOOD OR BAD GOD WILL JUDGE IT, WE MUST REALIZE WHOSE SPIRIT WE LIVE WITH,

EVERYTHING YOU DO IN LIFE IS RECORDED, BY THE MIND, THE EARS OR THE EYES, THEY ARE THE DIVINE WITTNESSES, WITHIN YOURSELF, THAT YOU DON'T REALIZE,

IF YOU ARE ON TRIAL FOR SOMETHING YOU DID NOT DO, YOU DON'T NEED AN OUTSIDE WITTNESS YOU JUST NEED YOU,

GOD IS STANDING BY AT ALL TIMES UPHOLDING YOUR TRUTH, WHEN OTHERS MAYBE CONGREGATING AGAINST YOU IN THEIR UNTRUTHS,

BUT BE NOT DISMAYED WHOEVER IS THE GUILTY ONE, GOD WILL JUDGE THEM FOR EVERY WRONG THEY HAVE DONE,

IT CAN BE ONE, OR IT CAN BE A TRILLION, THERE IS NO NUMBER THAT GOD CANNOT JUDGE TO COMPENSATE SOMEONE,

NEXT TIME YOU ARE THINKING OF DOING SOMETHING OUTSIDE OF THE CHARACTER OF GOD, REMEMBER WHOSE PRESENCE, YOU ARE DOING IT IN, OUR SAVIOUR OUR LORD,

WE THINK WE ARE RULED BY THE COURTS AND MAGISTRATES OF TODAY, AS THE PREACHER HAS SAID IN HIS HOLY BOOK THERE ARE THOSE HIGHER THAN THEY,

WHEN WE ARE SIDE TRACKED AND DERAILED AND KNOCKED OFF OR TAKEN OVER BY A FORCE, IT IS GOD'S DRIVING FORCE THAT PUTS US BACK ON COURSE,

HE'S SO MAJESTIC TO ME!

THERE ARE NO WORDS TO DESCRIBE THE UNDESCRIBILE,
THERE ARE SOME THINGS WE WILL NEVER KNOW,

I CAN SAY THAT ONE DAY I WILL SEE, THE ONE WHO IS SO
SPIRITUALLY MAJESTIC TO ME,

HE PAINTS AND IMBUES CREATION WITH COLORS WE DON'T
EVEN KNOW, SOME OF THESE COLORS ARE FAR BEYOND
OUR RAINBOW,

ALL OF CREATION ARE HIS HANDY WORKS, HE BREATHED
INTO THIS UNIVERSE, EVERY SPOKEN WORD HAS BECOME
A BIBLICAL VERSE,

FOR US TO KNOW AND READ WHAT OUR GOD HAS DONE,
HE PUT THEM INTO 66 BOOKS INTO A HOLY BIBLE AS ONE,

HE HAS INSPIRED MEN TO WRITE ALL THE COMMANDMENTS
AND ALL THE LAWS, HE ENTERED INTO A PERFECT COVENANT
WITH MANKIND WITHOUT FLAWS,

THROUGH THIS COVENANT WE WOULD HAVE SALVATION,
THROUGH HIS SON JESUS CHRIST BORN TO SAVE
EVERY NATION,

I CAN SAY THAT ONE DAY I WILL SEE, THE ONE WHO IS SO
SPIRITUALLY MAJESTIC TO ME,

NO ONE BUT GOD CAN TRULY SAY WHO, WHAT OR HOW,
THE LORD WILL SAVE IN THE END, BUT WE DO KNOW WE
ARE ALL HIS CHOSEN CHILDREN,

I THANK GOD FOR THE IMMACULATE GIFT OF LIFE, WE NOW KNOW AS JESUS CHRIST,

WITHOUT HIM I WOULD HAVE BEEN LOST, WITH NO-ONE TO PAY MY SIN DEBT COST,

YOU ARE OMNIPOTENT, OMNIPRESENT AND ENTERNALLY PLACED WITHIN THE HEAVENLY SPHERES, TIME HAS NO FACTOR IN YOUR EXISTENCE YOU ARE CREATOR OF ALL YEARS,

YOU CAN NEVER LEAVE YOURSELF NOR CAN YOU LEAVE YOUR HEALTH, BECAUSE YOU ARE EVERYTHING YOU ARE THE ENTIRE EARTH'S WEALTH,

WHEN I HERE EVIL DEMONS LIE AND SAY, JESUS CHRIST IS NOT HERE, I KNOW THAT THEY ARE LYING, BECAUSE THEY ONLY EXIST BECAUSE OF FEAR,

I KNOW THAT WHEN CHRIST IS NO LONGER HERE, EVERY EVIL ENTITIY WILL BE CAST INTO THE LAKE OF FIRE TO BURN FOR ETERNAL YEARS,

I CAN SAY THAT ONE DAY I WILL SEE, THE ONE WHO IS SO SPIRITUALLY MAJESTIC TO ME,

HEAVEN'S OWN

SOMETIME IT IS A CONFUSING PLACE, IN THE MULTITUDES OF THE HUMAN RACE,

THEN I HAVE TO REMEMBER THIS IS NOT MY HOME, GOD PLACE ME AS ONE OF HEAVENS OWN,

WE ARE IN THE WORLD, BUT NOT COMPLETELY OF IT, MY SPIRIT AND THE IS WORLD IS NOT A GOOD FIT,

GOD SOWED IN ME ANGELS AND LIGHT, THAT WHATEVER I DECIDED TO DO IN LIFE IT WOULD BE BLESSED AND RIGHT,

GOD MADE SURE I UNDERSTOOD, PART OF AN ANGELS JOB IS TO UNITE BROTHERHOODS,

AT ALL COST AN ANGELS ATTEMPTS AND INTENTS, MUST ALWAYS BE BLESSED BENEVOLENT,

IT IS A BLESSING TO BE OF THE ANGELIC HOST, WATCHING AND GUARDING YOUR ANGELIC POST,

I AM TRULY ONE OF HEAVEN'S OWN FULL OF GOD'S GLORY, A TESTIMENT IN HIS SACRED AND ETERNAL STORY,

IN THE END GOD'S CHILDREN WILL BE GATHERED AROUND HIS THRONE, BECAUSE ALL ANGELS ARE HEAVENLY SOWN,

I AM TRULY ONE OF HEAVEN'S OWN, ONE DAY GOD WILL TAKE ALL ANGELS TO THEIR HEAVENLY HOME,

HOLY THINGS ARE NOT MEANT FOR THE DEVILS

IT IS APPARENT WHAT IS GOOD AND WHAT IS BAD, HOLINESS IS SOMETHING THE DEVIL HAS NEVER HAD,

WHEN HE WAS IN HEAVEN HE WAS NOT PURE, THROUGH HIS JEALOUSY, OF GOD'S MAJESTY HE COULD NOT ENDURE,

HIS SCHEMES TO BECOME THE REIGNING AUTHORITY, REMOVED HIM FROM HEAVEN'S LIGHT AND HEAVEN'S IMMORTALITY,

HE WAS CAST INTO A NEGATIVE LIGHT, HE WILL ALWAYS BE KNOWN AS THE ANTICHRIST,

HE IS THE FATHER OF ALL FILTH PIGS AND HOGS, HE HAS AN UNHOLY ARMY OF HELL HOUNDS AND DOGS,

SATAN'S THOUGHTS ARE THE WORST, GOD SENTENCED HIM WITH AN ETERNAL CURSE,

ALL HE WILL EVER DO IS STEAL KILL AND DESTROY, BE DETESTIBLE, NEGATIVE, HATEFUL AND HE WILL ALWAYS ANNOY,

HE WILL NEVER LOVE YOU AND WILL ALWAYS HATE YOU, EVERYTHING ABOUT YOU HE JUST WANTS TO DAM YOU,

HE CANNOT LOVE WITH THE ESSENCE OF GOD'S DIVINE SOURCE, THAT IS THE ULTIMATE ESSENCE OF GOD'S DIVINE FORCE,

AS YOU SEE HOLY THINGS IS NOT MEANT FOR THE DEVIL, HE CAN NEVER AGAIN REACH GOD'S HOLY LEVEL,

GOD'S THOUGHTS ARE SPIRITUAL, PURE, RIGHT, LIGHT AND SUBLIME, WE SHOULD EXPECT NOTHING BUT THE BEST FROM THE DIVINE,

AS REPRESENTATIVES OF GOD'S DIVINE LIGHT, WE MUST BE ABLE TO UPHOLD WHAT IS DIVINE AND RIGHT,

WE CANNOT IGNORE WHAT IS HATEFUL, VENGEFUL AND UNJUST, BECAUSE OF THIS WORLDS EVILNESS, PROMISCURITY AND LUST,

AS YOU SEE HOLY THINGS ARE NOT MEANT FOR THE DEVIL, HE CAN NEVER AGAIN REACH GOD'S HOLY LEVEL,

YOU CANNOT FEED TWO OPPOSING FORCES, WITHOUT CATERING TO ONE AS A PRIMARY SOURCE,

YOU MUST LOVE ONE AND HATE THE OTHER, BECAUSE LOVE AND HATE OPPOSE EACH OTHER,

THE DEVILS PRIMARY SOURCE IS HATE, HE CANNOT LOVE WHAT GOD HAS MADE GREAT,

THOSE OF US WHO HAS CHOSEN TO LIVE FOR CHRIST, LIVE IN THE IMAGE OF HIS DIVINE LIFE AND LIGHT,

I AM NOT AN ATTENDANT OF HELL

LOOK DEEPLY INTO MY EYES CAN'T YOU SEE, THERE IS A GOD LIVING INSIDE OF ME,

I WAS MADE BY AND FOR GOD ALONE, TO BE BY HIS SIDE IN JUDGEMENT WHEN HE RULES FROM HIS THRONE,

I KNOW I AM PART OF HEAVEN'S BEST, I AM STRONG, FAITHFUL, AND ETERNALLY BLEST,

SO, I CAN NEVER BE AN ATTENDANT OF HELL, I HAVE TOO MUCH HEAVEN INSIDE IF YOU REALLY LOOK AT ME YOU CAN TELL,

GOD LET ME KNOW I AM A CHOSEN ONE, HE GAVE ME A KINGLY NAME, AFTER KING SOLOMON,

HE SAID IF MY PEOPLE, CALLED BY MY NAME WILL HUMBLE THEMSELVES AND PRAY, I WILL HEAL THEIR LAND AND REINSTITUTE THEIR DAY,

I HAVE NO DOUBT HEAVEN IS MY HOME, IT IS WHERE MY GOD RULE AND SITS ON HIS THRONE,

I DON'T HAVE TO THINK ABOUT IT TWICE, GOD DESIGNED MY LIFE TO BE AN ATTENDANT TO AND FOR JESUS CHRIST,

SO, I CAN NEVER BE AN ATTENDANT OF HELL, I HAVE TOO MUCH HEAVEN INSIDE IF YOU REALLY LOOK AT ME YOU CAN TELL,

YOU MUST FIRST EXCEPT ME FOR WHO I AM, AND STOP TRYING TO CURSE ME, AND MAKE ME DAMMED,

WHEN YOU EXCEPT ME FOR WHO GOD MADE ME, ONLY THEN WILL YOU BE ABLE TO SEE THE HIDDEN SIDE OF MY DESTINY,

I AM VERY GLAD THAT IT WAS GOD'S WILL, TO KEEP PART OF MY LIFE CONCEALED,

I WAS TOO MEEK AND HUMBLE FOR THIS WICKED WORLD OF OURS, TOO MANY THIEVES, HATRED, RUMORS AND WARS,

I AM MEEK AS GOD'S LAMB, BUT I CAN BECOME LIKE STEEL AND IRON,

GOD'S SECOND RETURN WILL BE AS A FEROCIOUS AND RAVENOUS LION,

I PREFER TO SEE GOD'S GENTLE SIDE, WHEN HE COMES AS THE LAMB I DON'T HAVE TO RUN AND HIDE,

IN MY HEART SOUL AND SPIRIT, I KNOW THAT IT'S RIGHT, TO ALWAYS BE AN ATTENDANT TO JESUS CHRIST,

I SHALL PASS THROUGH THEIR MIDST

SAFELY I SHALL PASS RIGHT ON THROUGH, ALL THE WALLS, ALL THE MOUNTAINS, THAT SEEM TO HINDER YOU,

TO MAKE A WAY FOR THE CHILDREN OF THE DAY, DESTINED FOR ALL OF THESE CHRIST DID PAY,

IT PLEASED THE FATHER TO MAKE HIM THE ONE AND ONLY LAMB, TO BECOME THE GREAT I AM,

THAT COULD NEVER BE STOPPED BY TRIBULATIONS OR STRIFE, HE WAS GIVEN AN UNSTOPPABLE LIFE,

WHILE IN THE TOMB AND GRAVE, EVEN THE GRAVE BEHAVED, WHEN HE DECIDED TO GET UP THE WHOLE EARTH OPENED UP,

HE ROSE WITH THE CHILDREN OF THE DAY, NOTHING IN HELL OR EARTH COULD GET IN HIS WAY, TO FULFILL A DESTINY OF THE WRITTEN BOOK, THAT CAUSED DEMONS TO TREMBLE AND THE WHOLE UNIVERSE SHOOK,

EARTHQUAKES, FLOODS, TORANADOS AND HURRICANES TOO, THAT IS WHAT HAPPENS WHEN MY GOD COMES AND PASSES THROUGH,

LIGHTINGS, THUNDERS AND FIRE, HAIL AND RAIN, ALL THE ELEMENT GREETED HIM WHEN HE CAME,

I SHALL PASS RIGHT THROUGH THEIR MIDST, NO DEMI GOD, DEMON OR ELEMENT SHALL EVER STOP THIS,

I AM THE ONE WHO WATERS MOTHER EARTH WHEN SHE THIRST, I MADE HER A SEA BECAUSE I WAS MADE FIRST,

I HAVE ALL THE ELEMENTS AND LIFE BALLED UP IN MY FIST, I SHALL NEVER LET A DEMON OR DEVIL STOP THIS,

I DEFEATED SATAN AND TOOK HIS SEAT, I LET MY CHILDREN WALK ON HIM EVERYDAY HE IS UNDER THEIR FEET,

I SHALL PASS RIGHT THROUGH THEIR MIDST, NO DEMI GOD, DEMON OR ELEMENT SHALL EVER STOP THIS,

THEY WANTED TO REMOVE YOUR PLACE LORD, LET THEM CELEBRATE DELUSIONS, SHOW THEM HOW YOU CAN SPIRITUALLY USE THEM,

TO BELIEVE EVERYTHING THEY SEE, WHICH IS ONLY THEIR OWN THEIR REALITY,

GOD SAYS NOTHING IN HEAVEN OR EARTH SHALL EVER HINDER ME, I HAVE CREAFTED EVERYTHING TO SERVE ONLY ME,

A CREATION WILL NEVER BE GREATED THAN ITS MASTER, LIKE A SCULPTOR GOD FASHIONED CREATED US AS OUR CRAFTER,

I SHALL PASS RIGHT THROUGH THEIR MIDST, NO DEMI GOD, DEMON OR ELEMENT SHALL EVER STOP THIS,

ILLUMINATED SUN

I KNOW THE REAL LIGHT OF THE SUN, IT IS NOT A MAGNIFIED LIGHT THAT THEY CALL THE SUN,

THE DIFFERENCE BETWEEN THE TWO, IS THAT WITH PROPER INSTRUMENTS ANYONE CAN BE ILLUMINATED EVEN YOU,

HOW IT IS DIFFERENT FROM THE SUN, IT'S POWER NEVER TIRERS, IT IS NOT JUST LIGHT IT IS COMPOSED OF PURE FIRE,

THEY CALL IT THE EMPYREAM, A PLACE OF PURE FIRE, WHERE THE ANGELS AND GOD HIMSELF RELAX AND REPOSE IN THE FIRE,

I HAVE SEEN ILLUMINATION, THAT WAS BRIGHTER THAN THE SUN, THAT STILL DID NOT POSSESS THE HEAT AND FIRE THAT SHOULD GENERATE FROM A SUN,

THIS ANIMATED TIME IN WHICH WE LIVE, IS ALL DIGITALLY CONSTRUCTED, BY A MACHINES WILL,

IT TAKES FIRE TO GENERATE LIFE AND GENERATIONS, NOT A MAGNIFYING GLASS FOR ILLUMINATION,

THE SUN WILL PRODUCE FIRE NO MATTER WHERE IT IS, THE SUN'S NATURE IS UNCHANGING AND ITS ALL HIS,

THE SUN REPRESENTS THE DAY AND IS CALLED DIURNAL TIME, THE MOON REPRESENTS THE NIGHT AND IS CALLED NOCTURNAL TIME,

IMAGES OF PAGANS

THERE HAS BEEN MANY DIFFERENT PEOPLE IN THE AGES, THAT HAS WRITTEN ABOUT EVIL IN VARIOUS BOOKS AND PAGES,

THEY WORSHIPPED THE CREATURES MORE THAN THE CREATOR, GOD WAS ALWAYS THEIR MEDIATOR,

THEY SERVED MANY PAGAN GODS TO ACQUIRE MATERIAL THINGS, NOT REALIZING THE TROUBLE DISEASE AND HARDSHIPS IT MAY BRING,

GOD WILL NOT BE MOCKED BY VESSELS OF CLAY, WOOD, AND STEEL, GOD IS THE ONLY GOD, WITH LIFE, BREADTH, AND A WILL,

WHEN GOD GETS READY, YOU CANNOT CALL ON MOLECH, IT IS NOT A GOD THAT PROTECTS,

IT IS A FALSE GOD OF FIRE AND BLOOD DEMANDS, OF SACRIFICED CHILDREN WITHIN GOD'S GIVEN LAND,

THE WORSHIPPERS ARE ABOMINIABLE, FILTHY, AND FLESH EATERS OF THE DEAD, THEY WORSHIP THE FILTH OF THE LAND, INSTEAD OF THE HEAVENLY BREAD,

BLOOD SUCKERS, WHOREMONGERS, BACKBITERS, AND ADULTERERS TOO, ALL THE VICES AND EVIL IN THE BIBLE THESE PEOPLE DO,

WITCHES, WARLOCKS, AND HOME MADE SIN, THE GATES OF HEAVEN, THESE WILL NOT ENTER IN,

THEY ROBBED GOD'S PEOPLE, AND ABRAHAM'S SEED, THEY TRIED TO POISION AND DEFILE EVERYTHING JESUS WOULD NEED,

THEY WANTED TO MAKE SURE JESUS COULD NOT MAKE IT BACK, I THINK THEY FORGOT GOD HAS INFINITE WAYS OF ATTACKS,

THEY DEFILED AND TRIED TO CLOSE EVERY DOOR, HOW CAN YOU SHUT OUT A GOD THAT MADE THE DOOR, THE WORLD, AND MUCH, MUCH, MORE,

A SPIRIT HAS NO LIMITS IN A MATERIAL WORLD, IT CAN INHABIT, A CAR, A HOUSE, A BOY OR A GIRL,

A SPIRITUAL ENTRANCE IS WHERE IT LISTS, IT MAY BE A SOLID FORM OR IT MAYBE A VAPOR, OR MIST,

IMITATING IMAGES TRYING TO BE LIKE GOD AGAIN, WHEN WILL THEY REALIZE THEY ARE JUST PAGANS,

JESUS I WILL NEVER GIVE YOU UP!

NO MATTER WHAT THE WORLD SAYS ABOUT YOU, I WILL NEVER LEAVE YOU,

THERE'S NOTHING THEY CAN DO, TO PERUADE AND SEPARATE ME FROM YOU,

I WAS TAUGHT TO NEVER GIVE UP, ON WHAT YOU KNOW IS RIGHT, ALWAYS BELIEVE IN THE TRUTH KEEP IT IN YOUR SIGHT,

THE OLD SAYING SAYS, KEEP YOUR EYES ON THE PRIZE, THEREFORE I DO SO AND KEEP MY MIND POSITIVE PRAYERFUL AND SPIRITUALLY REALIZE,

JESUS I WILL NEVER GIVE YOU UP, YOU HOLD THE REINS TO MY LIFE, AND SUPPLY MY SPIRITUAL STUFF,

I ESTEEM YOU AS THE ONLY TRUE SOURCE THAT CAN HEAL EVERYTHING, GOD VESTED IN YOU THIS RIGHT WHERE YOU CAN HEAL EVERY HUMAN BEING,

YOU MY LORD HAVE THE WORDS OF LIFE LIGHT AND LOVE, IF MANKIND WOULD FOLLOW YOU WE WOULD HAVE EVERYTHING WE COULD THINK OF,

ALL DISEASES WON'T AND DON'T HAVE A CURE, THEY ARE THE PERFECTIONS OF THE WORK OF GOD'S, TO SHOW HIS HOLY WORDS ARE PURE AND ARE THE CURE,

THAT IS WHY, JESUS I WILL NEVER GIVE YOU UP, YOU HOLD THE REINS TO MY LIFE, AND SUPPLY MY SPIRITUAL STUFF,

JESUS WILL NEVER DIE

OH! HOW THEY WANT ME TO BELIEVE, JESUS DIED LIKE A MORTAL MAN,

THEN THE MIRACLE OF SALAVATION AND HIS RESURRECTION COULD NOT STAND,

THAT WOULD MEAN THE WHOLE WORLD WOULD BE LOST, IF THEY COLD MAKE US BELIEVE CHRIST DID NOT PAY REDEMPTIONS COST,

I SPEAK FOR ME, MYSELF, AND I, I KNOW THAT CHRIST PAID FOR ME, AND THAT ON THE THIRD DAY HE ROSE, WITH ALL POWER, AND ALL THE SPIRITS HE CHOSE,

LET ME BE THE FIRST TO SAY, JESUS CHRIST CAN NEVER DIE A MORTAL DEATH,

HE IS THE EPITOME OF ALL LIFE , IT IS ALL IN HIS BREATH,

HIS VERY ESSENCE IS TOO POWERFUL FOR ANY GRAVE, EARTH WOULD PROBABLY LIFT HIM UP FROM THE GROUND,

OBEYING DIVINE ORDER, KNOWING HIS SPIRIT IS TOO SPIRITUALLY SOUND, TO BE IN ANY GROUND,

EVERYTHING IN EXISTENCE KNOWS WHO JESUS CHRIST IS, THEY MUST OBEY THIS WHY AND HOW THEY LIVE,

EVERYTHING IN EXISTENCE KNOWS WHERE JESUS CHRIST BELONGS, CREATION KNOWS HEAVEN IS HIS HOME,

JESUS WILL NEVER DIE LET ME TELL YOU THE REASON WHY, THERE WOULD BE NO ONTOLOGICAL EXISTENCE OF ANY LIFE EVERY SINGLE THING STARTS WITH CHRIST,

WE ALL KNOW THAT HE WAS HEAVEN SENT, HE UNDERSTOOD AND CONTROLLED ALL THE ELEMENTS,

GOD KNEW THAT MANKIND WAS CAPABLE OF BEING UNSOUND, THAT IS HOW THE BEGGARLY ELEMENTS KEPT MAN BOUND,

JESUS CHRIST CAN NEVER DIE SO LET ME TELL YOU WHY, HIS FATHER GAVE HIM ALL THE WORLD SEES, HE REMOVED SATAN AND SNATCHED AWAY HIS KEYS,

JESUS IS NOW KEEPER OF DEATH, HELL, AND THE GRAVE, HE HAS THE KEYS AND IT IS HIS CHOICE TO WHO HE SAVES,

JESUS CHRIST LOVE IS STONGER THAN DEATH, HE IS THE COMPOSITION OF ALL ETERNITY IN ONE ENDLESS BREADTH,

JUST BECAUSE

WE SHOULD BE THANKFUL EVERY SINGLE DAY, THAT GOD HAS ALLOWED US TO BE AND TO PRAY, TO REVERENCE HIM AS WE SAID WE WOULD, TO GIVE HIM HIS GLORY AS ALL HUMANITY SHOULD,

SOME THINGS WE NEED TO SAY, AND NEED TO DO JUST BECAUSE, GOD IS OUR SAVIOUR AND KEEPPER OF ALL SPIRITUAL LIFE AND LAWS,

GOD MOVES AT HIS OWN WILL, GOD UNCOVERS AND JUDGES ALL THINGS HE REVEALS, NEVER THINK THERE WAS ANYTHING GOD COULD NOT HEAL,

IT IS GOD'S PERROGATIVE TO HEAL OR NOT TO HEAL, IT'S NOT THAT HE CAN'T OVER-RULE DISEASE OR SITUATION, BY HIS SOVERIGN WILL,

THINK FOR A MOMENT AND REMEMBER YOUR TERRIBLE LIFE, BEFORE GOD CAME IN AND REMOVED THE STRIFE,

DRUG ADDICT, WHOREMONGER, AND HOMOSEXUAL TOO, THERE WASN'T MANY THINGS YOU DIDN'T DO,

WE ALL KNOW AND REMEMBER WHERE WE WAS, GOD'S LOVE SAVED AND CLEANSED US JUST BECAUSE,

I WANT TO THANK YOU LORD, FOR MY FAMILY AND MY HOUSE, THE MANY TIMES I DIDN'T SEE HOW YOU PAID THE COST,

LET ME NEVER FORGET, YOUR UNDYING LOVE WHEN MERCY AND GRACE MET, ON THE CROSS MY SALAVATION WAS SET,

MOST OF ALL I HUMBLY EXTEND MY GRATITUDE YOU PAID
FOR US NOT TO BE LOST, ALL OUR SALVATION AND SIN DEBT
WAS PAID ON THE CROSS,

JUST DON'T TAKE
NOTHING OF MINE

ME IS NOT WHERE YOU WANT TO BE,

YOU KNOW THEY SAY YOU ARE GOING AROUND, SAYING YOU ARE TIRED OF ME,

WITH HOW I FEEL ABOUT TELLING ME THE TRUTH,

I HAVE TRIED TO PRACTICE HONESTY, SINCE MY YOUTH,

IF WITH ME IS NOT WHERE YOU WANT TO BE, IT IS MY OBLIGATION TO TELL YOU THE TRUTH, THEN SET YOU FREE,

I WILL NOT BE ANOTHER WOMAN'S GOLD MINE,

WHILE SHE PLAYS WITH MY MAN, AND HAS HIM STEAL WHAT IS MINE,

AS I HAVE ALWAYS, SAID BEFORE I DENY YOU , I WOULD RATHER FREE YOU,

I WOULD JUST LIKE TO SAY FOR THE LAST TIME, YOU ARE FREE TO GO JUST DON'T TAKE WHAT'S MINE,

LIFTING UP THE NAME OF JESUS

FAR ABOVE EARTH, REALMS, AND SPHERES, THERE IS A NAME OF OUR GOD THAT EVERYONE FEARS,

HIS NAME IS ABOVE ALL BLOOD, HUMANS AND LIFE, HIS NAME IS HOLY AND EXALTED, IT IS JESUS CHRIST,

IT IS LIFTED ABOVE ALL OTHER THINGS, BECAUSE THROUGH HIM EVERY THING HAS MOVEMENT ITS BEING,

HE IS THE FIRST AND HE IS THE LAST, HE IS OUR PRESENT, FUTURE, AND HE HOLDS OUR PAST,

WE SHOULD ALL TAKE SOME TIME EACH DAY, TO LIFT UP THE NAME OF JESUS IN SOME SPECIAL WAY,

READING GOD'S WORD IS LIKE TAKING DAILY MEDICINE, IT CLEANSES, PROTECTS, AND DIRECTS AWAY FROM SIN,

EVERY SINGLE DAY WE SHOULD DRINK FROM THIS CUP, IT IS LIKE DRINKING THE BLOOD OF JESUS,

WE WILL BE FULFILLING THE LAWS OF THE HOLY ONE, EATING AND DRINKING OF HIM UNTIL HE COMES,

I DRINK SOME OF GOD'S WORD, EVERYDAY TO ASSURE ME I AM GOING THE RIGHT WAY,

IF BY CHANCE I SEEM TO FAIL OR FALTER, I GO TO GOD AND CAN PUT IT ON HIS ALTER,

FOREVER AS I LIVE, I WILL LIFT UP THE NAME OF JESUS CHRIST, HE IS GIVER, THE MAKER, AND SUSTAINER OF MINE AND ALL OTHER LIFE,

LORD HEAL THE WORLD OF DISEASES

LORD PLEASE FORGIVE US FOR ALL OUR SINS, WE COMMIT THEM WITHOUT CONSIDERING THE SINS END,

WE PAY HOMAGE TO YOUR GREAT AUTHORITY, WE MUST ADHERE TO YOUR HOLY WORD,

WE ARE YOUR SERVANT OF YOURS AND CREATED TO WORSHIP YOUR HOLY WORD,

HELP US LORD WHEN WE NEGLECT OR FAIL TO SEE WHATS BEST, OR WHEN WE FAIL YOUR TEST, DON'T CAST US AWAY IN DISGUST AND ANGER, REMEMBER THE PRICE CHRIST AND SUFFERED ALL THAT EARTHLY DANGER,

WE COME BEFORE YOU AGAIN LORD ASKING FOR MERCY, GRACE AND PEACE,

OUR WORLD IS SUFFEREING AND WE NEED YOU SEND US RELIEF,

YOU SAID IF YOUR PEOPLE WOULD HUMBLE THEMSELVES AND PRAY, YOU WOULD HEAL THE LAND AND RESOTRE THE DAY,

HERE WE ARE LORD, CRYING OUT TO YOU, FOR THE ONLY HELP WE KNOW, WE HAVE NO WHERE ELSE TO GO OR NO WHERE TO GROW,

WE EXPECT FOR YOU TO HEAL BLESS AND TO RESTORE, WE ARE THE DOWN TRODDEN IN THE WORLD AND SPIRITUALLY POOR,

LORD WILL YOU HEAL OUR WORLD OF ITS DISEASE, IT IS CONSUMING YOUR PEOPLE AND BRINGING THEM TO THEIR KNEES,

BUT YOU OH LORD CAN LIFT US UP AGAIN, AND PUT US BACK WHERE WE BEGAN,

NO DISEASE OR PROBLEM IS TOO HARD FOR YOU TO CURE, IT IS YOUR POWER THAT MAKES US ALL AND HELPS US ENDURE,

I BELIEVE IN YOUR EVERY SINGLE WORD AND YOUR DECRESS TO HEAL BY YOUR OWN WILL,

THANK YOU FATHER FOR HEALING OUR LAND, IT WAS ALL IN YOUR HOLY PLAN,

YOU GAVE AND HAVE THE ANSWER TO VIRSUSES, DISEASE AND CANCER,

MUTILATED, COVETED, AND GROUNDED

GOD NEVER INTENDED MAN TO BE INHUMANE TO MAN, HE NEVER INTENDED WARS TO BE THE CONQUERING DESIGN TO SECURE THE LAND,

BUT NONETHELESS THIS HOW WE LIVE, WE WILL FOREVER BE ASKING GOD TO FORGIVE,

THERE WAS SO MUCH BRUTALITY IN THE LAND, I FOUND MY OWN LIFE IN GREAT DEMAND,

IT WAS NOT FOR MY OWN GOOD, I WAS PILFERED ALMOST TO DEATH BY MY OWN BROTHERHOOD,

I WAS MUTILATED, COVETED, AND GROUNDED, THERE WAS HARDLY ANYTHING LEFT OF ME TO BE FOUNDED,

THERE WERE SO MANY MIND GAMES THEY PLAYED, WITH EVERY GAME SOMETHING THEY TOOK AND REMADE,

THEY PLUGGED ME INTO THEIR OWN REALITIES, SO THAT I COULD NEVER SEE THE REAL REALITY GOD GAVE TO ME,

THEY GAVE ME MEDICINE AND SHOTS TO MAKE ME LIKE THEM, GRUESOME LIVES THAT YOU SEE ONLY ON FILM,

SOME CUT INTO MY LIFE AND CARVED OUT A SUBSTANCE FOR THEMSELVES, WHAT THEY DID NOT USE THEY SOLE FOR WEALTH,

THEY MADE SURE I WAS IN THE DRAMA AND MOVIES THEY MADE, EVERYBODY BUT ME KNEW I WAS BEING PLAYED,

---

I WAS MUTILATED, COVETED, AND GROUNDED, THERE WAS HARDLY ANYTHING LEFT OF ME TO BE FOUNDED,

IN ESSENCE I DON'T FEEL THEY HAVE THE BEST OF ME, I CAN CREATED FOR THE REST OF MY DESTINY,

AS THE SCHOLOR RENE DECARTES SAID, "I THINK THERE FORE I AM, BUILDING UP ALL TRUTHS AND DISCARDING ALL FLAMS,

TO MAKE SURE YOU GET TO THE ROOTS, THEN YOU CAN DISCOVER ALL TRUTHS,

TODAY I AM REBUILDING MYSELF ON A SOLID FOUNDATION, THAT IS SPIRITUAL AND HOLY WITHIN ANY DEGRATIONS,

WITH THE FATHER AND THE SON, EVERY BATTLE HAS ALREADY BEEN WON, I MUST ALWAYS REMEMBER WHAT HAS ALREADY BEEN DONE,

MY CUBIC SPACE

WE SIT IN ROOMS OF GEOMETRIC DESIGN, SOMETIMES WORKING, PLAYING OR JUST PASSING TIME,

BUT DO WE REALLY KNOW ANYTHING ABOUT THIS ROOM, WHAT SECRETS IT MAY HOLD, OR WHAT SECRETS MAY LOOM,

A ROOM IS A VERY IMPORTANT PLACE, SOME ROOMS WERE STRICTLY BUILT FROM AND FROM AND FOR YOUR GRACE,

JUST REMEMBER THAT IN YOUR CUBIC SPACE, IT IS GOD THAT BUILT IT FOR YOUR PLACE AND GRACE,

I PRAY THAT MY CUBIC PLACE IS USED FOR MY WORSHIP OF DIVINITY, A PLACE THAT GOD KNOWS AND REMEMBERS ME,

WHEN I PRAY CRY OR HUMBLY PETITION, I DO IT ALL FOR GOD'S RECOGNITION,

I PETITION TO GOD TO CLEAN, AND KEEP MY CUBIC SPACE, SO THAT EVIL CANNOT STEAL OR CROWD ME OUT OF MY PLACE,

AS I WRITE THESE LINES I WRITE WITH CONFIDENCE AND TRUTH, KNOWING THAT GOD HAS GUIDED MY HAND FROM MY BIRTH AND MY YOUTH,

THOUGH IT MAY BE SMALL, I AM STILL IN HIS GRACE, I HAVE HIS REASSURANCE, IN SIX WALLS OF MY CUBIC SPACE,

HIS LEGACY, HIS LAND, HIS PEOPLE, WOULD BE MINE, HIS BIBLE, HIS JEWELS, AND HIS ETERNAL TIME,

MY FATHERS COAT IS THE COLOR OF ALL NATIONS, IT IS THE LIFE AND SUBSTANCE OF ALL GENERATIONS,

NO AUTHORITY OVER ME

I MAY LOOK DOCILE TIMID AND WEAK, BUT I KNOW THE TRUTH MY FATHER SPEAKS,

HE PROMISED TO TAKE GOOD CARE OF ME, WHERE I AM NO DEVIL SHOULD BE,

GOD NEVER GAVE EVIL AUTHORITY OVER ME, BECAUSE HIS SPIRIT RESIDES IN ME,

MY BODY IS THE TEMPLE OF THE HOLY GHOST, NOT THE DWELLING OF SATAN OR HIS EVIL HOST,

SATAN YOU HAVE NO AUTHORITY OVER ME, GOD MADE ME SUBLIME, WHEN HE FILLED ME WITH HIS SPIRIT, HE DESTINED MY TIME,

SATAN YOU HAVE NO AUTHORITY OVER ME, THIS BODY GOD CONTROLS, HE CAST OUT DISEASE AND KEEPS ME PURE AND WHOLE,

CHRIST GAVE ME THIS AUTHORITY, TO KEEP SATAN UNDER SUBMISSION, SATAN CAN NEVER BE OVER A SAINT IN HIS POSITION,

BE WARNED SATAN, I AM ARMED WITH THE HOLY GHOST, IT IS THE POWER THAT DEFEATED YOU AND YOUR SATANIC HOST,

YOU WILL NEVER HAVE AUTHORITY OVER ME, I HAVE THE POWER OF JESUS CHRIST LIVING INSIDE OF ME,

THE SAME POWER THAT CONQUERED DEATH, HELL AND THE GRAVE, TOOK ALL SATANS KEYS, FOR THIS PURPOSE, JESUS SAVES,

BE WARNED SATAN OF THIS ELECTION, I AM PART OF JESUS CHRIST'S HOLY RESSURECTION,

HE REMOVED YOU AND TOOK YOUR KEYS, MADE YOU SUBMIT AND FALL DOWN TO YOUR KNEES,

SATAN, JESUS TOLD YOU IT IS WRITTEN, YOU ARE A SERVANT TOO, WITHOUT GOD THERE IS NOTHING EVEN YOU CAN DO,

NO REPROBATE
SHALL BE GREAT

GOD MADE EVERYTHING FOR HIMSELF, HE IS THE EPITOME OF ALL OUR WEALTH,

WHEN WE OPPOSE GOD AND LIVE IN SIN, THE GATES ARE CLOSE FOR US ALL TO ENTER IN,

IF GOD GIVES US OVER TO BE REPROBATE, GOD HAS DEEMED THAT NO REPROBATE SHALL BE GREAT,

WITH A REPROBATE THE MIND HAS BEEN TAINTED, THE TRUTH, THE SPIRIT, AND THE ETHNIC COLORS HAS BEEN EVILLY PAINTED,

A REPROBATE HAS BEEN DEFILED IN THE WORST WAYS, HE OR SHE HAS NOTHING BENEFICIAL AT NIGHT NOR FOR THE DAYS,

WITH A REPROBATE WHAT GOD MADE MALE, THEY TRY TO SWITCH TO BECOME FEMALE,

WHAT GOD HAS DEEMED RELIGIOUS LAWS, A REPROBATE CONSIDERS RELIGIOUS FLAWS,

WITH GOD NO REPROBATE SHALL BE GREAT, THEY HAVE BEEN CONSUMMED BY EVIL AND IS FULL OF HATE,

WHEN ONE HAS A REPROBATED MIND, IT NO LONGER BELIEVES IN OR RESPECTS WHAT IS DIVINE,

THE CREATIVE AND INSPIRED ESSENCE OF GOD CANNOT ABIDE IN A REPROBATE, GOD WILL NOT LIVE WHERE THERE IS ONLY HATE,

ON AMERICA I STAND

THE PROMISE LAND IS WHAT GOD PROMISED US, IF WE WOULD BELIEVE, SEEK AND TRUST,

WE MUST KNOW GOD IS ABLE TO BRING US THROUGH, HE IS ABLE TO DELIVER ME AND DELIVER YOU,

IT IS NOT ABOUT GOLD, SILVER, OR NOT EVEN MONEY, GOD IS PLACING US IN A LAND OF RICHNESS, A LAND FLOWING WITH MILK AND HONEY,

THROUGH ALL GENERATIONS GOD HAS DEVISED A PLAN, THAT FOR HIS CHILDRED WE MUST DWELL IN THE PROMISED LAND,

WHEN GOD DECIDED TO WIPE AWAY ALL OF OUR TEARS, HE RAISED UP SOMEONE TO HELP ERASE ALL OF OUR FEARS,

IT WAS NOT AN ACCIDENT WHAT THE PRESIDENT HAD DONE, GOD WAS DIRECTING PRESIDENT ABRAHAM LINCOLN,

TO BRING HIS PEOPLE OUT OF BEING A SLAVES, HE MADE A PRESIDENT THAT WAS DARING BOLD AND BRAVE,

GOD MADE SURE THE PRESIDENT WOULD ADHERE TO GRACE, SO HE PICKED A PRESIDENT NAMED AFTER THE FATHER OF FAITH,

A LAND THAT SETS THE PRECIDENT FOR ALL OTHERS, A PLACE OF RESPECT FOR ALL CHILDREN, SISTERS AND BROTHERS,

IN THIS PLACE OF BLOOD, SWEAT AND TEARS, PEOPLE HAVE TOILED FOR TOO MANY YEARS,

NOW IT IS TIME FOR THE DOWN TRODEN, TO
VEHEMENTLY DEMAND,

WE TOO ARE HEIRS AND ON AMERICAN WE STAND,

AS CONSTITUTENTS TODAY WE DEPEND ON OUR
DEMOCRACY,

THE TRUTH IS WE HAVE A HIDDEN HIEROCRACY,

THE GOVERNMENT WAS DESIGNED AND MADE FOR
JESUS CHRIST,

TO RULE AS OUR KING, PRIEST, GOVENOR AND PRESIDENT
TO GIVE US BETTER LIVES,

AMERICA WAS DESIGNED AND MADE BY GOD, A LAND
FILLED WITH HIS BEST,

A LAND WHERE ALL INHABITANTS AND CHILDREN COULD
BE BLESSED AND FIND GOD'S REST,

PARALLEL UNIVERSES

ALL THE WORLDS WERE CREATED BY AND FOR HIM, AND NONE OF THE WORLDS EVEN KNEW OF HIM,

THEY WERE ALL CREATED FROM HIS BEST, IN THIS PHYSICAL WORLD THEY HAD TO BE HIS FLESH,

WORLDS WITHIN WORLDS, SOME SIDE BY SIDE, NO MATTER WHERE THEY ARE GOD IS STILL THEIR GUIDE,

THEY ARE LIKE PARALLEL UNIVERSES, READ IN THE BIBLE AS SINGLE LAWS, OF LINEAR VERSES,

EACH LINE A REPRESENTATIVE OF A POINT AND A PERIOD OF TIME, WHERE GOD HAS PLACED HIS HOLY GENETIC LINE,

EVERYWHERE A PROPHET HAS GONE THROUGH, GOD HAS DONE WHAT HE SAID HE WOULD DO,

WE ARE JUST LIKE PARALLEL UNIVERSES, IN A HOLY BOOK REPRESENTING ALL GOD'S HOLY COMMANDED VERSES,

ONE SIDE IS FOR THE MOON, ONE SIDE IS FOR THE SUN, WE MUST RIGHTLY DIVIDE OUR WORDS TO ACQUIRE AND SEPARATE THE POSITIVE ONES,

THE CONSCIOUS AND SUBCONSCIOUS MIND, CREATED TO DETERMINE OUR WAYS, TO SEE IF THEY ARE NIGHTS OR IF THEY ARE DAYS, SEPERATING GOOD DAYS FROM THE EVIL DAYS,

MAKE SURE YOU ARE ON THE SIDE OF THE GOD WHO IS FIRST, WHO HAS CREATED YOUR LIFE, BEING AND UNIVERSE,

IF THEY STAND AGAINST ME IN AS TRILLIONS, MY GOD IS STILL GREATER, THAN ANY NUMBERED TRILLIONS,

HE WILL ALWAYS BE THE EPITOME OF THE NUMBERS THEY HAVE SET, HE IS THE GOD OF CREATION THERE IS NO END HE HAS MET,

WHILE THEY ARE COUNTING AND LIVING IN SIN, THEY WILL NEVER ENTRAIN A GOD THAT HAS NO END,

ONE SIDE IS VISIBLE ONE SIDE IS CONCEALED, THEY WILL ONLY SEE WHAT THE SUPREME GOD HAS WILLED,

HOW CAN YOU SET WHAT YOU CANNOT SEE, IF YOU ARE NOT PURE, WHOLE HOLY AND GODLY,

POISIONED MINDS

BE CAREFUL OF WHOM YOU TRUST, SOME PEOPLE ARE FULL OF LUST,

ALL THEY REALLY WANT FROM YOU, IS TO CHANGE THE DIVINITY INSIDE OF YOU,

THEY CAN ONLY DO THIS BY POISIONING YOUR MIND, BREAKING YOUR SPIRIT AND STEALING YOUR TIME,

THEY MUST CHANGE YOUR ATTITUDE TOWARDS YOUR LOVED ONES, THIS IS WHERE THEIR ULTIMATE EVIL HAS BEGUN,

THEY WILL MAKE YOU HATE YOU MOTHER, FATHER, SISTER AND THIS BROTHER, THIS IS THE EVIL POWER EVIL SHARES WITH ONE ANOTHER,

THEY PLANT THEIR EVIL SEEDS WHERE GOD HAD PLACED GOOD, THEY CHANGED YOUR HERITAGE TO CULTIVATE WHAT EVIL THEY COULD,

SO, THEY POISIONED YOUR MIND AGAINST EVERYTHING THAT WAS BEST FOR YOU, SO THEY COULD CONTROL THE REST OF YOU,

THEY DID NOT WANT YOU TO KNOW THE TRUTH GOD HAD PREPARED FOR YOU, AS AN HEIR OF THE HIGHEST GOD THERE WAS NOTHING YOU COULD NOT DO,

THEY SCHEMED TO GET YOU TO LEAVE YOUR PLACE IN GOD, THEY MADE SURE YOU NEVER SAW ANY OF YOUR POSITIVE SIGHTS, SO THEY COULD FILL YOU WITH THEIR NEGATIVE LIGHT,

THE WHOLE WHILE THEY WERE CHANGING YOUR SEED AND DNA, TO CHANGE YOUR HOLY DAY TO AN EVIL DEVILS DAY,

JUST REMEMBER WHEN YOU SEEM TO GET ANGRY AND HATE YOUR LOVED ONES, IS IT YOU OR SOMETHING INSIDE OF YOU EVIL HAS DONE,

YOU MUST UNDERSTAND THAT THEIR ULTIMATE MISSION IS, TO REMOVE YOU FROM CHRIST AND LET THE DEVIL MAKE YOU HIS,

NO MATTER WHAT THEY SAY OR WHAT THEY DO, NEVER LET THEM CHANGE OR REMAKE YOU,

THEIR ULTIMATE WEAPON THAT THEY USE, IS LUST AND SEX A FLESHLY WEAKNESS MOST HUMANS CAN'T REFUSE,

I CAN TELL YOU THIS IS TRUE, BECAUSE THEIR WAS ONCE AT TIME I WAS PART OF THEIR CREW,

DON'T LET THEM POISION YOUR MIND AGAINST THE ONES WHO REALLY LOVE YOU, AND WANT TO KEEP YOU IN A RIGHT MIND SET AND HELP YOU MAKE IT THROUGH,

REFLECTION

IN MY MIND THERE ARE MANY INSTANCES OF YOUR SAVING GRACES, THAT RESCUED ME FROM MANY EVIL PLACES,

WHETHER IT WAS REAL OR IMAGINARY, I WAS SAVED FROM ALL EVIL THINGS TO GOD THAT WERE CONTRARY,

I KNOW FOR A FACT, THAT THE MOON IS CONTRARY TO THE SUN, AND THERE IS ONLY ONE SUPREME GOD, AND HE IS THE ONE,

JUST LIKE LOOKING IN A MIRROR, YOU WILL SEE YOUR REFLECTION, YOU ARE SEEING THE IMAGE GOD GAVE TO YOU, HE IS BEYOND YOUR PHYSICAL REFLECTION,

HAVE YOU EVER THOUGHT OF WHY TERM IS CALLED TO REFLECT, IT MEANS TO LOOK BACK UPON SOMETHING OR SOMEONE TO VIEW, REMEMBER AND OR DETECT,

I LIKE TO THINK OF IT AS MENTAL RECALL, ESPECIALLY WHERE MEMORY IS CONCERNED, PUTTING INTO ACTION RELIGIOUS PRAYERS AND, VERSES, YOU MAY HAVE LEARNED,

TO PRAY A UNIFYING PRAYER, WHEN PEOPLE ARE IN NEED, HELPS TO KNOW YOU ARE OF HOLY SEED,

THAT GOD HAS PROMISED NO MATTER WHAT YOU DO, HE HAS PROMISES HE MADE TO YOU,

JUST REMEMBER IN THIS LIFE TO KEEP HIS COMMAND, IT WILL TAKE YOU AND KEEP YOU IN ANY OTHER LAND,

LOOKING AT YOU WE ARE IN GOD'S IMAGE AND OUR REFLECTION, IS OUR GOD AND IS OUR PROTECTION,

REPEATING DEVIL'S

HAVE YOU NOTICED WHENEVER YOU START TO PRAY, A DEVIL GETS IN YOUR SPACE AND MIND GETS IN YOUR WAY,

THEY REPEAT NEGATIVE THOUGHTS AND EVIL STATEMENTS, THAT LEAVE YOU STRESSED OUT AND UNCONTENT,

JUST KNOW THEM FOR WHO THEY ARE, THEY ARE THERE TO PROHIBIT YOU FROM GOING TOO FAR,

BECAUSE THEY KNOW YOU HAVE A DESTINY, ONE THAT THEY DON'T WANT YOU TO KNOW, THEY DON'T WANT YOU TO SEE,

IF YOU FOUND OUT WHO YOU REALLY ARE IN THE LORD, THEY WOULD HAVE TO BOW DOWN EVERYDAY TO YOUR SWORD,

SO DON'T LISTEN TO THOSE WHO TRY TO DEFAME YOU, BUT CONNECT TO THOSE WHO WON'T TRY TO FRAME YOU,

THEY CAN ONLY REPEAT THE SAME NEGATIVE MIND SET, YOU MUST CONTOL WHAT YOU LISTEN TO THEY HAVE NOT CONQUERED YOU YET,

THEY WILL TELL YOUR MIND IT'S ALL OVER AND YOU ARE LOST AND A CAST AWAY,

THAT'S ONLY BECAUSE THEY ARE ALL USING YOUR DAY,

YOU KEEP YOUR MIND ON YOUR SAVIOUR AND LORD JESUS CHRIST,

HE IS THE BEGINNING AND ENDING OF YOU LIFE,

DON'T WORRY ABOUT THOSE REPEATING DEVIL'S AND WHAT THEY TRY TO DO, JUST REMEMBER GOD HAS ALREADY MADE IT THROUGH FOR YOU,

JUST FOLLOW GOD'S FOOTSTEPS RIGHT PAST WHERE SATAN WAS SEATED, RIGHT TO WHERE SATAN WAS DEFEATED,

ISN'T IT IRONIC THEY SEEM TO HAVE FORGOTTON THIS, WHERE THEIR MASTER WAS DEFEATED THEY WON'T REPEAT THIS THEY SEEM TO MISS,

THE OBJECT OF EVIL IS TO OCCUPY YOUR MIND, TO BRAIN WASH YOU AND KEEP YOU BLIND,

EVERYDAY THE SAME NEGATIVE LIES MUST BE REPEATED IF YOU ARE TO BE DEFEATED,

YOUR MIND WITH THEM THEY HAVE SET TO A CLOCK, TO MAKE SURE EACH HOUR YOUR MIND HAS A BLOCK,

THEY CAN'T ALLOW YOU TO THINK FOR YOURSELF, BECAUSE GOD'S TRUTH IS NOT GOOD FOR THEIR HEALTH,

RETURNING YOUR WORDS TO YOU (GOD)

SOME OF US DON'T KNOW WHERE WE COME FROM, IN CREATION WE MUST KNOW THERE IS ONLY ONE,

IT PAYS TO BE CONSCIOUS SOMETIMES, AND JUST TAKE A LOOK, IN GOD'S SACRED BOOK,

YOU MAY FIND YOU ARE JUST LIKE THE REST, CREATED AS ONE OF GOD'S BLESSED AND BEST,

A WORD AMONG MILLIONS, JUST LIKE YOUR GENETIC SEED INSIDE, YOUR HAVE TRILLIONS,

YOU AND I ARE VOLUMES JUST LIKE A BOOK, GOD DESIGNED US HE IS OUR AUTHOR, WHEN EVER HE CHOOSES, HE TAKES A LOOK,

I KNOW LORD THAT I AM CREATED JUST FOR YOU, WHEN EVER YOU SAY I WILL RETURN YOUR WORDS BACK TO YOU,

WHAT EVER I DO, SAY, OR WRITE, IT IS DONE THROUGH YOU, BY A SACRED RITE,

NONE OF US HAVE A PERSONAL BEING, IT IS THROUGH YOU WE DO EVERYTHING,

WE BORROW TIME, LIFE AND LOVE AND STRENGTH, ALL OF IT BELONGS TO YOU BECAUSE YOU ARE IMMENSE,

EVERY CELL IN ME IS ONE OF THE CHARACTERS YOU PLACED, YOU PLANNED MY LIFE FILLED ME AND GAVE ME GRACE,

SO, I COULD BE THE BEST I COULD BE, YOU HAD YOUR SON TO PAY FOR ME TO BE FREE,

I HAVE NO LIMITS ON MY LIFE, BECAUSE MY GUARANTOR, IS JESUS CHRIST,

HIS AWESOME LOVE FOR ME PAID THE PRICE, ONLY ONCE, NOT TWICE,

I KNOW LORD THAT I AM CREATED JUST FOR YOU, WHEN EVER YOU SAY I WILL RETURN YOUR WORDS BACK TO YOU,

JESUS HAS THE WHOLE WORLD IN HIS HANDS

SATAN TAKE YOUR HANDS OFF MY FINANCE

I MY FATHER IS RICH IN HOUSES AND LAND, HE CREATED THE GROUND ON WHICH WE ALL STAND,

WHEN MY RESOURCES ARE LOW, I AM NEVER POOR, THEN MY FATHER OPENS A SPIRITUAL DOOR,

WHERE THERE ARE TREASURES OF HEALTH, THOUGHT AND DEED, HE HAS IN HIS HANDS WHATEVER WOULD NEED,

I KNOW THAT GOD IS THE WEALTH OF THIS WHOLE UNIVERSE, WITHOUT HIM THIS WORLD BE UNDER AN UNAVOIDABLE CURSE,

YOU CANNOT UNDUE WHAT IS REALLY TRUE, GOD HAS MADE A WAY OUT FOR ME AND FOR YOU,

WE WERE BORN INTO SIN, THERE WAS NO WAY WE COULD WIN OR SPIRITUALLY ENTER IN,

OUR FLESH WAS THE PRISON THAT SEPARATED OUR SPIRIT, ENTOMBED IN THESE FLESHLY CELLS EVERYDAY WE HAD NO REASON TO FEAR IT,

UNTIL GOD SHOWED US BY HAVING JESUS PAY THE PRICE, FOR OUR FLESH TO RELEASE US TO OUR SPIRITUAL CHRIST,

SO, SATAN OUR SIN DEBTS HS BEEN PAID, YOU ARE THE ONLY ONE LOST, CHRIST HAS REDEEMED US AND PAID, SALVATIONS REQUIRED SPIRITUAL COST,

CHRIST BLOOD FILLED ME AND MADE ME RICH, IT GAVE MY LIFE ANOTHER CHANCE,

SATAN, I REBUKE YOU AND WARN YOU KEEP YOUR HANDS OFF OF MY FINANCE,

THE BLOOD THAT LIVES IN ME IS MY TOTAL WEALTH, IT IS THE EPITOME OF ALL MY PAST, PRESENT AND FUTURE HEALTH,

EVERYDAY THAT I LIVE I HAVE BEEN GIVEN ANOTHER CHANCE, I WARN YOU SATAN KEEP YOUR HANDS OFF OF MY FINANCE,

SODOM AND GOMMORAH

DON'T BE LIKE THE CITY THAT GOD HAD TO BURN, BECAUSE OF THEIR SINS THEY WOULD NOT TURN,

FROM ILLICT SEX AND IGNOBLE DEEDS, THE WHOLE WORLD WAS LYING IN FLESH ON WHICH SPIRIT DOES NOT FEED,

THEY MOCKED AND RIDICULED GOD AND MADE FUN OF HIS LAWS, CREATING FOR THEMSELVES PROBLEMS AND FLESHLY FLAWS,

SODOM AND GOMMORAH FOUND OUT FLESH WILL NEVER RULE OVER SPIRIT, GENERATIONS LATER WE ARE THE ONES TO HEAR IT,

GOD TOLD LOT JUST FIND ME 10 (TEN), AND THIS CITY I WILL SAVE AND I WILL NOT END,

LOT SET OUT TO FIND 10 THAT WERE NOT UNJUST, THAT GOD COULD FIND WORTH HIS PURCHASE,

STILL THEY SINNED WITHOUT A THOUGHT, ABOUT THEIR GOD AND WHAT HE HAD TAUGHT,

THE MOST HUMILATING SEXUAL ACTS THAT COULD BE COMMITTED, USING ORGANS THAT GOD CREATED FOR PURPOSES THAT THEY SHOULD NOT HAVE PERMITTED,

SODOM AND GOMORRAH WOULD YOU NOT ADHERE, TO WHAT THEY KNEW WAS RIGHT,

GOD HAD GIVEN THEM HIS DIVINE LAWS, THAT GAVE THEM LIGHT,

YET THEY SINNED WITHOUT A CARE, EVEN IN THE PRESENCE OF GOD WHILE HE WAS THERE,

IT WAS A DIVINE COMMAND THAT ALL VILE SINNING AND MURDER CEASE, SO THAT GOD COULD INTRODUCE, HARMONY, LOVE AND PEACE,

THEY WANTED TO CONTINUE SIN AND VILENESS, EVEN TODAY IN THE 20TH CENTURY, THAT SIN TRYS TO DEFILE US,

LORD KEEP US IN YOUR GRACE AND FAVOR, REMOVE VILE SIN WITH YOUR SWORD, LET IT CUT LIKE A RAZOR,

THEN WE WILL BE FREE FROM VILE AFFECTIONS, AND KEPT BY GOD'S HOLY PROTECTION,

SPOKEN FOR, I BELONG TO GOD

IN THIS TEMPORAL WORLD, MEN AND WOMEN ARE BETROVED, BUT IN A SPIRITUAL REALM GOD IS THE HIGHEST FORM OF LOVE, EVERYONE KNOWS,LOVE IS THE PURE ESSENCE OF GOD'S ULTIMATE BEING, HE IS THE MANIFESTOR OF EVERYTHING,

I AM NOT FOR SALE, I AM NOT AVAILABLE, I AM NOT ALONE, I AM NOT FREE, I BELONG TO GOD AND HE BELONGS TO ME,

I WAS SPOKEN FOR LONG BEFORE I WAS EVEN ON THIS EARTH, GOD CHOSE MY NAME, GOD ADORNED MY LIFE AND PLANNED MY BIRTH,

GOD FINALIZED AND MADE MY WORTH, AND SEALED IT WITH HIS SEAL AND HID IT IN MY BIRTH,

GOD IS MY BELOVED, AND HE IS MINE, HIS ESSENCE REACHES INFINITY AND FAR BEYOND ALL TIME,

HE IS THE SOUL SOURCE OF MY BEING HE IS SUPERNAL, A LOVE BEYOND MEASURE, PASSING THROUGH TO ETERNAL,

IN A WORLD WHERE EVERYTHING MANIFEST FROM THE MIND, WE CREATE FROM EACH OTHER AND CREATE ALL TIME,

JUST KNOW THAT I AM SPOKEN FOR EVEN IF YOU DON'T SEE, I BELONG TO GOD HE HAS SPOKEN FOR ME,

I AM NOT FOR SALE, I AM NOT AVAILABLE, I AM NOT ALONE, I AM NOT FREE, I BELONG TO GOD AND HE BELONGS TO ME,

---

STILL HOLDING ON TO YOU

LORD NO MATTER HOW GREAT THE TRIAL, I AM STILL TRYING TO SMILE,

NOTHING IS TOO GREAT FOR YOU, SO HOLDING ON IS WHAT I HAVE TO DO,

I AM ATTACHED TO YOUR INFINITE SPIRIT, LORD YOU KNOW ME AND HOW MUCH I FEAR IT,

SO, I'LL JUST KEEP HOLDING ON TO YOU, I AM STILL HOLDING ON TO YOU,

I KNOW THIS IS YOUR POOREST AND YOUR LOWEST, WHERE ALL NATIONS WILL EVENTUALLY JOIN MANKINDS SLOWEST,

WHERE ALL MEN ARE CREATED EQUAL NO ONE BUT GOD WILL ASSIGN, EARTHLY OR HEAVENLY TIMES,

LORD I AM STILL HOLDING ON TO YOU, INSPITE OF WHAT THIS HATEFUL WORLD WILL DO,

DESPISED AND HATED BECAUSE OF YOU, FORGIVE THEM FATHER FOR THEY KNOW NOT WHAT THEY DO,

IN ME THEY CONGREGATED AND JOINED INTO ONE MIND, TO CHANGE AND ALTER MY DIVINE TIMES,

IN ME THEY REDIRECTED AND CONFUSED THE WAYS, YOU HAD PLANNED TO FOR REDEMPTIONS DAYS,

THEY ALTERED MY COURSE AND PILFERED MY LIFE, STOLE MY HERITAGE AND DENIED ME CHRIST,

YET FATHER, I AM STILL HOLDING ON, ONE DAY THIS WILL ALL BE GONE,

WHAT IS TODAY WILL AT SOME POINT BECOME TOMORROR, HOW WE LIVE WILL DETERMINE IF IT IS LIVED IN SORROW,

SO BE CAREFUL OF HOW YOU TREAT EACH OTHER, IT WILL BE A DETERMINING FACTOR IF WE REALLY LOVE ONE ANOTHER,

MAN'S INHUMANITY TO MAN, HAS A DIRECT EFFECT ON OUR LIVES AND OUR TRENDS,

IF WE WANT OUR LAND RESTORED AND HEALED, WE MUST FIRST START BY HOW WE TRULY LOVE AND WHAT WE REVEAL,

GOD DID NOT ASK FOR MUCH, WHAT HE DID ASK WAS OBTAINABLE AND JUST,

HE JUST ASKED THAT WE LOVE ONE ANOTHER JUST LIKE A SISTER OR BROTHER,

THIS IS HOW WE WILL BE IN HEAVEN FILLED FULL OF GOD'S LOVE, NOTHING NEGATIVE TO FEEL OR EVEN THINK OF,

SO, FATHER I AM STILL HOLDING ON TO YOU, I KNOW YOU HAVE THE ONLY TRUTH,

YOU ARE THE ANSWER TO ALL OUR DISEASES, AND SCIENTIFIC FAILURES AT THEIR ROOTS,

EACH ONE OF US MUST HOLD ON TO YOU, BECAUSE IN THE WHOLE UNIVERSE YOU ARE THE ONLY TRUTH,

I AM WATCHING AS THINGS TAKE THEIR COURSE, 1000 OR 10,000 GOD IS REMOVING THEM BY SOME FORCE,

WE MUST NOT UNDERESTIMATE OR DEFILE, BECAUSE WE WHO BELIEVE ARE GOD'S CHILD,

WHEN GOD CALLS FOR HIS CROWN, WHERE WILL YOU BE STANDING, WHERE WILL YOU BE FOUND,

MAKE AMENDS AND REPENT, CHRIST IS DEFINITELY COMING IT IS EVIDENT,

WE HAVE A CHANCE TO GET IT RIGHT BEFORE GOD REMOVES HIS UNIVERSAL LIGHT,

STOP INTERFERRING WITH MY MIND

GOD GAVE US ALL OUR OWN SPIRITUAL GIFTS, SOME PEOPLE ARE A PROBLEM TO DEAL WITH,

THEY WANT WHAT BELONGS TO EVERYONE THEY USURP EVERYBODY ELSES TIME, AND ROB, STEAL, AND KILL AND COMMITT SPIRITUAL CRIMES,

THEY CLAIM AND CHANGE ALL MY CREATIONS, BECAUSE THEY HAVE A STRONGHOLD ON MY IMAGINATION,

I KNOW EVERYTHING THAT THEY TOOK, FROM MY SPIRITUALS SHOES TO MY GOD'S HOLY BOOK,

STOP INTERFERRING WITH MY MIND, AND STEALING MY FUTURE LIFE, AND YESTERDAYS TIME,

GOD GAVE ME THE WISDOM TO WRITE INTO BEING, BY FAITH THE THINGS I HAVE NOT BEEN SEEING,

THE CHANGES IN MY WORLD WILL START WITH ME, IT WILL ALL COME DOWN TO WHAT I BELIEVE AND WHAT I SEE,

THE MIND IS THE CLOSEST ORGAN TO A SPIRITUAL UNION WITH THE HEAVENLY HOST, AND THE DIRECT INTERACTION WITH THE HOLY GHOST,

SO, STOP INTERFERRING WITH MY MIND, AND DISTANCING MY CONNECTIONS, WITH MY GOD AND HIS SPIRITUAL RESURRECTIONS,

GOD GAVE ME MY PRIVATE TELEPHONE TO CALL HIM TO REBUKE EVIL FROM MY PHONE AND FROM MY HOME,

I KNOW THAT THE PHONE IS MINE, I KNOW THE HOME IS MINE, I KNOW MY HERITAGE AND I KNOW MY TIME,

SO, STOP INTERREFERING WITH MY MIND, TRYING TO ALTER AND CHANGE MY HEART, HOPING TO GAIN A FELONIOUS START,

ONLY FOR A MOMENT YOU MAY HAVE CAUSED A RIFT IN MY MIND, BUT GOD HAS YOU IN HIS HANDS AND HOLDS ALL YOUR TIME,

IT IS A TERRIBLE THING TO BE IN THE HANDS OF AN ANGRY GOD, HE CONTORLS EVERYTHING YOU DO AND CAN MAKE YOUR LIFE QUITE HARD,

WHO CAN YOU CALL AND WHO CAN YOU TELL, WHEN IT IS THE SUPREME GOD YOU HAVE FAILED,

MY ADVICE TO YOU WOULD BE TO ASK FOR FORGIVENESS AND REPENT, AND LEARN TO RESPECT THOSE THAT ARE HEAVEN SENT,

NO MORE LIES, NO MORE DECEIT, NO MORE VISCIOUSNESS AND NO MORE CONCEIT, THIS YOU MUST DO IF IT IS GOD YOU WANT TO MEET,

STOP INTERFERRING WITH MY MIND, THE PLACE WHERE ME AND MY GOD SPENDS SPIRITUAL TIME,

TAKE A DOLLAR FOR EVERY WORD

I BELIEVE IN SELF WORTH, GOD HAS GIVEN US ALL AT OUR BIRTH,

WHAT EVER YOU CREATE BECOMES YOUR PERSONAL PROPERTY, A PART OF YOU THE WORLD CAN SEE,

CREATION COMES FROM WITHIN OR FROM THE INSIDE, A PART OF YOU NONTHE LESS, WHENEVER WHATEVER YOU CREATE IS ALREADY BLESSED,

GOD'S WORD HAS SAID, WHATEVER YOU PUT YOUR HANDS TO, HE HAS ALREADY BLESSED WHATEVER YOU DO,

I HAVE WRITTEN MANY LITERARY BOOKS OF MY OWN, EACH ONE WAS PERSONALLY AND SPIRITUALLY SOWN,

THEREFORE I WILL TAKE A DOLLAR FOR EVERY ONE OF MY INTELLECTUAL WORDS,

THAT OTHERS ARE USING I HAVE HEARD,

THEY TAKE CREDIT FOR EVERYTHING THAT I DO, THEY PLAGIARIZE MY CREATIONS AND STEAL MY HERITAGE TOO,

IN CASE THEY WANT TO KNOW, WRITING IS PART OF MY DAY,

I CAME HERE WRITING, I CAN WRITE MY WAY,

I AM TRULY FULLY VESTED IN SPRITUAL CONTENT,

LOOK AT MY WORKS, IT IS ALL EVIDENT, SINCE EVERYBODY WANTS TO USURP MY DAY, I THINK THEY ALL SHOULD CONSIDER THEIR FAULT AND THEY SHOULD PAY,

AT LEAST A DOLLAR FOR EVERY SINGLE WORD, I HAVE EVER PUT ON PAPER AND WROTE,

I HAVE WRITTEN AND DESIGNED ENOUGH WORDS, TO FASHION AND DESIGN A BIBLICAL COAT,

THE BOOK IS MINE

EVERY SINGLE PAGE IN GOD'S HOLY BOOK, IS TIME TESTED AND PROVEN FOR ALL OF US TOO TAKE A LOOK,

AT WHAT GOD HAS ALREADY DONE FOR HIS CHOSEN ONES, IF WE CHOOSE HIM HE WILL DO THE SAME FOR ME AND YOU,

I CAN SPIRITUALLY HEAR GOD SAYING THE BOOK IS MINE, A BOOK THAT ENCOMPASSES ALL MATTER AND ALL TIME,

THE BOOK MANIFEST AND BRINGS FORTH SACRED KEYS, TO ALL GENERATIONS, REGENERATING ALL HIS PEOPLE, INCLUDING YOU AND ME,

IT IS GOD'S PROVIDENCE AND SOVERIGN RIGHT OF OUR FATHERS WILL, TO LET THIS WHOLE UNIVERSE KNOW THIS BOOK IS HIS WORDS AND IT IS REAL,

GOD IS GRACIOUS AND GOD IS MERCIFUL, EVERYDAY HE SHOWS THAT HE CARE, BY YOU AND EVERYONE BREATHING HIS DIVINE AIR,

WITH THE SNAP OF HIS FINGER HE CAN CHANGE OR CUT ANYTHING OFF, GOD IS THE EPITOME OF MERCY, AND DOSEN'T WANT US TO BE LOST,

WE MUST DO BETTER AND LEARN TO RESPECT GOD'S MERCY AND RULE, AND NOT TAKE HIM FOR GRANTED AND USE HIM AS A TOOL,

GOD IS WAITING FOR HIS BOOK TO RETURN, ALL HIS PEOPLE WERE WRITTEN FOR US TO REVERE AND LEARN,

BEFORE GOD THERE IS NO-OTHER, HE IS OUR HOLY FATHER,
AND THE FEMININE SIDE OF THE HOLY MOTHER,

I CAN SPIRITUALLY HEAR GOD SAYING THE BOOK IS MINE,
A BOOK THAT ENCOMPASSES ALL MATTER AND ALL TIME,

THE LORD'S HOUSE

I KNOW A PLACE I CAN GO IN THE NIGHT OR THE DAY, THE KEY TO THE DOOR IS TO BE HUMBLE AND PRAY,

THIS HOUSE IS CALLED THE HOUSE OF PRAYER, WHENEVER YOU GO GOD WILL MEET YOU THERE,

IN HIS HOUSE IS THE KING, WHO IS OVER EVERYTHING, THERE WILL BE NO EXALTED PLACE BUT HIS, HE IS THE BUILDER AND KEEPER OF HIS OWN HOUSE, EVERYONE MUST WORSHIP HIM, WE ALL KNOW WHO HE IS,

WHEN YOU ARE DOWNTRODDEN, BROKEN, AND MISUSED, THERE IS A PLACE TO GO WHERE YOU WON'T BE ABUSED,

IN THE PRESENCE OF GOD, HE CAN RESTORE YOU, HE IS THE ONLY SPIRITUAL DOCTOR THAT CAN REPAIR YOU,

WHEN THE WORLD HAS YOU BATTERED, TATTERED AND TORN, YOU NEED JESUS, YOU NEED HIS FORM,

YOU CAN RECOVER IN THE LORD'S HOUSE TO REGAIN YOUR SPIRITUAL HEALTH, TO KEEP PULLING DOWN THE STRONG HOLDS THAT THE WHOLD WORLD FELT,

WE ARE OVERCOMERS AND WARRIORS FOR THE LORD, TO BE WEAK AND VOID WE CANNOT AFFORD,

WE MUST BE FILLED WITH STRENGTH AND GLORY OF GOD, THEN WHEN WE CAN FIGHT THE GOOD FIGHT IT WON'T BE HARD,

CAUSE THE POWER OF OUR GOD HAS ALREADY WON, WE JUST HAVE TO TAKE CHARGE, IN THE NAME OF JESUS CHRIST HIS SON,

MY FATHER'S HOUSE IS THE HOUSE OF PRAYER, WHEN YOU PRAY GOD WILL MEET YOU THERE

THERE IS ONLY ONE GOD, OVER US ALL IN THE EARTH,

MANY PEOPLE WORSHIP PAGAN GOD'S AND THINGS, NOT WORSHIPING THE GOD OF EVERYYHING,

THEIR GOD IS CLAY, STONE, AND WOOD, A GOD THAT HAS NO CONCEPTION OF THE TRUTH OR WHAT IS HOLY AND TRULY GOOD,

MY GOD IS MERCIFUL, LOVING AND JUST, HE HAS CREATED THIS ENTIRE UNIVERSE THEY ALL BREATHE HIS BREADTH,

I KNOW THAT THERE IS ONLY ONE GOD OVER US ALL IN THE EARTH, HE CAN STAND ALONE AS ONE, OR AS CREATIONS COMPLETED AND FINISHED BIRTH,

WE MUST REMEMBER CHRIST ONLY BORROWED, BLOOD BONE AND SKIN, TO PAVE A WAY FOR MANKIND TO BE REDEEMED FROM SIN,

GOD GAVE US HIS BEST, WHEN HE SENT CHRIST, AS SALVATION TO REDEEM US FROM SIN IN CREATED IN THE FLESH,

NOTHING IN HUMANITY CAN COME NEAR IT, CHRIST REAL ESSENCE IS PURE AND UNDEFILED AND HOLIEST OF SPIRIT,

RATHER WE EXCEPT HIM OR NOT THERE IS ONLY ONE GOD OVER US ALL IN THE EARTH, HE CAN STAND ALONE AS ONE, OR AS CREATIONS COMPLETED AND FINISHED BIRTH,

EVIL HAS BEEN TRYING SINCE THE INCEPTION OF TIME, TO UNDO THE CURSE GOD PUT ON THEIR FAMILY LINE,

SATANS PEOPLE ARE MARKED THEY HAVE WOUNDED HEADS, THEY ARE THE LEADERS AND TEACHERS OF THE LOST AND THE DEAD,

KEEP YOUR MIND ON CHRIST AND THE BONDAGES IN YOU HE FREED, YOU WILL FIND YOU CAN RESIST ALL THE DEVILS SEED,

MEDITATE ON GOD AND ALL THINGS ABOVE , HE WILL KEEP YOUR MIND SURROUNDED BY HIS INFINITE GODLY LOVE,

I KNOW THAT THERE IS ONLY ONE GOD OVER US ALL IN THE EARTH, HE CAN STAND ALONE AS ONE, OR AS CREATIONS COMPLETED AND FINISHED BIRTH,

THOUGHTS ARE SPIRITUALLY ACTIVE LIFE FORCES

HAVE YOU EVER REALLY THOUGHT ABOUT HOW SPIRITUALLY GREAT GOD MADE YOU, HE MADE YOU A THINKING ENTITY SOMETHING NO OTHER CREATION CAN DO,

GOD GAVE YOU AN THE ATTRIBUTE NO OTHER MAMMAL OR CREATION POSSESS, HE EQUIPPED YOU AND PREPARED YOU FOR HISTORY AND THE WORLDS CONQUEST,

IN HIS IMAGE HE GAVE YOU THE RIGHTS TO EVERYTHING YOU WOULD NEED TO DO, HE GAVE YOU THE COMMANDMENTS AND RIGHTS TO ALL ANIMALS TO SUBDUE,

THINKING IS A SPIRITUAL ACTIVITY AND RIGHT TO A GOD MADE MAN OF A DIVINE SOURCE, THOUGHTS ARE SPIRITUALLY ACTIVE AND IS A DIVINE FORCE,

THOUGHTS ARE ESSENTIAL TO YOUR LIFE AND TIME, THEY ARE THE GOVENORS OF YOUR FUTURE THROUGH THE DIVINE,

YOUR STATE OF MIND CONTROLS YOUR ATTITUDE, GOD GIVES YOU BREADTH AND LATITUDE,

WHERE EVER IT IS THAT YOU ARE HEADED, YOU BETTER BELIEVE IN GOD IT IS ALREADY EMBEDDED,

WITHOUT GOD THERE IS NOTHING YOU CAN DO, HE IS THE ESSENCE OF EVERTHING OLD AND EVERYTHING WE THINK IS NEW,

EVERYTHING OF GOD'S THAT HAS A COURSE, IS HELD TOGETHER, BY HIS SPIRITUAL FORCE,

THAT IS WHY ILL BEGOTTON WEALTH AND THINGS THAT EVENTUALLY WILL FALL, THEY ARE OUT OF GOD'S WILL SOMETHING GOD DID NOT CALL,

THERE WILL BE TIMES WHEN THE WORLD WILL SEEM INVERSE, WRONG WILL BE RIGHT, AND THE WORLD WILL SEEM A CURSE,

THE KEY TO ANY STATE OF MIND IS RIGHT THINKING, AND A SPIRTUALLY POSITIVE ATTITUDE,

TO CREATE THIS WHOLE UNIVERSE THIS THE POWER THAT OUR GOD USED,

SO WHEN EVIL DEEDS AND ACTIONS SEEM TO BE WINNING, JUST REMEMBER GOD DOES NOT APPROVE OF WICKEDNESS AND SINNING,

THEY WILL HAVE THIEIR DAY TO ANSWER FOR ALL THEIR SIN, THAT'S THE DAY ALL VICTIMS WILL RECOVER AND GOD WILL CAUSE THEM TO WIN,

I AM REMINDED OF THE GREAT MIND THAT SAID, THESE WORDS THAT THE WORLD HAS HEARD,

HE SAID I THINK THEREFORE I AM, ISN'T I WONDERFUL TO KNOW YOUR THOUGHTS CAN'T BE AND ARE NOT DAMMED,

THOUGHTS ARE A SPIRITUALLY ACTIVE LIFE FORCE, RIGHT THOUGHTS PUTS YOUR LIFE ON A RIGHT COURSE,

UNBROKEN

LORD YOU GAVE ME THE RIGHT TO LIFE, LOVE AND LIBERTY, TO BE WHATEVER IN THIS WORLD I COULD ASPIRE TO BE,

YOU ENRICHED ME WITH WHAT I WOULD NEED, YOU SUPPLIED ME WITH TRILLIONS OF GENETIC SEED,

THEN YOU EQUIPPED ME WITH YOUR SACRED PRESCENCE, AN ETERNAL GIFT AND AN UNENDING ESSENCE,

THE ONLY TRUE RICHNESS, THAT IS ALWAYS FULL A FOUNT OF PURE HEALTH, WHERE WE ALL CAN DRINK AND FIND UNTOLD SPIRITUAL WEALTH,

I KNOW THAT YOUR GIFTS AND PROMISES WILL ALWAYS BE UNBROKEN, BECASUSE THE TRUE ESSENCE OF ALL YOUR WORDS ARE UNSPOKEN,

UNTIL YOUR WORDS ARE WRITTEN, FOR THE WHOLE WORLD TO READ, THEY ARE SECRETELY HIDDEN LIKE ROOTS AND UNPLANTED SEED,

THE RICHNESS IS UNTOLD AND THE SUPPLY IS IMMEASUARABLE, ONLY WHEN THEY ARE MANIFESTED CAN THE WORLD ABLE TO BEHOLD,

YOU CANNOT BREAK WHAT HAS NO PERMANENT SUBSTANCE, YOU MIGHT USURP ITS TIME AND HOARD ITS PLACEMENT,

THE TRUTH IS SPIRIT IS NOT SOMETHING YOU CANNOT STEAL, SPIRIT CAN NOT BE MANIFESTED BY THE HUMAN WILL,

THE SPIRIT IS DIVINELY DIRECTED, PROTECTED AND DISPENSED BY THE FATHER OF THE HOLY SEAL, NOTHING IN HEAVEN OR ON EARTH CAN STOP THE FATHERS WILL,

GOD AND HIS CHILDREN WILL NEVER BE BROKEN, WE ARE NOT SUBSTANCES OF PHYSICAL MATTER THAT CAN BE BROKEN,

NO MATTER WHAT IT LOOKS LIKE OR WHAT YOU ARE SEEING, THE TRUTH IS WHAT IS SUSTAINING YOU AND CAUSING YOU TO HAVE YOUR BEING,

STOLEN WATERS WILL STILL STATISFY A THIRST, BUT WHERE DID THE WATERS COME FROM FIRST,

IF IT HAPPENS THAT SOME OF OUR ATTRIBUTES OR GIFTS CHANGE, IT IS ONLY THAT THEY HAVE BEEN REARANGED,

TRUE POWERS ARE NOT CREATED OR MADE BY MAN, THEY MIGHT BE CONVERTED, INVERTED, AND REVERTED,

THEY ARE STILL THE SAME POWERS, THEY JUST ARE SOME WHERE OR SOMETHING ELSE,

THIS IS THE TRUTH I KNOW, WE ARE USING THE POWERS JESUS USED 2,000 YEARS AGO,

CHRIST WAS ABUSE DENIED ACCUSED AND SMITTEN, IT WAS DIVINE DESTINY TO HAVE ALL HIS HISTORY WRITTEN,

WHEN EVIL DEEDS AND THOUGHTS TELL YOU, YOU ARE NOTHING AND THAT YOU ARE BROKEN, JUST REMEMBER THE LOVE MANIFESTED ON THE CROSS, THE WORDS THAT WERE WRITTEN AND SPOKEN,

VINDICATION

I PRAY FOR THOSE WHO HAS BEEN ASSOCIATED WITH THE NEGATIVE THINGS IN LIFE,

WHOSE UNDERSTANDING IS SEPARATE FROM THE LIFE OF CHRIST,

THEY THINK THEY ARE THE CREATORS AND KEEPERS OF THEMSELVES,

NEVER GIVING GOD THE CREDIT FOR CREATING THEIR HEALTH,

GOD MAKES POOR AND HE MAKES RICH, IT IS YOUR AND BELIEF THAT DETERMINES WHICH,

A MAN CAN BE MONTARILY POOR, BUT CAN BE SPIRITUALLY RICH, HEAVEN IS HIS HOME HE HAS FOUND HIS NICHE,

A MAN CAN BE MONETARILY RICH, BUT SPIRITUALLY POOR, HE CANNOT EVEN ENTER HEAVEN'S DOOR,

NO MATTER WHAT YOUR POSITION, YOU HAVE TO TRUST GOD TO HAVE CONTROL OF YOUR CONDITION,

WHEN THERE IS TOO MUCH EVIL, AND TOO MUCH HATE, GOD WILL INTERVENE AND START TO REASSOCIATE,

SEPARTING THE TRUTH FROM THE LIES, SEPERATING DECEIT AND FALSEHOOD FROM LOVE AND BROTHERHOOD,

THAT'S THE TIME WHEN HUMANITY NEEDS AN OVERHAUL, GOD TO NEEDS TO REVALUE PEOPLE AND SPIRITUALLY CALL,

GOD INITIATES VINDICATION, FOR ALL LIFE, ORGANISMS AND ALL CREATED NATIONS,

TAKING AWAY FROM GOD YOU TAKE AWAY, FROM YOUR FUTURE DAY, HE CONTROL THE FIRST AND THE VERY LAST,

YOU CANNOT HAVE A TODAY WITHOUT A YESTERDAY, YESTERDAY PAVED ALL THE WAYS FOR TODAY,

BETWEEN TODAY AND YESTEREDAY, GOD PLACED THE PRESENT, THE GIFT OF LIFE THAT WAS HEAVEN SENT,

THE PRESENT TIME IS THE ONLY TIME YOU REALLY HAVE RIGHT NOW, YESTERDAY IS OVER AND DONE THE PAST IS WHERE THE FUTURE IS CREATED COMES FROM,

VIOLATED STATE

ONE DAY I WILL BE FREE AT LAST, AND ALL MY TROUBLES WILL ALL BE A THING OF THE PAST,

I CAN TRULY SAY THAT I HAVE NOT LIVED MY TIME, BECAUSE THEY HAVE ALL VIOLATED MY MIND,

MY STATE OF MIND IS WHAT MAKE LIFE WORTH LIVING, HOW CAN YOU DO THAT IF PAIN AND GRIEF IS ALL YOU WILL BE GIVING,

IF I CANNOT GIVE THE LOVE GOD GAVE ME TO GIVE, THEN FOR HIM HOW CAN I LIVE,

I AM VERY AWARE WHERE I LIVE BECAUSE IN A VIOLATED STATE, THAT FOR ME IS FULL OF JEALOUSY AND HATE,

I KNOW GOD DID NOT PLACE ME HERE, THIS WAS DONE DECEITFULLY WITH MALICE AND WITHOUT FEAR,

GENETICALLY THEY SOWED ME IN A PLACE, WHERE THEY COULD ROB AND CHANGE MY GRACE,

TO DENY ME OF MY DIVINE RIGHTS AND LIFE, TO SEPARATE ME FROM MY FUTURE WITH JESUS CHRIST,

I LIVE IN A VIOLATED STATE, THAT SPAWNS NOTHING BUT JEALOUSY AND HATE,

I BELIEVE IN JESUS CHRIST AND THAT HE WILL CHANGE MY FATE, HE HAS ALREADY CONQUERED THIS WORLD TO UNDO VIOLATED STATES,

WE SHALL LIVE AND SHALL NOT DIE

GOD'S COVENANT WITH HIS PROPHETS, HIS PEOPLE AND ALL LIFE HE CREATED, WAS A COVENANT, AND A PROMISE THAT COULD NOT BE NEGATED,

THE COVENANT OF LIFE WAS ON THE RIGHT, A CURSE AND PATHWAY OF DEATH WAS ON THE LEFT,

GOD GAVE US SURE MERCIES AND BENEFITS EVERYDAY, OUR PROMISE OF LIFE HAS ITS OWN PATHWAY,

THAT LEADS US TO CHRIST AND ETERNITY, SALVATION, AND BLESSEDNESS FOR YOU AND ME,

GOD MADE US SPECIAL, DON'T STOP, DO NOT HALT, GOD ALSO GAVE YOU A COVENANT OF SALT,

YOU ARE SPECIAL IN THIS EARTH, SALT GIVES LIFE AND PURIFIES IMPURE BIRTHS,

ALWAYS REMEMBER GOD'S PURPOSE, AND REMEMBER HE TOLD US WHY, WE SHOULD LIVE AND WE SHALL NOT DIE,

HE MADE A SACRIFICE JUST FOR YOU AND ME, HE SENT HIS SON JESUS FOR THE WHOLE WORLD TO SEE,

OUR SIN DEBT HAS BEEN PAID CHRIST BLOOD HAS BEEN SHED, CHRIST SUFFERED AND DIED FOR US AND PAINFULLY BLED,

I HAVE MANY MANY REASONS TO JOYFULLY PROCLAIM, I BELONG TO JESUS CHRIST HE DIED FOR MY NAME,

YES, I AM ONE OF HIS OWN I AM HIS HEIR, JESUS CHRIST IS MY SAVIOUR, HE HAS PROVEN TO ME HOW MUCH HE CARES,

ALWAYS REMEMBER GOD'S PURPOSE, AND REMEMBER HE TOLD US WHY, WE SHOULD LIVE AND WE SHALL NOT DIE,

WHEN I FALTER

LORD YOU KNOW EVERYTHING THERE IS TO KNOW ABOUT ME, YOU CREATED ME WITH YOUR IDENTITY,

YOU DESTINED MAN TO BE CREATED IN YOUR IMAGE, ALL MANKIND IS CREATED FROM YOUR DIVINE LINEAGE,

KNOWING HOW I WAS MADE, MADE ME EXCEPT MYSELF CREATED WITH YOUR DIVINE GRADE,

YET I SEEM SOMETIMES TO FALL SHORT, OF YOUR GRACE, MERCY, AND PEACE, I AM WIDE AWAKE AND SOMETIMES MY SPIRIT SEEMS TO BE IS ASLEEP,

LORD FORGIVE ME IF AND WHENEVER I FALTER, REMIND ME TO ALWAYS TAKE IT TO YOUR ALTER,

WHERE MERCY AND GRACE KNOWS MY NAME, THEY WILL ONLY SEE JESUS, IN ME WHERE THERE IS NO BLAME,

HIS REDEMPTION PAID FOR ME AND HIS BLOOD COVERS ME, HIS BLOOD HAS SET ME FREE, HALLELUJAH!

HIS BLOOD HAS RESSURECTION POWER, I NEED IT EVERY HOUR,

I WILL NEVER THINK OF GIVING IN, TO ANY OF SATAN'S MORTAL SINS,

LORD I AM ONLY PERFECT THROUGH JESUS CHRIST, ONLY WHEN HE EXIST IN MY LIFE,

THEN THIS WHOLE WORLD CAN SEE, THAT IT IS HE WHO REDEEMED ME,

LORD FORGIVE ME IF AND WHENEVER I FALTER, REMIND ME TO ALWAYS TAKE IT TO YOUR ALTER,

WHOSE SEED!

WHEN GOD COMMANDS US TO NOT DO SOMETHING, IT IS USUALLY BECAUSE HE KNOWS WHAT IT WILL BRING,

YOU AND I DON'T KNOW WHAT WILL BE, BUT GOD'S WILL ALWAYS SPIRITUALLY SEES,

CULTIVATE YOU LIFE AND PLANT GOOD SEED, THAT WILL ONE DAY DETERMINE EVERYTHING YOU NEED,

DO NOT INTERCOURSE WITH EVIL SEED, THEY WILL CORRUPT AND MINGLE YOUR GOOD SEED,

IF YOU FORNICATE IT ALLOWS THE EVIL ONE TO SOW HIS SEEDS, WITHIN YOUR BODY THEY WILL DEGRADE AND FEED ON YOUR GOOD SEED,

ONCE THEY HAVE CORRUPTED AND POSSESSED WHAT THEY NEED, YOU ARE NO LONGER THE SEED THEY NEED,

THEY WANT TO INFECT AND CHANGE YOUR BIRTH RIGHTS TO YOUR RIGHTFUL PLACE, THEY CAN ONLY DO THAT BY CHANGING YOUR GODLY RACE AND PLACE,

PLEASE DON'T LET THEM DESTROY, POSSESS AND INFECT, FOR ONE NIGHT OF PLEASURE HAVING ILLICIT SEX,

NOW YOU KNOW WHY GOD COMMANDED NOT TO FORNICATE, IT GIVES SATAN A CHANCE TO ENTER INTO YOUR HOLY GATE,

GOD CREATED YOU AS A SACRED TEMPLE, YOU MUST BE DISCREET, WHO YOU LET IN PLACES WHERE GOD HAS PLACED A HOLY SEAT,

KEEP YOURSELF PURE AND CLEAN, ESCHEWING, AND REBUKING EVIL THINGS,

MOST OF ALL TO FOLLOW THE HOLY GHOST LEAD, THEN THEY WILL NOT HAVE TO ASK WHOSE SEED,

LET IT BE KNOWN WHERE YOU BELONG, MAKE SURE WE KNOW HEAVEN IS YOUR HOME,

WORD'S THAT ROUT THE DEVIL AND DEMON'S OUT

I WRITE THE WORDS OF POWER TRUTH AND LOVE, THE VERY WORDS THE FATHER IS MADE OF,

THE SUBSTANCES THAT CAUSES ABUNDANT LIFE, THE SUBSTANCES THAT VESTED JESUS CHRIST,

THAT GAVE JESUS THE SPIRITUAL FORCES, TO STOP EVIL IN ALL IT'S COURSES,

THE FATHER AND THE SON OUR ETERNAL HEAVENLY TEAM, HERE FOR ALL ETERNITY TO CLAIM FREE AND REDEEM,

WE USE SPIRITUAL WORDS WE KNOW ABOUT, WORD'S THAT WILL ROUT DEVILS DEMONS, ROUT THEM ALL OUT,

THE KEY TO THE VERY FIRST STEP, IS TO PRAY AND TO LET EVIL IN,

ALWAYS KEEP GOD HIS SON FIRST IN YOUR LIFE, THEN YOU ARE FULFILLING, THE PRINCIPLES OF FIGHTING THE GOOD FIGHT,

GOD HAS AN AVENUE TO CONNECT YOU WITH HIS DIVINE LINE,

CAUSE YOU HAVE SOWN SOME SPIRITUAL TIME,

ALL THE THINGS WE PRAY ABOUT, WE SHOULD BE ASKING GOD FOR THE WORDS THAT ALL ROUT DEMONS OUT,

IT PROTECTS AND KEEPS US WHILE WE ARE ASLEEP,
ESPECIALLY WHEN WE PRAY,

YOUR WORDS ARE THE KEYS TO ALL OUR NEEDS,

THEY ARE THE DETERMINANTES TO ALL OUR HOLY DEEDS,

THEY ARE THE WISDOMS OF ALL TIME,

THEY HOLD THE ANSWER TO THE DEEPEST OF ALL OUR MINDS,

CHRIST WORDS ARE DIFFUSED THROUGHOUT THE LAND,

IN THE END ONLY WHAT YOU DO FOR CHRIST WILL STAND,

TO A NATURAL MAN IT DOSEN'T MAKE SENSE,

HOW A HOLY GOD'S LIFE CAN BE A NATIONS
ULTIMATE DEFENSE,

YESTERDAY, TODAY, OR TOMORROW, HE IS STILL THE SAME,

ALL THE POWER AND SECRETS ARE IN JESUS NAME,

ALL FAMILIES MAKE UP THE WORLD ONE GOD MAKES UP THE UNIVERSE

JESUS CHRIST HAD TO BE FIRST, TO MAKE A WORLD, THEN MAKE A UNIVERSE, ALL HUMAN FAMILIES MAKE UP THE WORLD, EVERY BLOOD BOUGHT BOY AND EVERY GIRL,

EVERY SINGLE LINE WE READ IN GOD'S WORD EACH DAY, REPRESENTS A DIRECTION AND A PATHWAY, THAT WE CAN TRAVEL TO REACH A DESTINY IN LIFE, THAT IS SURE TO LEAD US TO JESUS CHRIST,

WALKING THROUGH THE BIBLE IN TIMES PAST AND GONE, HELPS US TO SEE OUR ANCESTORS WERE NO ALONE,

HELP US ALSO TO BE ABLE TO SEE, OUR OWN FUTURE DESTINY, ESPECIALLY IF WE ARE LIVING THE LIFE, WE WILL ONE DAY SEE JESUS CHRIST.

ALL FAMAILIES MAKE UP THE WORLD, GOD MAKES UP THE UNIVERSE, THAT IS WHY JESUS CHRIST HAD TO BE FIRST,

DID YOU KNOW THAT THE WHOLD WIDE WORLD IS ENCIRCLED BY A CURSE, BUT IT COULD BE CURED BY THE ONE WHO CREATES THE WHOLE UNIVERSE,

WE HAVE TO KNOW THERE IS A PENALTY EVEN TO THOSE THINGS WE CANNOT SEE, IT HAS BEEN SPOKEN AND PUT INTO MOTION SPIRITUALLY,

WHAT EVER WE DO IN THE DARK, OR BEHIND CLOSED DOORS, GOD HAS ALREADY MADE A RESOLUTION, AND WHAT HE CREATED IT FOR,

NEVER THINK SIN WILL EVER WIN, IT IS JUST A MATTER OF TIME BEFORE THE CURSE OF JUDGMENT WILL ENTER IN,

THEREFORE SEEK TO DO WHAT IS RIGHT AND APPROPRIATE AT ALL TIMES, THEN YOU WON'T HAVE TO WORRY ABOUT WHAT GOD'S JUDGEMENT WILL FIND,

ALL FAMAILIES MAKE UP THE WORLD, GOD MAKES UP THE UNIVERSE, THAT IS WHY JESUS CHRIST HAD TO BE FIRST,

CHRIST LIFE IS OUR DEFENSE

LOOKING BACK OVER THE ANNALS OF TIME AND HISTORY,

I REALIZE MY LIFE AND EXISTENCE IS BOUND TO YOUR
SACRED STORY,

THERE IS REALLY NOTHING OUTSIDE OF YOUR WORD,

OUR ANCESTORS AND PARENTS, TAUGHT US EVERYTHING
WE'VE HEARD,

YOUR WORD MANIFEST EVERYTHING WE HEAR AND SEE,

YOUR WORDS ARE THE EPITOME OF ALL DESTINY,

YOUR WORDS KEEPS US HEALTHY, UPRIGHT, WISE,
AND STRONG,

YOUR WORDS MAKES US WEALTHY, WORTHY,

GIVING ALL OUR HEARTS NEW SONGS,

WHO WOULD KNOW AND BELIEVE THE LIFE AND
HEALING PROPERTY,

OF JUST YOUR UTTERED AND WRITTEN HOLY WORDS FOR
ALL HUMANITY,

SOMETIMES TO THE NATURAL MIND IT DOESEN'T
MAKE SENSE,

HOW A HOLY GODS'S LIFE CAN BE OUR
ULTIMATE DEFENSE,

YES, YOUR WORDS GIVE LIFE EVERY SINGLE DAY,

IT PROTECTS AND KEEPS US WHILE WE ARE ASLEEP,
ESPECIALLY WHEN WE PRAY,

YOUR WORDS ARE THE KEYS TO ALL OUR NEEDS,

THEY ARE THE DETERMINANTES TO ALL OUR HOLY DEEDS,

THEY ARE THE WISDOMS OF ALL TIME,

THEY HOLD THE ANSWER TO THE DEEPEST OF ALL
OUR MINDS,

CHRIST WORDS ARE DIFFUSED THROUGHOUT THE LAND,

IN THE END ONLY WHAT YOU DO FOR CHRIST
WILL STAND,

TO A NATURAL MAN IT DOSEN'T MAKE SENSE,

HOW A HOLY GOD'S LIFE CAN BE A NATIONS
ULTIMATE DEFENSE,

YESTERDAY, TODAY, OR TOMORROW, HE IS STILL THE SAME,

ALL THE POWER AND SECRETS ARE IN JESUS NAME,

GREAT NAME

LORD I HAD TO MAKE A DECISION HOW I WOULD LIVE MY LIFE, WOULD IT BE FOR ME OR WOULD IT BE FOR JESUS CHRIST,

I HAD TO REALIZE I WOULD BE NOTHING UNTIL YOU CAME, AND CONNECTED ME TO YOUR GREAT NAME,

NO MATTER WHAT I DID OR WHAT I SAID, IT DIDN'T MEAN ANYTHING IF IT WAS NOT SPIRIT LED,

I HAD THE CHANCE TO OBSERVE MEN OF HONOR AND PRAISE, I HAD A PANORAMIC VIEW OF WHAT IT LOOKED LIKE TO BE GODLY RAISED,

YOUR PEOPLE WERE IMBUED WITH GRACE AND STRENGTH, WITH AN UNFAILING CONFIDENCE, THAT WAS ALWAYS VISIBLE AND THEIR VISIONS WERE GREAT AND IMMENSE,

YOUR LOVE AND JUSTICE WOULDN'T LET ME BE BLAMED, BECAUSE I AM A CHILDBEARING YOUR GREAT NAME,

I FOUND OUT WHEN EVIL CAME, ALL I NEEDED TO DO WAS CALL YOUR GREAT NAME,

I CAN BIND THE DEVIL IN BONDS AND CHAINS, BY REBUKING HIM IN YOUR GREAT NAME,

WHAT EVER I DO AND WHAT EVER I SEE, IS NOTHING COMPARED TO YOUR DIVINITY,

I WOULD NOT TRADE YOU FOR THIS WHOLE WIDE WORLD, YOU ARE THAT PRICELESS TREASURE, YOU ARE MY UNIVERSAL PEARL,

AS LONG AS I HAVE YOU, I AM NEVER LOST, YOUR LOVE ENCOMPASSED EVERYTHING UPON THE CROSS,

LET THEM THINK WHAT EVER THEY WILL, AND DO WHAT EVER THEY FEEL, BECAUSE I KNOW THAT IN TIME, YOU WILL CAUSE A LIGHT IN ME TO SHINE,

I HAD TO REALIZE I WOULD BE NOTHING UNTIL YOU CAME, AND CONNECTED ME TO YOUR GREAT NAME,

NO CHAINS

I WAS HELD BACK IN LIFE, BECAUSE I DID NOT KNOW JESUS CHRIST, I DECIDED I WANTED TO BE SET FREE, THAT'S WHEN JESUS CHRIST CAME TO ME,

HE TOOK AWAY THE PAIN, AND WIPED AWAY ALL MY TEARS, AND SAID TO ME I WILL RESTORE ALL YOUR YEARS,

THAT WAS CONSUMED BY THE CATAPILLARS, LOCUSES, AND WORMS, WHAT THE INSECTS DID NOT EAT MY ENEMIES BURNED,

JESUS SET ME FREE, FREE INDEED, HE REMOVED ALL MY CHAINS, HE SAID NOW VICTORY, IS YOURS TO CLAIM,

I WANT THE WHOLE UNIVERSE TO KNOW, I AM UNHINDERED AND FREE, THERE ARE NO MORE CHAINS BINDINGS ME,

I AM A CHILD OF GOD'S, JESUS CHRIST HAD MERCY ON ME AND SET ME FREE,

NOW I HAVE MORE CHAINS BINDING ME,

THERE ARE DIFFERENT KINDS OF CHAINS THAT BIND IN DIFFERENT WAYS, SOME CHAINS THAT BIND ARE IN PEOPLE'S DNA,

THESE KIND OF CHAINS ARE SPIRITUALLY BROKE, THEY WERE ON PEOPLE NECKS AS A BONDAGE AND YOKE,

GOD'S PEOPLE SHOULD HAVE NO STRANGE CHAINS, IF IT ISN'T IN OUR HEAVENLY FATHER'S NAME,

GOD WATCHES US AND KEEPS US CONNECTED, HE SHIELDS US AND KEEPS US PROTECTED,

THE ONE THING GOD ASK US TO DO THAT IS THE SPIRITUALY WAY, HE ASK US TO PRAY EACH AND EVERY DAY,

DAY'S ARE MADE ANEW EACH DAY BY OUR KING, EVERY DAY IS A NEW DAY WE HAVE NEVER SEEN,

SO THERE IS NO MORE CHAINS FOR ME, BECAUSE MY FATHER HAS COME AND SET ME FREE,

GOD'S COVENENT RAINBOW/
BLESSINGS AND PROMISES TO MANKIND

THE SILENT FIGHT FOR LIFE

THERE IS A WAR THAT RAGES EVERYDAY, THAT PAVES AND OPENS EVERY WAY,

FOR EVERY HUMAN TO HAVE THEIR BEING, THIS WAR IS ON THE OPPOSITE SIDE OF EVERYTHING AND CANNOT BE SEEN,

THIS WAR RAGES BETWEEN THE MOON AND THE SUN, THEY FIGHT FOR THEIR PLACES, THE RIGHT TO SHINE FORTH AS ONE,

THE SUN AND THE MOON OCCPUY THE SKY, BUT IT IS THE TIMING OF THE HEAVENLY BODIES THAT SEPERATES THE TRUTH FROM THE LIE,

THERE ARE SPECIFIC HOURS MOVEMENTS FOR THE SUN TO SHINE,

GOD GRANTED TWELVE HOURS A DAY AS THE SUN'S TIME,

GOD ALSO GAVE GLORY TO THE MOON TO SHINE AT NIGHT, A TIME WHEN DARKNESS REALLY NEEDED SOME LIGHT,

THERE IS ALSO A FIGHT BETWEEN THE EARTH AND THE PLANTED SEEDS, THE DAISIES, THE FLOWERS, AND THE TREES, ARE BATTLING TO PUSH THROUGH THE EARTH TO BE FREED,

ALL AROUND US EACH HOUR OF THE DAY, SOMETHING IS BATTLING AND FIGHTING FOR ITS RIGHTFUL COURSE TO COME FORTH THROUGH ITS NATRUAL WAY,

THE POSITIVE FORCES ARE FIGHTING TO CONTROL THE POSITIVE SIDE, WHILE THE NEGATIVE FORCES TRY TO STEAL, CONVERT, AND DERIDE,

GOD IS FIGHTING FOR YOUR SOUL, SPIRIT AND LIFE, TO MAKE SURE YOU ARE JOINED TO JESUS CHRIST,

WHILE SATAN IS SEEKING YOUR SOUL, YOUR LIFE, TO DEVOUR, CONSUMING YOUR LIFE-TIME RIGHT DOWN TO THE VERY LAST HOUR,

TEMPTING YOU WITH ALL HIS SEDUCERS HOPING YOU CAN NOT TELL, THEY ARE THERE TO HELP DIRECT YOU RIGHT TO HIS HELL,

GOD CREATED OUR ENTIRE ANATOMY WITH BOARDERS PATHS,

EACH ORGAN HAD A SPECIFIC WAY TO IT'S PLACE FROM THE FIRST TO THE LAST,

OUR WHOLE BODY WAS DESIGNED WITH ORDER KEEP, SO THAT WE DON'T CONFUSE OUR HEAD WITH OUR FEET,

ALL OUR ORGANS HAVE THEIR OWN PLACE, THEY FIGHT AND PROTECT THEIR OWN GOD GIVEN SPACE,

THIS IS ALL DONE TO PERPETUATE THE SILENT FIGHT FOR LIFE, KEEPING OUR BODY IN ORDER FOR THE INDWELING SPIRIT OF JESUS CHRIST,

TOO WRONG TO BE RIGHT

WHY LET EVIL KEEP YOU BOUND TO YOUR INSECURITIES, BY THE THINGS YOU DO AND THE REASONS WHY YOU HATE ME,

HOW CAN YOU MAKE AMENDS WITH DIVINITY, WITH THE CHAINS OF JEALOUSY AND HATE THAT I CAN SEE,

THE WORDS THAT I WRITE ARE TRUE, AND DIRECTED RIGHT TO YOU,

HOPING TO CHANGE YOUR EVIL WAYS, FROM WHAT HATES TO WHAT PRAYS,

GOD DID NOT MAKE A MISTAKE, WHEN HE MADE YOU IT WAS NOT FROM THE ESSENCE OF HATE,

WHEN DID YOU CHOOSE HATE OVER GOOD, BELIEVE IT OR NOT GOD KNEW THAT YOU WOULD,

WHEN YOU ARE FEELING BROKEN, MISUSED AND CONTRITE,

SOMETIMES IT MAKES YOU FEEL TOO WRONG TO BE RIGHT,

GOD'S MERCY AND CARE FOR THE HUMAN RACE, CAUSED HIM TO HAVE HIS SON TAKE OUR PLACE,

NO MATTER HOW YOU SEARCH, YOU WILL NEVER FIND ANOTHER LOVE LIKE THIS, IT IS SPIRITUAL A REDEMPTIVE, DIVINE, ETERNAL GOD GIVEN GIFT,

WHEN YOU ARE FEELING BROKEN, MISUSED AND CONTRITE,

SOMETIMES IT MAKES YOU FEEL TOO WRONG TO BE RIGHT,

JUST ONE

LORD I STARTED OUT WITH A MULTITUDE THAT PROMISED TO BE USED, BY YOU AND THE HOLY SPIRIT AND TO BRING ABOUT SPRITUAL THINGS TO CAST EVIL THINGS OUT,

DECADES LATER I MUST CONFESS, I ONLY SEE ONE THAT HAS SUSTAINED ALL THE DURESS,

YET LORD YOU KNOW MY HEART AND MY SOUL, AND ALL IT TOOK TO MAKE ME WHOLE,

I AM STILL STANDING AS JUST ONE, BELIEVING ON ALL THE THINGS YOU HAVE SAID, AND YOU HAVE DONE,

A TRUE GIFT JUST HAS TO HAVE A RECEIVER, HERE I STAND FATHER AS YOUR ONE TRUE BELIEVER,

YES, I IN TOTAL JUST ONE, BUT I AM EQUIPPED AND ABLE TO RECEIVE EVERYTHING CHRIST HAS DONE,

I KNOW THAT I AM QUALIFIED WHY ELSE WOULD EVIL AND HATRED WANT TO RUN AND, THEY KNOW THE TRUTH ABOUT ME AND WHAT YOU INVESTED,

WITH ALL THEIR COVERINGS I HAVE STILL NOT BEEN CONVERTED,AND, INFESTED,

I WILL REMAIN TO STAND FOR TRUTH, JUSTICE, AND RIGHT, UNTIL JESUS COMES AND CHANGES DARKNESS TO LIGHT,

THE TRUTH AND BEGINNING OF WISDOM, IS TO KNOW THE TRUE GOD AND TO FEAR, AND NOT TO WORRY ABOUT TIME, A DAY, YOUR LIFE, OR ANOTHER YEAR,

I HAVE SEEN THE PARTS OF ME LEAVE, IT WAS NOT ALL BECAUSE OF DEATH, EVEN DEATH LEFT,

FATHER YOU KNOW EVERYTHING HOU HAVE EVER MADE, YOU VESTED IN MY LIFE TO MAKE BETTER GRADES,

YOU CAN SEE ALL THE THINGS I HAVE DONE, MULTITUDES OF LIFE COMING FROM JUST ONE,

I UNDERSTAND MORE NOW I HAVE PRAYED, THE CREATOR OF LIVES CANNOT BE REMADE,

I AM SO MUCH BETTER THAN ANYTHING I HAVE EVER MADE, I AM THE PURE ESSENCE OF EVERY SINGLE GRADE,

FATHER WHEN DEATH LEFT I WAS THERE STANDING AS ONE PROFESSING AND COMMANDING THE THINGS CHRIST HAD DONE,

I REMEMBERED THE LIFE CHRIST GAVE, AND THAT I HAD THE POWER TO MAKE DEATH BEHAVE,

A TRUE GIFT JUST HAS TO HAVE A RECEIVER, HERE I STAND FATHER AS YOUR ONE TRUE BELIEVER,

YES, I IN TOTAL JUST ONE, BUT I AM EQUIPPED AND ABLE TO RECEIVE EVERYTHING CHRIST HAST DONE,

FATHER OUT OF TRILLIONS, I AM ALONE AS JUST ONE, WILLING AND ABLE TO RECEIVE ALL THE THINGS CHRIST HAS DONE,

STOP STEALING MY STUFF

IT IS APPARENT EVERYTHING THAT YOU DO, I HAVE REALLY HAD ENOUGH OF YOU,

STEALING MY LIFE, MY TIME AND MY MIND, YOU HAVE STOLEN MY EVERY BELIEF YOU COULD FIND,

I KNOW NOW WHY YOU DO THESE THINGS, EVERY THING YOU STOLE HAS A FORM OF LIFE IT BRINGS,

SO YOU LIVING OFF OF ME, IS NOT THE WAY GOD PLANNED IT TO BE,

STOP OPENING MY SEED TO FEED YOUR GREED, AND DENY MY OWN LIFE BLOOD AND NEED,

I AM TELLING YOU NOW TO STOP STEALING MY STUFF, ALL THESE YEARS YOU SHOULD HAVE HAD ENOUGH,

I AM PRAYING EVERYDAY THAT YOU CAN STEAL NO MORE, AND THAT GOD WILL NOT LET YOU OPEN MY LIFE'S DOOR,

SATAN COMES TO ROB STEAL AND KILL, I KNOW YOU ARE ONE OF HIS, BECAUSE YOU ARE DOING HIS WILL,

I KNOW I AM THE CHILD OF THE KING, BECAUSE WHAT YOU STEAL MY GOD CAN REPLACE EVERYTHING,

GOD HAS PROMISED ME THERE WOULD BE NO LACK, WHAT EVER IS TAKEN I CAN GET IT BACK,

STOP STEALING MY STUFF, YOU SHOULD REALLY HAVE ENOUGH, GOD IS SEEING ME THROUGH, AND HE WILL TAKE EVERYTHING BACK FROM YOU,

MY ANATOMICAL GARDEN

GOD HAS GIVEN ME THIS ABILITY, TO CULTIVATE WHAT IS INSIDE OF ME,

I CAN GROW JEWELS THAT ARE GREAT, OR DEMONS OF LUST AND HATE,

YES, MY BODY IS THE GARDEN THAT GOD HAS SPIRITUALLY MADE, I CAN ASCEND TO BE THE BEST OF GOD, OR DESCEND TO THE DEVILS DEGRADED,

I THROUGH GOD CAN GROW ALL THINGS GOOD AND RIGHT, I CAN SEPARATE THE DAY FROM THE NIGHT,

WEATHER I AM BOY OR GIRL, I CAN GROW EVERYTHING IN MY OWN WORLD,

IN MY WORLD WHAT EVER YOU CAN SEE, WILL HAVE COME FROM ME FROM THE OCEANS TO THE LAND OF FOREST AND TREES,

OF ALL THE THINGS TO BE DESIRED I PREFER, CHRIST TO BE MY PEARL OF GREAT PRICE, MY SACRED OYSTER,

FROM THE TOP OF MY HEAD TO THE BOTTOM OF MY FEET, GOD HAS ALLOWED ME TO CULTIVATE WHATEVER I WOULD NEED,

EVERYONE OF MY CULTIVATED CELLS ARE A PART OF ME, AND HAS A HIDDEN ASPECT OF MY DESTINY,

CELLS WERE MADE TO FUNCTION IN SPECIFIC DOMAINS, IF STOLEN, WHAT GOOD ARE THEY IF DIVINITY DOES NOT REMAIN,

CELLS ARE ONLY WHAT IS CREATED FROM THE HOST, THEY DONOT INCORPORATE EVERYTHING THEY ARENOT HE MOST,

THEY FUNCTION IN RECORDED SPACE, IN ORDER FOR THE SOVERIEGN HOST TO REPLACE,

LIKE PEOPLE CELLS GENERATE, SOMETIMES THEY HAVE TO REGENERATE,

A FRUITING BODY IS LIKE A FRUITFUL TREE, GROWING FRUIT LIKE YOU AND ME,

WHEN WE BEGAN TO GROW AND REALLY UNDERSTAND, LIFE WILL TAKE ON A NEW MEANING, AND A NEW PLAN,

YOUR WORLD WILL TAKE SHAPE, FORM, AND PURPOSE, YOU WILL SEE THE BEAUTY OF BEING CREATED FROM THE EARTH'S DUST,

NOTHING GROWS WITHOUT WATER AND EARTH, YOU ARE THE EARTH YOU GIVE ALL YOUR CELLS BIRTH,

GOD GAVE ME THIS ANATOMICAL GARDEN OF LIFE, TO CULTIVATE EVERYTHING TO LIVE FOR CHRIST,

WORDS TO LIVE BY

EVERYDAY THAT WE LIVE THERE ARE THINGS WE CAN GIVE IN LIFE, WHETHER THEY ARE PHYSICAL OR SPIRITUAL TO HONOR THE PROMISE OF JESUS CHRIST,

WE ARE CREATED IN THE IMAGE OF GOD, WHICH MEANS THERE ARE THINGS WE CAN DO,

WE ARE THE KEEPERS OF THE BLOOD OF JESUS CHRIST, AND HIS RESURRECTION TOO,

I AM A TRUE BELIEVER IN THE POWER AND REGENERATION OF THE HOLY WORD, THE ONLY ONES THAT ARE IN DOUBT ARE THE ONES THAT HASN'T HEARD,

THE GOOD NEWS OF THE GOSPEL AND THE SALVATION OF JESUS CHRIST, HOW HIS SACRIFICE AND REDEMPTIVE GOODWILL SAVED MANKIND'S LIFE,

GOD GAVES US THE BIBLE AS WORDS, LAWS, STATUTES TO LIVE BY, WORDS THAT ARE TIMELESS, BLESSED, CONSTRUCTED WITH SPIRITUAL ESSENCE THAT CANNOT DIE,

THOSE OF US THAT ARE TRUE BELIEVERS, MUST BE THE VICARS IN THE EARTH UNTIL CHRIST COMES,

HE WILL THEN JUDGE ALL THE THINGS IN HIS NAME WE HAVE DONE, TO EXALT THE NAME OF JESUS CHRIST THE HOLY SON,

IF YOU KNOW YOU HAVE HONORED HIM WITH YOUR WHOLE HEART, YOU WILL HAVE AN INHERITANCE IN HIM, HE WILL DESIGNATE YOU A PORTION AS YOUR PART,

BECAUSE IN THIS WORLD ONLY WHAT YOU DO FOR CHRIST WILL LAST, EVERYTHING ELSE WILL DISSOLVE AND BECOME SOMETHING AS IF IT HAD NEVER BEEN CAST,

GOD GAVES US THE BIBLE AS WORDS, LAWS, STATUTES TO LIVE BY, WORDS THAT ARE TIMELESS, BLESSED, CONSTRUCTED WITH SPIRITUAL ESSENCE THAT CANNOT DIE,

I AM FREE FROM DISEASE

MANY TIMES, IN LIFE TROUBLES AND PERILS COME, BUT NONE OF THEM ARE GREATER THAN WHAT CHRIST HAS DONE,

FOR ONLY A MOMENT WE ARE AFFLICTED AND PUNISHED, FOR A LIFETIME WE HAVE BEEN REDEEMED AND ASTONISHED,

AT THE MIRACLES AND BENEFITS GOD HAS GIVEN TO US, ESPECIALLY TO THOSE THAT BELIEVE IN HIM AND TRUST,

NO PROBLEMS, DEMONS, OR ANATOMICAL CONSTRAINTS HAVING INFESTED SEED,

CAN HINDER THE SAINTS AND THE GREAT I AM WHO IS FREED FROM ALL DISEASE,

BECAUSE OF MY INHERITANCE I CAN CLAIM THE RIGHT AND EXEMPTIONS, THAT CHRIST SACRIFICED FOR MANKIND REDEMPTIONS,

JESUS FREED ME FROM ALL THE VISSITUDES OF LIFE, THAT I MIGHT BE BLAMELESS HAVING HIS DIVINE RIGHTS,

I CAN NOW EAT FROM THE SACRED TREE OF LIFE, BECAUSE OF THE LOVE OF JESUS CHRIST,

NOTHING IS TOO GREAT FOR THE GREAT I AM, BECAUSE EVERYTHING CAME FROM THIS PASCHAL LAMB,

WHEN GOD CREATED THE SEVEN DAYS, HE CREATED THE ENTIRE WORLD, HE CREATED ALL GOOD DAYS NONE WITH TURMOIL,

THEY WERE ALL GOOD DAYS FOR MANKIND TO HONOR, ENJOY, AND SHARE, TO LIVE OUT LIFE AS SAINTS AND BELIEVERS, THROUGH A HEAVENLY FATHER WHO CARES,

IN GOD'S HANDS IS ALL TIME, ALL LIFE, AND ALL GENERATIONS TO COME, WE MUST LEARN TO RESPECT OURSELVES, OUR ELDERS AND THE SOVEREIGN ONES,

WE CANNOT DENY THAT GOD LIVES INSIDE OF EACH ONE AND THE OTHER, WITH THAT BEING SAID THEN YOU SHOULD KNOW HOW TO TREAT YOUR SISTER AND BROTHER,

HOW YOU TREAT THEM IS HOW YOU ARE TREATING THE GOD INSIDE, YOU MAY HAVE TO FACE HIM ONE DAY, WILL HE BLESS YOU OR WILL YOU BE DENIED,

NO PROBLEMS, DEMONS, OR ANATOMICAL CONSTRAINTS, HAVING INFESTED SEED,

CAN HINDER THE SAINTS AND THE GREAT I AM WHO IS FREED FROM ALL DISEASE,

GOD'S DEMOCRACY

GOD CHOSE HIS SON TO BE THE SOVEREIGN GOVERMENT, TO REDEEM THE SOULS OF MANKIND WAS THE SPIRITUAL INTENT,

JESUS CHRIST IS THE PEOPLE'S GOVERNMENT, HE IS SOVEREIGN HE IS ALSO THE PRESIDENT,

WE ARE LIVING IN TIMES PEOPLE ARE VERY UNSURE, ESPECIALLY WITH THEIR SICKNESSES

AND SEEKING FOR CURES,

I PERSONALLY KNOW SOME SICKNESS IS BROUGHT ABOUT BY SIN, ESPECIALLY WHEN THEY CHANGE THE COURSE OF THINGS GOD DESIGNED, SIN ENTERS IN,

WE MUST LEARN TO LET THINGS BE AS GOD DESIGNED THEM, WHO WOULD BETTER KNOW WHAT IS BEST BETTER THAN HIM,

THERE WILL COME A TIME WHEN THERE WILL BE NO DEMOCRACY, WE WILL BE RULED BY GOD'S HEIROCRACY,

ALL HOLY PEOPLE, WHOM GOD HAS CHOSE, PEOPLE SPIRITUAL AND UPRIGHT MOST OF ALL WHO GOD KNOWS,

WE WON'T HAVE TO WORRY ABOUT LIES, THIEVES, AND SIN, OR PEOPLE ROBBING AND KILLING, FAMILY OR OUR FRIENDS,

WE WILL BE HAPPY, CONTENT, AND FREE, CAUSE HEAVEN PROTECTS BOTH YOU AND ME DIVINITY,

WE MUST BE IN ANTICIPATION OF GOD'S DEMOCRACY, DESTINED TO BE RULED BY HEIROCRACY,

WEATHER WE ARE ABSENT OR PRESENT, GOD WILL DO WHAT HE SAID HE WILL DO,

THERE IS NO DIMENSION GOD CANNOT TAKE YOU THROUGH,

I CAN'T WAIT TO LIVE IN GOD'S PERFECT WORLD, CREATED FOR THE HUMBLE, THE JUST, WITHOUT TURMOIL,

THE BLESSED, THE ARCH ANGELS AND THE ANGELIC BEINGS, ARE ALL IN RANKS PRAYING AND SITTING AROUND OUR SOVEREIGN KING,

JESUS CHRIST IS THE PEOPLE'S GOVERNMENT, HE IS SOVEREIGN HE IS ALSO THE PEOPLE'S PRESIDENT,

GOD PREDESTINED ME

WHILE I WAS YOUNG, FOOLISH AND UNRULY, I FOUND OUT
THERE WEREN'T MANY THAT DID NOT TRY TO FOOL ME,

INTO DOING THINGS THAT WERE NOT SPIRITUALLY RIGHT,
THERE WERE ALL SATAN'S CHILDREN OF THE NIGHT,

I THOUGHT PARTYING, STEALING, AND USING DRUGS, WAS
ALL THERE REALLY WAS,

UNTIL GOD HAD TO GET MY ATTENTION SO THAT I COULD
SEE, HE WAS MY ONLY REAL DESTINY,

EVERYTHING ELSE WAS JUST IMATATIONS, IMAGES AND
FALSE REALITIES, THAT HE COULD USE TO MAKE A REAL
WORLD FOR ME,

MY PAST, MY FAILURES, AND ALL MY ACCOMPLISHMENTS,
BECAME MY FUTURISTIC PATHWAYS CREATED WITH GOD'S
DIVINE INTENTS,

GOD CALLED ME IN THE WOMB AND GAVE ME HIS NAME,
BEFORE I WAS EVEN BORN IN THIS WORLD MY GOD CAME,

BETTER IS THE PERSON WHO HAS NOT SEEN THE EVILS IN THIS
WORLD, WHO HAS NOT BEEN BORN IN SIN AND TURMOIL,

THAT GOD HAS ALLOWED TO CHOOSE TO BE BORN IN A
DAY, THAT EVIL HAS BE MOVED OUT OF THEIR WAY,

THEY WHO HAS BEEN CHOSEN TO BE BORN IN PEACE, A
TIME WHEN TROUBLE AND HATRED HAS CEASED,

I BELIEVE THAT GOD PREDESTINED THIS FOR ME, IN MY HEART
GOD'S PEACE, AND GOD'S JOY IS THE ONLY SOLACE FOR ME,

I DON'T WORRY ABOUT THIS WORLD AND WHO THEY SUE,
I LEAVE THAT TO GOD AND HIS JUDGEMENT TO DO,

I KNOW THAT AGAINST SOME THINGS GOD HAS NOT MADE
A LAW, THE FRUITS OF HIS HOLY SPIRIT, THEY HAVE NO FLAWS,

I BELIEVE THAT GOD PREDESTINED THIS FOR ME, IN MY HEART
GOD'S PEACE, AND GOD'S JOY IS THE ONLY SOLACE FOR ME,

CONFUSED

LORD I AM IN A QUANDRY STATE, NOT KNOWING IF THIS MY FATE,

I DESIRE TO DO WHATEVER IS EXALTING, TO THE GOSPEL AND FOR YOU,

RIGHT NOW, I AM EXPERIENCING, TROUBLES THAT WON'T LET ME THROUGH,

I KNOW THAT YOU ARE GREATER, AND HAVE THE LAST SAY,

NO DEVIL OR DEMON IN HELL CAN STOP YOUR WAYS,

I NEED TO KNOW THE TRUTH OF WHAT I AM DOING,

IS IT WORTHY AND WORTH MY TIME OR AM I JUST FOOLING,

LORD I REALLY NEED YOUR HELP, I AM SPIRITUALLY CONFUSED,

I FEEL, LET DOWN, WORN OUT AND PHYSICALLY AND MENTALLY MISUSED,

LORD YOU KNOW EVERYTHING ABOUT ME THERE IS TO KNOW, YOU KNOW MY FUTURE AND WHERE I AM TO GO,

IF I AM FALTERING IN MY MIND BODY OR SOUL, YOU CAN INSTANLY TELL, IT IS MY DESIRE TO PROGRESS SPIRITUALLY AND DO WELL,

LORD, I REALLY NEED YOUR HELP, I AM SPIRITUALLY CONFUSED,

THEN, WHY DO I FEEL LET DOWN, PHYSICALLY AND MENTALLY MISUSED,

---

WHEN I AM WEAK, I KNOW YOU CAN TELL, IT'S BECAUSE THE FORCES OF EVIL ARE SENDING ME THROUGH THE PITS OF HELL,

I WON'T COMPLAIN BECAUSE I KNOW IT IS TRUE, EVEN IN HELL YOUR TRUTH COMES THROUGH,

WHEN THEY TRY TO CAST ME INTO DARKNESS, YOUR WORDS OF TRUTH ARE MY LIGHTS,

THEY STRENGHTEN ME AND REMIND ME THIS IS ALL YOUR FIGHT,

TO PROVE EVEN IN HELL GOD WORDS REIGNS SUPREME, IT CAN CHANGE A NIGHTMARE OF HELL INTO A HEAVENLY DREAM,

LORD I NEED YOUR ASSURANCE TO KEEP ME IN MY RIGHT MIND, TO GIVE SUBTLY THE REMINDER THAT ONLY YOU HOLD ALL TIME,

LET SATAN AND HIS DEMONS KNOW THE ONLY THINGS THAT REALLY STAND, ARE THE WRITTEN LAWS, YOUR WORDS, AND YOUR COMMANDS,

THERE IS NOTHING SATAN OR HIS HORDES OF HELL CAN DO, WITH GOD ALMIGHTY SATAN MUST BOW DOWN TOO,

DEMONIC POSSESSION

I BELONG TO GOD AND I WANT THE WHOLE WORLD AND UNIVERSE TO KNOW,

INSPITE OF THE PROTECTION RIGHT NOW THAT DOES NOT SEEM TO SHOW,

IT IS NOT BECAUSE I FALTERED, IT IS BECAUSE I HAVE BEEN PHYSICALLY AND SPIRITUALLY ALTERED,

THEY WANTED TO POSSESS MY VERY BEING, THEY WANTED TO RECONSTRUCT MY CONNECTION TO JESUS CHRIST MY HOLY KING,

THEY TRIED TO CONDITION MY MIND TO BELIEVE THAT I WAS DEAD, AND THAT GOD WAS NOT MY SPIRITUAL GODHEAD,

WHILE I WAS ASLEEP SATAN AND HIS HORDES SOWED THEIR EVIL TARES, GOD MADE ME REMEMBER HOW MUCH JESUS CARED,

EVIL MAY SOW SEEDS OF DISCORD AND DEMONIC POSSESSIONS, JUST REMEMBER TO WHOM YOU OWE YOUR PROFESSIONS AND CONFESSIONS,

WORDS CAN BE THE PATHWAYS AND BUILDING BLOCKS OF TOMORROW, THEY CAN BE THE EVIDENT SPIRITUAL GUIDES TO QUELL THE PAINS AND SORROWS,

RIGHT WORDS CAN BE THE WARRIORS YOU NEED IN A SPIRITUAL WARFARE,

THEY CAN PROTECT AND UPHOLD ALL YOUR GOD DIRECTED PRAYERS,

ONLY FOR MOMENT WILL EVIL HARRASS YOUR LIFE, YOU MUST CONTINUE THE QUEST TO SECURE A PLACE IN JESUS CHRIST,

NEVER GIVE UP ON WHAT GOD HAS PROMISED YOU, HE WILL FULFILL YOUR PROMISE AND YOUR DESIRES TOO,

IT IS UP TO YOU IF YOU NEVER TRY, GOD WILL STILL BE GOD YOU CANNOT MAKE GOD A LIE,

KNOW YOUR PURPOSE IN SPEECH AND KNOW YOUR REASON, YOU HAVE THE RIGHT WORDS OF POWER, WORDS THAT CAN BE SPOKEN IN DUE SEASONS,

EVIL MAY SOW SEEDS OF DISCORD AND DEMONIC POSSESSIONS, JUST REMEMBER TO WHOM YOU OWE YOUR PROFESSIONS AND CONFESSIONS,

BE LIKE DAVID

HOW CAN YOU FIND SOMEONE TODAY ANYWHERE, THAT HAS WRESTLED WITH AND KILLED A LION AND A BEAR,

HE DID THIS WITH HIS BARE HANDS, WHILE HIS SPIRIT WAS UNDER GOD'S COMMAND,

THE HISTORY OF DAVID LETS YOU I AND KNOW, IT WAS GOD'S SPIRIT THAT MADE HIS SPIRITUALLY GROW,

GOD DID GREAT THINGS IN THE BIBLE FOR KING DAVID,

IF WE HAD HALF OF HIS SPIRIT, WE WOULD ALL MAKE IT,

DAVID WAS A MAN OF TRANSCENDING PRAYERS, HIS INCESSANT, SPIRITUALITY AND HOMAGE, IN PRAYER GOD WOULD ALWAYS MEET HIM THERE,

GOD ASSOCIATED DAVID TO THE MOST SACRED PART, DAVID WAS CONSIDERED A MAN AFTER GOD'S OWN HEART,

WE ALL KNOW ABOUT THE GIANT, IT WAS NO MYTH,

DAVID ACTUALLY SLEW THE GIANT, WHO WAS NAMED GOLIATH,

DAVID'S HEART WAS THE EQUIVALENT OF IT'S WEIGHT IN GOLD,

TO GOD DAVID WAS THE EPITOME, OF WHAT IT MEANT TO BE PRAYERFULLY AND SPIRITUALLY WHOLE,

THE BOOK OF PSALMS AND PRAISES IS ONE HUNDRED AND FIFTY CHAPTERS,

WITHIN THEM EVERYONE CAN FIND A SPIRITUAL PRAYER THEY ARE AFTER,

DAVID'S PRAYERS ARE THE LONGEST CHAPTERS IN THE WHOLE SACRED BOOK,

EVERYONE HAS READ THEM OR AT LEAST TOOK A LOOK,

GOD DID GREAT THINGS IN THE BIBLE FOR KING DAVID,

IF WE HAD HALF OF HIS SPIRIT, WE WOULD ALL MAKE IT,

EVERYONE CAN'T BE LIKE DAVID, HE WAS SPIRITUALLY PURE, THAT'S HOW GOD MADE HIM, THAT HIS PRAYERS WOULD ENDURE,

HIS PRAYERS TRANSCENDED RIGHT DOWN TO TODAY, WHEN WE WANT TO GET A PRAYER THROUGH IT IS THE BOOK OF PSALMS WE PRAY,

ONE THING I CAN SAY THAT I THINK ABOUT KING DAVID,

THE LOVE OF GOD WAS IN HIS HEART, THAT'S HOW HE MADE IT,

DON'T TEAR ME DOWN

PEACE MY SISTER, MY BROTHER, I AM JUST LIKE YOU, THE SAME GOD DWELLING IN ME, DWELLS IN YOU TOO,

SO BE CAREFUL HOW YOU TREAD MY WATERS, GOD INSTILLED THEM IN ME AS PART OF OUR HOLY FATHER,

HE MADE ME A TEMPLE JUST LIKE YOU, FOR THE HOLY GHOST TO HELP ME GET THROUGH,

PLEASE DON'T TEAR ME DOWN WITH YOUR WORDS OR HANDS,

GOD HAS A FUTURE FOR ME TOO, HE HAS A PLAN,

SO, DON'T TEAR ME DOWN, I AM ALSO PART OF THE FATHERS CROWN,

WE ALL FILL A PLACE AND SPACE THAT GOD HAS FOUND, ERECTED AND PLACED ON SPIRITUAL GROUND,

FOR THE LOVE OF CHRIST, DO IT EVEN IF YOU HATE ME, GOD IS THE INDWELLING TRINITY, IT IS NOT EVEN ABOUT ME,

IF YOU WANT TO SEE JESUS CHRIST, YOU WILL HAVE TO CHECK YOUR ACTIONS NOT ONCE, BUT TWICE,

ARE YOU REALLY DOING WHAT YOU SHOULD, OR ARE YOU DOING WHAT OTHERS WOULD,

GOD SAID YOU MUST LOVE YOUR SISTER AND BROTHER,

BEFORE YOU CAN BEGAN TO SAY YOU HAVE LOVE FOR ANY OTHER,

I THINK WHEN IT COMES TO DIVINE LOVE AND BEING DIVINELY CONNECTED,

WE AS HUMANS ARE SHORT SIGHTED, AND PHYSICALLY, MENTALLY, AND FLESHLY AFFECTED,

THE WORD OF GOD WILL NOT WALK AFTER THE FLESH, THERE IS NO GOOD THING IN THAT PHYSICAL MESS,

THE TRUTH CAN STAND ON ITS OWN EVERYONE HAS HEARD,

TO FULFILL GOD'S LAWS WALKING AFTER THE SPIRIT IS GOD'S WORDS,

WITH YOUR HARSH WORDS AND HATE DON'T TEAR ME DOWN,

I AM ALSO A PART OF THE HEAVENLY FATHER'S CROWN,

TEACHER OF ALL MANKIND

GOD HAS ALREADY GIVEN THE COMMAND, FOR HIS HOLY SPIRIT TO DIRECT THE INHABITANTS IN THE LAND,

WE SHOULD BE LED BY GOD'S HOLY SPIRIT, THROUGH WISDOM AND UNDERSTANDING WE SHOULD HUMBLY FEAR IT,

BECAUSE IT IS THE REPROVER, TEACHER AND JUDGE OF ALL MANKIND, CAPABLE OF DESTRUCTION BEYOND OUR MINDS,

IMAGINE FOR A MOMENT ONE SUPREME UNIQUE SPIRITUAL BEING, HAVING THE POWER TO SEAL EVERYTHING AND HUMAN BEING,

HIS AWESOME SPIRIT, IS TANTAMOUNT TO HIS DAILY TASKS, EQUAL JUDGEMENT FROM THE FIRST PERSON TO THE VERY LAST,

YES, THE HOLY SPIRIT IS THE TEACHER OF ALL MANKIND, THE DIRECTOR OF OUR SOULS, THE SEALER OF OUR SPIRITUAL TIMES,

I BELIEVE THE HOLY SPIRIT IS ALSO THE KEEPPER OF ALL WISDOM, AND IS THE PROMOTER OF OUR SPIRITUAL MINDS AS ONE,

THE HOLY SPIRIT IS NOT BOUND BY HUMAN, TIME, PLACE, OR ENVIRONMENTS,

HE IS SELF SUFFICIENT AND CAPABLE OF ENDURING ALL WITHIN HIS GUIDELINES AND INTENTS,

IT IS NOT WISE TO UPSET, REBUKE, OR CAUSE DERISION, WHERE THE HOLY SPIRIT IS CONCERNED YOU CANNOT BE FORGIVEN,

THEREFORE BE HUMBLE, AND RESPECT ALL GOD'S CHOICES CONCERNING THE TRINITY, IT IS THE SUPREME GOVERNING PRINCIPLES OF THE LAND THE HIGHEST AUTHORITY,

YES, THE HOLY SPIRIT IS THE TEACHER OF ALL MANKIND, THE DIRECTOR OF OUR SOULS, THE SEALER OF OUR SPIRITUAL TIMES,

THAT ONE BLOOD STAINED DAY

WHEN WILL THE BLOOD SHED END, WILL WE EVER REALLY FIND THE TRUE MEANING TO GRACE,

WHEN CHRIST PAID THE COST, AND WAS THE SUBSTITUTE IN EVERY ONE'S PLACE,

IF WE REALLY UNDERSTAND WHAT IT ALL ACTUALLY MEANT, WHY IS OUR WORLD STILL RACIALLY BENT,

WE ARE BENT TOWARDS, WHITES KILLING BLACKS, BLACKS KILLING WHITES, WE EVEN COMMITT GENOCIDE, WHERE WE KILL EACH OTHER NO NATION SEEMS RIGHT,

CHRIST BLOOD WAS SHED FOR A NOBLE PURPOSE THAT DAY, FOR ALL PEOPLE HE PAVED A BETTER WAY,

I BELIEVE WE HAVE TAKEN FOR GRANTED OR FORGOTTON, ABOUT THAT ONE BLOOD STAINED DAY,

THE BLOOD WAS SHED TO MAKE US BETTER THAN WE ARE, TO CLEAN UP A SIN SICK WORLD, CHRIST BECAME OUR VICAR,

OUR SOULS WERE DARKENED WITH MUD AND PITCH, GOD'S PEOPLE WERE SOLD, FOR A PAIR OF SHOES TO THE POOR OR TO THE RICH,

WHAT I THINK WE DON'T UNDERSTAND IS THAT WE ARE NOT OUR OWN, CHRIST BLOOD WAS TO BE FOR US AS ATONED,

THAT BLOOD THAT WE ARE CONTINUING TO SPILL, IS JESUS'S BLOOD THAT THE ROMAN GOVERNMENT KILLED,

FROM THE CROSS RIGHT DOWN TO TODAY, CHRIST THROUGH US, NEVER STOPPED SHEDDING HIS BLOOD TO PAY,

ARE WE TOO IGNORANT TO SEE EVERY HUMAN BEING, IS A BLOOD BOUGHT PURCHASE, WHOSE BLOOD CAME FROM A HOLY KING,

EVERY TIME YOU SLAY OR KILL YOUR SISTER OR BROTHER OR SOMEONE, YOU DISAVOW THE SACRED THINGS CHRIST HAS DONE,

TO GOD OUR BLOOD AND OUR SOULS ARE PRECIOUS, IT IS A LIFE GIVING SOURCE, TO DIVINITY FOR US,

THINK ABOUT IT THAT IS CHIST BLOOD YOU ARE SPILLING, IT MAY LOOK LIKE JUST ANOTHER HUMAN BEING IN ESSENCE IT IS CHRIST BLOOD YOU ARE STILL KILLING,

CHRIST BLOOD WAS SHED FOR A NOBLE PURPOSE THAT DAY, FOR ALL PEOPLE HE PAVED A BETTER WAY,

I BELIEVE WE HAVE TAKEN FOR GRANTED OR FORGOTTON, ABOUT THAT ONE BLOOD STAINED DAY,

MADE FOR TRAVEL

WITHIN THE HUMAN BODY IS MANY PATHWAYS,

LEADING TO DIFFERENT STATES OF EXISTENCE WHERE SOMETIME BACTERIAL PREYS,

THE HUMAN ANATOMY IS TRULY A WORLD WITHIN ITSELF,

FULL OF GENETIC SEED AND VITAL HEALTH,

WHY DO YOU THINK MOST OUR BLOOD VESSELS AND VEINS,

AND OUR INTERCONNECTED ARE VEINS ARE LIKE PASSAGES IN OUR ANATOMICAL FRAME,

FROM THE BOTTOM OF OUR FEET, TO THE THE ONLY ETOP OF OUR HEAD, IT IS A JOURNEY THAT CAN BE SPIRITUALLY LED,

THE FOUNDATION FOR EVERY MAN WOMAN AND CHILD,

IS TO HAVE CHRIST AS OUR FOUNDATION, SO WE WON'T BE DEFILED,

CHRIST WILL BUILD US UP WITH TRUTH AND LOVE,

THE ONLY ESSENCE THE FATHER KNOW AND IS MADE OF,

YES, YOUR BODY WAS TRULY MADE FOR TRAVEL WITH GODLY INTENTS,

ONE SIDE FOR REBELLIONS, THE OTHER SIDE FOR THOSE WHO ASCEND,

GOD SEPERATED THE SHEEP FROM THE GOATS, THEY CLEARLY DO NOT WEAR THE SAME COATS,

YOU MUST LEARN WHAT YOU ARE INSIDE, WHEN USED BY CHRIST THERE ARE MANY PLACES TO HIDE,

MAKE YOU ARE ON THE RIGHT JOURNEY AND THE RIGHT QUEST,

IT'S ALL ABOUT REACHING CHRIST AND DOING YOUR BEST,

WE ARE FEARFULLY AND WONDERFULLY MADE TO LIVE LIFE,

WE MUST ADHERE TO THE TRUE PRINCIPLE AND PROMISES OF JESUS CHRIST,

ERASE THE DEVILS FACE

THERE ARE SO MANY LIES BEING TOLD, THE DEVIL HAS GOTTEN TO BE TOO DIABOLICALLY BOLD,

HE HAS NO RESPECT FOR THE GOD'S AUTHORITY,

SO, HE DOES HIS DIRTY WORK THROUGH EVERYONE HE SEES,

NEVER GIVE ROOM TO THE DEVIL, HE WILL DISTORT YOUR PLACE, HE WILL TRY TO STEAL YOUR FACE,

IF THE DEVIL HAPPENS TO OCCUPY AND POSSESS YOUR PLACE, YOU HAVE TO ASK GOD TO ERASE AND REMOVE THE DEVIL'S FACE,

HE WILL BRING NASTY HORDES OF DEMONS TO DEFILE AND ABUSE YOU,

BUT YOU MUST STAY PRAYERFUL AND TRUE, NEVER LET EVIL GET THE BEST OF YOU,

JUST REMEMBER GOD IS TRUE TO HIS WORD, HE WILL REMEMBER THE PROMISE TO YOU AND WHAT YOU HAVE HEARD,

IF YOU LOOK IN THE MIRROR AND DON'T LIKE WHO YOU SEE, JUST REMEMBER GOD KNOWS AND CAN ALWAYS MAKE YOU WHO YOU SHOULD BE,

IF THE DEVIL HAPPENS TO OCCUPY AND POSSESS YOUR PLACE, YOU HAVE TO ASK GOD TO ERASE AND REMOVE THE DEVIL'S FACE,

MY BODY OF EVIDENCE

GOD GAVE ME MY OWN DAY, IN ORDER FOR ME TO COME IN MY OWN WAY,

GOD HAS ALL AUTHORITY, AND NOBODY ELSE HAS ANY RIGHTS OVER ME,

HE DESIGNED ME FROM MY HEAD RIGHT DOWN TO MY TOES,

MY PROOF IS MY BODY OF EVIDENCE, CREATED FOR ME THROUGH GOD'S HOLY PROVIDENCE,

HE KEPT MY TIME SECRET AND OUT OF THE WAY, SO IT WOULD NOT BE EASY FOR EVIL TO STEAL MY DAY,

HE HID ME IN PLACES THE DEVIL COULD NOT GO,

SO THAT THE DEVIL WOULD NOT EARTHLY KNOW,

GOD HAS SPECIAL TIMES, AND SPECIAL CODES, GOD HAS SOME VERY SPECIAL ABODES,

WHERE NO DEVIL OR HUMAN BEING CAN EVERY GO,

ONLY GOD HAS THE KEY A PLACE WHERE ONLY GOD CAN SOW,

MY PROOF IS MY BODY OF EVIDENCE, CREATED FOR ME THROUGH GOD'S HOLY PROVIDENCE,

MY PERIOD OF TIME

EVERYDAY I REALIZE GOD HAS MADE A WAY, FOR US ALL TO BE AND TO KNOW WHO HAS MADE THIS DAY,

EVEN TIME WINDS AND UNWINDS, MOVES AND STOPS AT HIS COMMAND IN HIS MIND,

HE HAS CREATED ALL PERIODS OF TIME GENELOGICALLY AND GEOLOGICALLY WE WILL FIND HIS DIVINE WORD IN EVERY SINGLE LINE,

GOD HAS GIVEN ME A PERIOD IN TIME, THAT I MIGHT EXPERICENCE DIVINITY AND BELIEVE IN HIS DIVINE MIND,

WE LOVE YOU LORD WITH AN UNCEASING LOVE, PERSISTING THROUGH ADVERSITIES REACHING TO HEAVEN ABOVE,

YOU ARE THE GIFT WE ALWAYS THINK OF, A LOVE THAT SURPASSES ALL PHYSICAL THINGS THERE IS NO HIGHER LOVE,

WE LOOK TO AND COUNT ON HEAVENLY THINGS, AND THE ABUNDANT JOY, LIFE, AND LOVE THEY BRING,

IF YOU ARE UNSURE OF WHAT TO DO OR TO THINK TODAY,

GIVE IT TO GOD HE HAS ALREADY PAVED THE WAY,

EVERYONE HAS A SPACE AND A PLACE, GOD HAS GIVE THEM, ALONG WITH A MEASURE OF GRACE,

WINDOWS OF MY SOUL

OPEN THOU LORD MY PATH, THAT MY SOUL MAY REST AT LAST,

AND BE REMOVED FROM THE SINS OF THE PAST,

LIFT ME LORD THAT MY SOUL MY TAKE WINGS,

AND BE A PART OF YOUR HEAVENLY THINGS,

YOU ARE MY CROWNING KING,

YOUR LOVE MAKES MY SPIRIT SING,

THE PRAISES OF YOUR POWER AND MIGHT, KEEPS AND TEACHES OUR FINGERS AND MIND TO FIGHT,

FIGHTING FOR THE PROMISES, TRUTH, FAITH AND GOD'S LOVE,

THAT WAS ONCE DELIVERED TO THE SAINT'S BY ANGEL'S FROM UP ABOVE,

ORDAINED BY LAW, SECURED BY GRACE,

FOR US TO DWELL IN CHRIST BODY AS A SPECIAL PLACE,

HEIRS OF TRUTH AND GRACE, THE MOST POWERUL GIFT,

PROCEEDING THROUGH THE ANNUALS OF HISTORY AND TIME,

PROCLAIMING CHRIST IS NO MYTH,

A PROMISED SAVIOR FOR ALL MANKIND,

THE RULER OVER LAND, SEAS, AND ALL MEN MINDS,

IN THE SPIRITUAL REALM, CHRIST HAD TO BE FIRST,

HE UPHOLDS AND CAUSES TO REVOLVE THIS WHOLE UNIVERSE,

WORD BY WORD ONE THING I KNOW,

OUR WHOLE UNIVERSE IS FULL OF WINDOWS

WHEN GOD LOOKS AT ME HE SEES, THROUGH THE WINDOWS OF MY SOUL,

WHERE CHRIST DIED FOR ME TO CLEANSE ME AND MAKE ME WHOLE,

GOD'S SPIRIT IS NEVER DEPLETED

HOW CAN THEY(YOU) THINK A GOD THE WITH THE ABUNDANT LIFE YOU HAVE IN YOU,

CAN EVER GET LOW IN SPIRITS OR THE TRUTH,

I KNOW YOUR SPIRIT IS NEVER DEPLETED, BECAUSE IT WILL ALWAYS BE NEEDED,

AS OUR KING, YOU ARE HIGHLY AND PERMANENTLY SEATED,

YOUR SPIRIT CAN NEVER BE SPIRITUALLY DEPLETED,

I THANK YOU FATHER, FOR YOUR LOVE AND CARE,

YOU HAVE ALWAYS BEEN SPIRITUALLY THERE,

I KNOW YOUR SPIRIT CAN NEVER BE DEPLETED,

BECAUSE IT WILL ALWAYS BE SPIRITUALLY NEEDED,

AS OUR KING, YOU ARE HIGHLY AND PERMANENTLY SEATED,

YOUR SPIRIT CAN NEVER BE SPIRITUALLY DEPLETED,

GOD RULE'S

LORD I ASK FORGIVENESS FOR MY WORLD, FOR EVERY WOMAN, MAN, BOY AND GIRL,

I PRAY THAT ONE DAY WE WILL ALL SEE, YOUR LOVE AND PROMISED DIVINITY,

FOR YOUR PEOPLE WHO HAS LABORED FAITHFULLY ALL THEIR LIFE,

EXPECTING YOU TO RELEASE THEM FROM EVIL AND STRIFE,

LORD YOU RULE IN EVERYTHING YOU DO,

WE CANNOT DO ANYTHING WITHOUT YOU,

PLEASE KEEP OUR MINDS IN A SAFE PLACE

A PLACE FULL OF LOVE AND FULL OF YOUR GRACE,

THAT WE MAY NEVER DEPART, THAT WE WILL ALWAYS REMEMBER,

YOU ARE OUR KEEPER, YOU ARE OUR MENDER,

LORD YOU RULE THE DAY, AND YOU RULE THE NIGHT,

LORD YOU RULE EVERY PATHWAY, YOU RULE ALL POWER AND ALL MIGHT,

GOD RULES THAT'S GOD'S RIGHT, THAT'S GOD'S AUTHORITY, THAT'S GOD'S MIGHT THAT'S GOD'S LIGHT,

EVERYDAY WE SEE YOUR LIGHT AND DIVINITY,

SHINING FOR US ALL GIVING LIFE, THROUGH SPRING, SUMMER AND FALL,

FORGIVE US LORD FOR FAILING TO ALWAYS SEE,

YOUR LOVE AND EXTENSIONS OF PEACE,

KEEP US LORD AND TEACH US LORD LIKE YOUR CHILDREN WE ARE,

EVEN THOUGH WE HAVE GROWN, WE ARE NEVER OUT OF YOUR REACH TOO FAR,

HELP US TO UNDERSTAND IN ALL THINGS YOU RULE,

THE HEAVEN'S THE EARTH, EVERY ORGANISM EVERY MAN,

ONLY WHAT YOU DO FOR CHRIST WILL LAST

MEN BUILD GREAT PALACES OF WOOD AND STONE, GOD
DESIGNS MEN, WOMEN, AND CHILDREN OF FLESH AND BOND,

MEN AND WOMEN SEEK FORTUNE AND FAME AND WEALTH,
GOD ISSUES US SPIRIT LIFE, LOVE, AND HEALTH,

ONLY WHAT YOU DO FOR CHRIST WILL LAST, JUDGEMENT
IF ON YOUR PRESENT LIFE AND ON YOUR PAST,

WE ARE CHILDREN OF GOD'S PURPOSE,

THE SACRIFICE OF HIS ONLY SON WON US,

WE MAKE THE CHOICE TO SERVE THE ONLY TRUE GOD OF
THIS HEAVEN AND OF THIE EARTH,

TO VALID JESUS CHRIST'S MIRACULOUS BIRTH,

SEED'S FROM A KING THAT'S WHAT'S WITHIN HIS HAND,

SOWN IN A GODLY FIELD, A BLESSING GOR THE KING IS
WHAT IT WILL YEILD,

READY TO BE SOWN WHERE HE CHOOSES WITHIN
CHOSEN LANDS,

A SEED IN THE GROUND THAT ONE DAY WILL STAND,

ONLY WHAT YOU DO FOR CHRIST WILL LAST, JUDGEMENT
IF ON YOUR PRESENT LIFE AND ON YOUR PAST,

WE ARE THE GODLY FIELDS OF JESUS CHRIST, WE ARE FERTILE, HOLY GOOD GROUND AND HIS FRUIT,

SOWN IN GODLY, FIELDS, A BLESSING TO THE KING HOLY FRUIT IS WHAT IT WILL YEILD,

ONLY WHAT YOU DO FOR CHRIST WILL LAST, JUDGEMENT IF ON YOUR PRESENT LIFE AND ON YOUR PAST,

SERVANT IN THE MIDDLE

LORD I BELIEVE THAT EVERYTHING YOU ALLOW HAS A REASON,

JUST LIKE EACH AND EVERY YEAR WE HAVE FOUR SEASONS,

I KNOW YOU SAID LORD YOUR SHEEP ARE ON THE RIGHT,

AND THE GOATS ARE ON THE LEFT, THERE ARE TWO KINGDOMS ONE OF LIFE AND ONE OF DEATH,

ALL BELONGS TO YOU LORD THE LIVING AND THE DEAD,

AT SOME POINT IN LIFE THEY HAVE ALL HEARD THE WORDS AND LAWS YOU'VE SAID,

LIKE APOSTLE PAUL WHOSE NAME MEANT LITTLE,

I AM CONSTANTLY USED AS A BURDEN BEARER FOR ALL PEOPLE,

I AM YOUR SERVANT IN THE MIDDLE,

BECAUSE OF THE HAND OF GOD WHO MADE ME,

EVIL AND WICKEDNESS AND TROUBLE WILL ALWAYS HATE ME,

BECAUSE I WILL NEVER BE LIKE THEM,

THEY KEEP TRYING MAKE MY LIFE INTO A TREACTEROUS, EVIL, LUSTFUL, FILM,

GOD MADE SURE SATAN COULD NOT SAY,

HE HAD ANYTHING TO DO WITH MAKING ANY PART OF ME OR MY DAY,

MY GOD IS LOVING, PURE AND A GOD YOU CAN TRUST,

HE IS NOT DECEITFUL, LUSTFUL, AND UNJUST,

THEY DRAW FROM ME ON THE LEFT, THEY DRAW FROM ME ON THE RIGHT,

THEY HIDE ME IN THE MIDDLE, OUT OF EVERYONE'S SIGHT,

NO MATTER WHAT THE CASE LORD I AM STILL YOUR SERVANT,

I DON'T MIND BEING USED FOR GODLY INTENTS,

I PRAY THAT YOU WATCH AND MAKE SURE YOUR GOODNESS, PURITY, AND SPIRITUALITY,

IS NOT USED FOR HELL AND ALL OF IT'S FATALITIES,

JUST IN CASE EVIL HAPPENS TO POSSESS SOMETHING OF MINE,

IT IS ONLY POSSIBLE THROUGH MY FATHER AND ONLY FOR A TIME,

THE TRUE HEIRS ARE UNDER GOD'S COVENANT,

THEY ARE NOT LIKE OTHER PEOPLE, THEY WILL BE HEAVEN SENT,

UNTIL THEY COME THE WORLD CAN ONLY SHARE,

WHAT BE LONGS TO THEM UNTIL THEY GET THERE,

YOUR WORD SAID DON'T LOOK TO THE LEFT, DON'T LOOK TO THE RIGHT,

KEEP YOU EYES LOOKING STRAIGHT AHEAD, TIL YOU REACH GOD'S ABUNDANT, BOUNDLESS, LIMITLESS LIGHT,

LORD YOU ARE THE ONLY WINDOW TO MY SOUL,

ALL OTHER WINDOWS ARE JUST FOR THE EYES TO BEHOLD,

MY WINDOW WAS MADE FOR ONLY ONE,

FOR JESUS CHRIST YOUR HOLY, UNDENIABLE SANCTIFIED SON,

TRUTH ONLY COMES FOR ME FROM SEEING THROUGH HIS EYES,

THEN I CAN SEE EVIL AND THE GOOD AND WHO SPIRITUALLY LIES AND DEFIES,

LORD I KNOW YOU PLANTED MY SEEDS IN THE GROUND,

EVERY SEED A MEASURED A CHAIN OF LIFE FOR ME TO BE FOUND,

THEY ARE YOUR TRUE WORLDLY HARVEST, THAT YOU GAVE TO ME AND THAT YOU SPIRITUALLY INVEST,

LIKE APOSTLE PAUL WHOSE NAME MEANT LITTLE,

I AM CONSTANTLY USED AS A BURDEN BEARER FOR ALL PEOPLE,

I AM YOUR SERVANT IN THE MIDDLE,

ILLEGAL PENETRATION

I WANT MY GOD TO KNOW WHEREVER I WENT,

IT WAS USUALLY WITH MY OWN CONSENT,

IF I WAS EVER FORCED TO DO WHATEVER SOMEONE ELSE WANTED ME TO,

THAT SHOULD NOT BE COUNTED AGAINST

THE THINGS THAT I ALLOW AND DO,

EVIL KEEPS TRYING TO PENETRATE MY LIFE, WITH EVIL DEEDS,

TO INFILTRATE MY HOST WITH DEMONIC SEEDS,

I CHARGE ALL SANTANIC WORKS WITH ILLEGAL PENETRATION,

WITHHOLDING MY LIFE, FROM MY FAMILY AND WITH GENERATIONAL SEGREGATION,

I AM NOT AND I PROCLAIM, VERY LOUD,

I AM A CHILD OF GOD'S AND VERY PROUD,

I WILL NEVER BE PROFANE, EVIL, AND SCUM,

LIKE THE THINGS I KNOW HAVE ALLOWED AND DONE,

I WILL NEVER WILLINGLY CONSENT TO ANY OF THEIR EVIL INTENTS,

THAT'S ALL IN THE WAY I WAS MADE,

I AM NOTHING LIKE THE ENEMIES EVIL GRADE,

I KNOW MY GOD IS WATCHING ME TO SEE WHAT I WILL DO,

I CANNOT PLEASE THE LUSTFUL, ONLY THE ONLY GODLY THE TRUE,

YOU WILL NEVER BE TOTALLY COMFORTABLE IN MY SPACE,

BECAUSE YOU KNOW IT TRULY BELONGS TO MY GOD GIVEN GRACE,

YOU MAY ROB, STEAL, AND KILL, BUT ONE THING IS A FACT,

WHEN GOD GETS READY GOD GETS EVERYTHING BACK,

SO WHEN EVERY ONE OF GOD'S CHOSEN TAKES A FALL,

GOD HAS ALREADY MADE A WAY FOR US TO RECOVER ALL,

ONE THING IS FOR SURE WHAT EVER THEY SAY OR DO,

IT CAN NEVER COMPARE TO YOUR TRUTH,

THEY WORSHIP IDOLS OF WOOD, STONE, AND HAY,

AN IMAGE THAT WAS CREATED IN A MATERIAL WAY,

THAT WAS NEVER CREATED IN GOD'S DAY,

DON'T COME IN MY SPACE, AND WASTE YOUR TIME,

TRYING TO ROB, STEAL, AND COMMIT EVIL CRIMES,

YOU ARE A SERVANT OF EVERYTHING BAD, EVIL, AND ASSOCIATED WITH WASTE,

TRYING TO MAKE ME LIKE YOU,

AND TAKE MY PLACE AND REMOVE MY GRACE,

THESE WORDS ARE WRITTEN AGAINST YOU AND ALL YOUR EVIL DEEDS,

WE STAND FIRMLY ON GOD'S TRUTH, AND GOD'S HOLY SEEDS,

I CHARGE ALL SANTANIC WORKS WITH ILLEGAL PENETRATION,

WITHHOLDING MY LIFE, FROM MY GOD, FAMILY, AND GENERATIONAL, SEGREGATION,

GOD'S TIME WARRIOR

LORD YOU GAVE ME THE RIGHTS, TO BATTLE IN ANY TIME PERIOD, TO BRING THROUGH THE LIGHT,

THERE IS NO TIME I CANNOT GO THROUGH,

TO RIGHT THE WRONGS THAT HAS BEEN DONE TO YOU,

YOU DESIGNATED ME AS YOUR WARRIOR OF LIGHT AND TIME,

I CAN SLAY DARKNESS WITH LIGHT AND RESTORE ALL SPIRITUALLY GENUINE MINDS,

LIGHT CANNOT BE CULTIVATED, DESTROYED, OR EVEN MADE,

GOD IS IT'S CREATOR AND DETERMINES IT'S MAGNITUDE AND GRADE,

LIGHT CANNOT BE CUT, SHOT, OR MAINED, IT IS NOT A FLESHLY SUBSTANCE THAT CAN BE BRUTALLY TAMED,

IT IS THE FASTEST ELEMENT KNOW TO MAN, TRAVELLING DISTANCES FAR BEYOND THIS EARTH, UNIVERSE, AND ORIONS BANDS,

WHAT NIGHT, IF ANY CAN FIGHT THE LIGHT, EVERYTHING IT KNOWS WILL BE EXPOSED, UNCOVERED, PUT IN PLAIN SIGHT,

GOD'S LIGHT IS DESIGNED TO REVEAL ALL THINGS, FROM A THE POOREST PAUPER TO THE RICHEST KING,

TIME WAS MEANT TO BE LIVED AND SHAPED, NOT TO BE STOLEN, SQUANDERED, AND RAPED,

THAT IS WHY I AM YOU TIME WARRIOR, FOR ALL THE PRECIOUS SOULS THEY STOLE,

I HAVE COME TO TRANSCEND THROUGH TIME TO MAKE YOU WHOLE,

I KNOW WHAT THEY HAVE ARE SHADOWS OF THINGS TO COME,

AND THAT YOU HAVE ALL THE ORIGINALS AND ALL THE REAL ONES,

YOU CAST TO THEM IMAGES, FIGURES AND CARBON COPIES,

FIGMENTS OF MY LIFE THINGS THAT ARE ONLY SENTIMENTS OF ME,

THOSE THINGS WON'T LAST, NOR CAN THEY TOTALLY FILL MY SHOES,

THEY ARE PARTICLES OF MY DREAMS, THEY HAVE ALREADY BEEN USED,

I DESIGNED THEM, I OWN THEM, CREATED FROM MY MIND, THEY EXIST BY MY SPIRIT AND BY MY TIME,

LIKE TIME FATHER YOU PLACED ME EVERYWHERE, PAST, PRESENT, AND FUTURE, TIME STARTS WHEN I GET THERE,

LORD YOU GAVE ME THE RIGHTS, TO BATTLE IN ANY TIME PERIOD, TO BRING THROUGH THE LIGHT,

THERE IS NO TIME I CANNOT GO THROUGH,

TO RIGHT THE WRONGS THAT HAS BEEN DONE TO YOU,

SPIRITUAL BREECHES

LORD I PRAY TO YOU EVERYDAY, THAT I MAY BE IN ALIGHMENT WITH YOUR HOLY WAYS,

THAT I MAY FAR FROM EVILS AND UNTRUTHS, THAT HAS DISTORTED MY WAYS SINCE MY YOUTH,

NOW THAT I AM MATURE AND ALL GROWN UP, I DENIE THEM THE SATISFACTIONS OF CONTINUING TO MESS ME UP,

I REMEMBER THE SPIRTUAL THINGS I HAVE BEEN TOLD, EVIL COMES AND TEARS THEM UP AND LEAVE THEM FULL OF HOLES,

NONETHELESS, I STILL EARNESTLY SEEK FOR YOU UNENDING PROMISES,

THAT YOU HAVE DESIGNED AND PAVED FOR THE DILIGENT SEEKERS OF YOUR JUSTICES,

FATHER MY REQUEST IS THAT YOU REMOVE ALL SPITITUAL BREECHES,

THAT HAS ATTACHED THEMSELVES TO ME LIKE EVIL, DEMONIC, WICKED LEECHES,

THEY USURP MY LIFE, POWER, AND SPACE, SO THAT I MIGHT NOT HAVE ANY SPIRITUAL GRACE OR PLACE,

I BELIEVE I AM STRONG IN YOU WORD AND IN YOUR STRENGH,

IT TAKES A UNIVERSE OF THEM TO QUELL MY FAITH, THIS IS EVIDENT,

I LOVE YOU WITH A GENTLE AND QUIET LOVE THAT SURPASSESS TIME IT SELF,

IT GIVES TO ME THE CONFIDENCE I NEED, THE TENACITY TO CARRY ON IN BELIEF AND HEALTH,

AS YOU HAVE WRITTEN, WE MUST CAST THEM OUT IN THE NAME OF YOUR SON,

WE MUST BE BELIEVERS, I KNOW I AM NOT THE ONLY ONE,

I KNOW THERE MUST BE MORE THAT HAS NOT COMPLETELY GIVEN IN,

WE MUST BE OVERCOMERS IN YOUR NAME TO CAST OUT SIN,

THE HOLY THREE/THE MAJESTIC TRINITY

MY GOD REVERSED IT

LORD I WAS ALWAYS PUT IN UNCOMPROMISED POSITIONS,

UNDER VERY EVIL AND WICKED CONDITIONS,

NOTHING I HAD DONE TO DESERVE THIS TREATMENT,

OTHER THAN BEING A CHILD OF GOD'S HEAVEN SENT,

I WAS HATED IN THE WORST OF WAYS, I WAS DENIED TO LIVE MY DAYS,

ONE DAY EVIL WAS GONE, I DIDN'T KNOW WHAT IT ALL MEANT,

A BEAUTIFUL ANGEL CAME TO MY MIND, AND SAID YOUR GOD HAS REVERSED IT,

SHE SAID YOUR FATHER, WILL NO LONGER STAND FOR THIS ABUSE,

YOU WERE CREATED FOR BETTER, THINGS AND SPIRITUAL USE,

YOU HAVE A DESTINY AND YOU HAVE A RIGHT, TO LIVE AND LOVE IN A ETERNAL LIGHT,

I AM NOW LIVING IN A DIFFERENT STATE, MY FATHER HAS GIVEN ME MY OWN GATE,

I CAN COME AND GO AS I CHOOSE, WITH GOD BY MY SIDE I CAN NEVER LOSE,

I COULD HAVE BEEN CHAINED UP TO THIS DAY, BUT MY FATHER WOULD NOT HAVE IT THAT WAY,

ONE DAY EVIL WAS GONE, I DIDN'T KNOW WHAT IT ALL MEANT,

A BEAUTIFUL ANGEL CAME TO MY MIND, AND SAID YOUR GOD HAS REVERSED IT,

MY HOUSE IS YOUR HOUSE

FATHER MY HOUSE IS YOUR HOUSE, NO MATTER
WHERE WE ARE,

IT CAN BE NEAR BY OR CLOSE, OR VERY VERY FAR,

I AM GLAD TO BE A PART OF YOUR HOUSE,

YOU PAID THE PRICE YOU PAID THE COST,

TO DWELL HERE FOREVER, IF YOU CHOOSE TO DO SO,

YOU ARE ALWAYS WELCOMED HERE, I WANT
YOU TO KNOW,

MY HOUSE IS YOUR HOUSE, YOU PAID THE RANSOME,
YOU PAID THE COST,

IT IS AN AWESOME BLESSING, TO BE IN THE PRESENCE, OF
GOD'S ETERNAL SPIRIT,

JUST YOUR PRESENCE, ISSUES FORTH HEALING, TO
ANYONE NEAR IT,

MY HOUSE IS YOUR HOUSE, I PRAY THAT YOU WILL KEEP
ME ALWAYS,

THROUGH THE TUMULTOUS TIMES, AND THE WICKED AND
EVIL DAYS,

MY HOUSE IS YOUR HOUSE, YOU PAID THE RANSOME,
YOU PAID THE COST,

ETERNAL LIGHTS

ONCE YOU HAVE FOUND YOUR LIGHT,

YOU NO LONGER LIVE IN THE NIGHT,

YOU CAN BE A BEACON FOR GOD'S HOLY CHILD,

SO HOLY MEEK AND MILD, SO PURE GIFTED AND UNDEFILED,

LORD LET US BE AN ETERNAL LIGHTS,

OF YOUR LOVE AND PURE ESSENCE SHINING BRIGHT,

FOR THIS WHOLE WORLD TO SEE,

WE ALREADY HAVE THE VICTORY IN THEE,

WE ARE ETERNAL LIGHTS TO PAVE THE WAY,

TO REPRESENT OUR GOD'S CHOSEN DAY,

FOR SIN SICK SOULS AND LOST CHILDREN, IN BY GONE TIMES,

THAT HAS BEEN CAST ASIDE AND CAST OUT OF ALL
PEOPLE'S MINDS,

WE ARE ALL SHARING A TIME IN SPACE,

THAT ONLY GOD HAS AUTHORITY TO ERASE,

GOD HAS A PLACE FOR ALL GENETIC LINES, EVEN THOSE
WHO WERE FORGOTTEN, AND LEFT BEHIND,

ETERNAL LIGHTS SHINING BRIGHT, TO MANIFEST GOD'S LOVE,

REPRESENTED BY A PERFECT HOLY DOVE,

TO KEEP US AND SPREAD HIS INFINITE, UNIVERSAL LOVE,

I FOUND OUT ABOUT YOUR RESENTMENT

WHY DO YOU HATE ME SO, WHEN I WAS THE ONE TO ALWAYS THERE,

TO THE BAT FOR YOU, WHEN YOU WERE IN TROUBLE AND DESPAIR,

I THOUGHT YOU LOVED ME LIKE I LOVED YOU, THERE WAS NOTHING I WOULD NOT TRY TO DO,

TO MAKE YOUR DAY A HAPPY AND JOYFUL ONE,

NO MATTER WHAT THE ENEMY MIGHT HAD BEEN DONE,

BUT THEN ONE DAY I FOUND A NOTE AND HEART-FELT LETTER,

YOU WERE WRITING THINGS TO MAKE YOU FEEL BETTER,

THAT DAY I FOUND OUT, YOU WERE EXTREMELY JEALOUS OF ME,

BECAUSE OF MY LOVE FOR YOU, THIS I COULD NOT SEE,

I PRAYED AND CRIED UNTIL I WENT TO SLEEP, I HAD A DREAM ABOUT THE GOOD THINGS, I COULD STILL KEEP,

I REFUSED TO LET JEALOUSY BE THE END OF OUR CONNECTION,

I VOWED EVEN IN TRUTH I WOULD STILL TRY TO MAKE IT END WITH GODLY PERFECTION,

THIS ONE THING I KNOW, IN THE BEGINNING FRIENDSHIP WAS YOUR INTENT,

FOR SOME REASON AS WE GREW, IT TURNED INTO RESENTMENT,

I CAN ONLY SAY, I HAVE ONLY THE GIFTS GOD HAS GIVEN ME,

TO SHARE WITH THE PEOPLE WHO LOVE AND REALLY EXCEPT ME, FOR WHAT GOD MADE ME TO BE,

NO MATTER HOW YOU FEEL ABOUT ME,

I WAS MADE TO LOVE AND EXCEPT YOU STILL,

BECAUSE I AM A LIGHT, FROM GOD'S HEART AN INTIMATE PART OF HIS WILL,

THIS ONE THING I KNOW, IN THE BEGINNING FRIENDSHIP WAS YOUR INTENT,

FOR SOME REASON AS WE GREW, IT TURNED INTO RESENTMENT,

WORD OF FAITH CHURCH

I KNOW A PLACE WHERE WE SHOULD ALWAYS GO,

THIS PLACE IS WHERE THE HOLY SPIRIT SOWS,

IT IS A PLACE OF HOLINESS AND TRUTH,

WHERE YOU GET THE WORD AND ITS WORTH,

THE NAME OF THIS PLACE, IS THE WORD OF FAITH CHURCH,

IF YOU COME HERE EMPTY, THE PASTOR IS BLESSED AND ABLE TO FILL US,

GOD HAS NAMED HIM AND CALLED HIM, HIS NAME IS PASTOR BILL GILLIS,

IN THIS HOUSE OF GOD'S, THE PASTOR PREACHES GOD'S HOLY WORD WITH GRACE,

GOD HAS DESIGNATED HIS HOUSE TO BE THE MOST HOLY PLACE,

WHERE ALL PEOPLE CAN GO EACH DAY OR EVERY SUNDAY,

TO HONOR GOD'S HOLY SABBATH DAY,

GOD WORKS THROUGH HIS PROPHETS, TO HELP US TO UNDERSTAND,

HE IS SOVEREIGN, IN EVERY STATE IN EVERY, EVEN IN NO MAN'S LAND,

WE MUST RESPECT, HONOR AND OBEY,

GOD'S LAWS, COMMANDMENTS, IN ORDER TO WALK IN HIS HOLY WAYS,

COME TO WHERE THE WORD IS PURE, AND PREACHED FOR IT'S WORTH,

THIS IS AT GOD'S HOUSE, THE WORD OF FAITH CHURCH,

THE PASTOR IS FULL OF COMPASSION FOR GOD'S WORD, HE MAKES SURE YOU HAVE UNDERSTOOD AND HAS HEARD,

HEALING IS A FRUIT OF THE SPIRIT GIVEN BY GOD, TO THE PREACHER WHO IS OUR LEADER AND TEACHER,

RIGHTEOUS IS AN ATTRIBUT OF ALL SAINTS, WE ARE TAUGHT AND DESIGNED TO FACE ADVERSITY AND NOT TO FAINT,

INSISTANCE TO PERFORM THE WORKS OF CHRIST, IT IS OUR DUTY, IT IS OUR RIGHT TO EXAULT JESUS'S LIFE,

SALVATION IS OUR ANTICIPATED REWARD, WHY WE WORSHIP, SERVE, AND REVERE OUR LORD,

THANKFULNESS FOR MERCY, LOVE, AND GRACE, FOR GOD SENDING HIS SON, JESUS CHRIST TO DIE IN OUR PLACE,

THE MESSAGE ABOVE IS ACROSTICALLY SPELLING OUT CHRIST,

THE RANSOME, BENEFACTOR, AND PURPOSE FOR ALL OF HUMAN LIFE,

YOU MUST RESPECT ME FOR WHO I AM

I KNOW YOU HAVE YOUR DERROGATORY
OPINIONS ABOUT ME,

BUT NONETHELESS I AM WHO GOD MADE ME TO BE,

I WAS NOT CREATE TO APPEASE YOUR DESIRES, OR TO
PLEASE YOUR TASTE,

I WAS CREATED TO SERVE JESUS CHRIST, WHO DIED
IN MY PLACE,

I TOOK ON A NEW LIFE IN CHRIST, WHEN HE DIED FOR ME,

YOU MUST LEARN TO RESPECT, ME FOR WHO
GOD MADE ME,

GOD HAS FLOCKS OF SHEEP, THEY ARE ALL HIS LAMBS,

YOU MUST LEARN TO RESPECT ME JUST FOR WHO I AM,

GOD MAKES NO MISTAKES ON HIS CHOSEN VESSELS,
OR SERVANTS,

WE ARE MIGHTY IN GOD, WISE, ADEPT, AND FERVENT,

I WILL ALWAYS LOVE YOU WITH THE LOVE OF CHRIST,

NOTHING YOU DO CAN CHANGE THAT BECAUSE OF
CHRIST IN MY LIFE,

THE LESSON FOR ME, IN MY LIFE WAS TO LEARN,

THAT LOVE IS NECESSARY AND NEEDED EVERYWHERE, I
HAD TO LEARN TO DISCERN,

LOVE IS THE CONQUERING ESSENCE OF OUR FATHER,
GOD ALMIGHTY,

THERE IS NO GREATER LOVE, OR GREATER QUALITY,

YOU MUST LEARN TO RESPECT, ME FOR WHO
GOD MADE ME,

GOD HAS FLOCKS OF SHEEP, THEY ARE ALL HIS LAMBS,

YOU MUST LEARN TO RESPECT ME JUST FOR WHO I AM,

A FAMILY OF PRAISE

LORD YOU MADE US FOR THE CROWN OF YOUR HEAD,

LET US NEVER BE ERRONEOUSLY MISLED,

KEEP US AS A FAMILY OF PRAISE IN YOUR TRUTH AND FAITH,

WE WERE RAISED WITH THE PROMISE TO BE SAVED BY YOUR SON'S GRACE,

AN ENSIGN OF HIS REIGN, EVEN IF THE WHOLE WORLD IS GONE,

WE WILL STILL BE A FAMILY OF PRAISE TO OUR GOD, DESIGNED FOR HIS CROWN ALONE,

YOU ARE SO SPECIAL AND PRECIOUS TO US, TAUGHT TO PRAY, SEEK, BELIEVE AND TRUST,

TO GIVE TO YOU, MEANS REACHING BEYOND PHYSICAL TIME AND SPACE,

PLEASE HELP US LORD, REMEMBER YOU ARE ETERNALLY PLACED,

NO MAN, WOMAN, BEAST OR CHILD, CAN INFILTRATE, REPLACE, REMOVE OR EVEN DEFILE,

THE SPECIAL ABODES, THAT GOD HAS FOR HIS OWN,

A PLACE PREPARED FOR CHOSEN ONE'S ALONE,

AN ENSIGN OF HIS REIGN, EVEN IF THE WHOLE WORLD IS GONE,

WE WILL STILL BE A FAMILY OF PRAISE TO OUR GOD, DESIGNED FOR HIS CROWN ALONE,

---

YOU SHOULD ASK YOURSELF WHY

WHEN YOU ENCOUNTER THINGS YOU DON'T UNDERSTAND,

CONSIDER THE HUMAN BODY AS GOD'S SACRED LAND,

HAVE YOU BEEN TREATING OTHERS, LIKE YOU KNOW YOU SHOULD,

OR HAVE YOU BEEN DOING TO OTHERS WHAT EVER YOU COULD,

SO, WHEN YOU START HAVING, TROUBLE AND DIFFICULTIES IN LIFE,

REMEMBER THAT BROTHER AND SISTER'S LIFE BELONGS TO JESUS CHRIST,

WHENEVER, YOU TREAT A CHILD OF GOD'S WITH ILL CONTENT,

GOD WILL INFLICT, UPON ALL HIS DIVINE PUNISHMENT,

IT WAS CHRIST BLOOD BOUGHT SACRIFICE, THAT CAUSED US NOT TO DIE,

SO WHEN YOU MISTREAT YOUR SISTER OR BROTHER, YOU SHOULD ASK YOURSELF WHY,

WHY ARE YOU OFFENDING THE CROSS, THROUGH YOUR SISTER OR BROTHER,

WHEN CHRIST DIED FOR US TO LOVE ONE ANOTHER,

BE SURE HEAVEN IS WHERE YOU WANT TO SPEND THE REST OF YOUR TIME,

GOD WILL NOT ALLOW HATRED, AND EVIL TO COEXIST, WITH THE DIVINE,

WHEN YOU SEE THERE ARE THINGS YOU CANNOT ENJOY, LIKE OTHERS,

ASK YOURSELF HAVE I BEEN FAIR TO MY SISTERS AND MY BROTHERS,

THE FINALITY OF THESE WORDS, I AM PRAYING YOU CAN SPIRITUALLY SEE,

IN HEAVEN GOD AND ALL ANGELS AND HEAVENLY THINGS WE ARE ONE BIG FAMILY,

NEVER USELESSLY SIN, AGAINST YOUR SISTER OR BROTHER,

LET'S EARNESTLY TRY TO LOVE ONE ANOTHER,

HONESTLY, ASK YOURSELF WHY,

WOULD I HARM OR TROUBLE,

A LIFE FOR WHICH CHRIST CHOSE TO DIE,

WRITE THROUGH/ RIGHT THROUGH

I HEARD A MINISTER ONCE SAY, THE WORDS YOU SPEAK AND BELIEVE TODAY,

WILL BE THE WORDS THAT WILL ULTIMATELY SET YOU FREE,

THEY WILL BECOME YOUR REALITY,

THUS, WE SHOULD ALWAYS SPEAK TRUTH, AND SPEAK PEACE,

THAT WAY WE ARE SURE TO HAVE A DAILY FEAST,

EVERYDAY INCORPORATE POSITVE MEDITATION, THAT WAY WE WILL KNOW WE HAVE GIVEN GOD OUR UNDIVIDED CONSIDERATIONS,

THEY CAN BE STEPPING STONES FOR US TO PRAY, AND FOLLOW GOD'S HOLY WAY'S

FROM THIS DAY ON I VOW TO ENHANCE MY DISPOSITION,

TO REARRANGE MY LIFE, MY WORDS, AND MY POSITIONS,

I WILL SPEAK THESE WORDS TO MY SOUL, MY MIND, SPIRIT AND LIFE,

TO COME FORTH AND BE THE TRUE BLESSING GIVEN TO ME BY JESUS CHRIST,

IF I REALLY BELIEVE I CAN WRITE MY LIFE OUT OF ANY SITUATION,

BY DOING SO I CAN AVERT EVIL AND DEVASTATIONS,

I CAN WRITE A DOORWAY OUT OF DESPAIR,

I WRITE MYSELF, INTO THE LOVING HANDS OF SOMEONE THAT REALLY CARES,

SO, WHEN THE SITUATION SEEMS BLEAK,

I WILL BE PROMOTING THE SITUATIONS I TRULY SEEK,

I WILL WRITE ABOUT YOUR HATE AND JEALOUSY,

I WILL WRITE ALL THE POSITIVE THINGS THAT SHOULD BE,

I WILL KEEP WRITING UNTIL I CAN SEE,

SOME OF THE PROMISES GOD GAVE TO ME,

RIGHT ON MY SISTER, MY BROTHER, I AM A SOLID BELIEVERS,

THAT GOD BLESSES ALL OF US AS HIS PROMISED RECEIVERS,

AS A WRITER I HAVE COMMANDED TO WRITE ON BY,

PASSING THROUGH YOUR MIDST TO REACH GODLY PROMISES ON HIGH,

INSUFFICIENT FUNDS

I AWOKE THIS MORNING TO ULTIMATELY FIND,

GOD HAD GRANTED ME ANOTHER DAY SOME MORE TIME,

TO SEEK AND SEARCH HIS TRUTH TO SEE,

THAT HE HAD ALREADY GIVEN ME A DESTINY,

I PRAYED EACH DAY, I THOUGHT THAT WAS ENOUGH,

I FOUND, PUTTING IN TIME WITH GOD WAS BUILDING A SPIRITUAL TRUST,

YOU CAN GET OUT WHAT YOU PUT IN,

ONLY IF YOU HAVE REFRAINED FROM PURPOSELY COMMITTING SINS,

I BELIEVED, I WAS DOING EVERYTHING RIGHT, AND OVER EVIL I HAD WON,

UNTIL I QUESTIONED SPIRITUALLY WHAT I HAD DONE,

UNTIL ONE DAY I WENT TO PRAY,

AND GET SPIRITUAL ENERGY FOR THAT DAY,

I FOUND I HAD INSUFFICIENT FUNDS,

THERE WAS NOTHING THERE, OF WHAT I FELT I SPIRITUALLY DONE,

I HEARD YOU GET OUT ONLY WHAT YOU PUT IN,

I REALLY BELIEVED I WAS LIVING ABOVE SIN,

WHAT I THOUGHT WAS THE KEY TO MY FAITH, TRUTH, AND DAILY ACTS,

HAD TO LINE UP WITH GOD'S WORD AND HIS JUSTIFIED FACTS,

IN SEARCHING FOR GOD'S TRUTH,

I HAD TO REMOVE AND TAKE OUT THE I'S,

AND LOOK TO THE SACRAFICE OF JESUS CHRIST, TO KNOW, UNDERSTAND, RESPECT, THE REDEMPTIVE REASONS OF WHY,

NOW, IT IS NO LONGER ME, THINKING WHAT I BELIEVE IS RIGHT,

I CAN GO TO GOD'S WORD AND FIND ME A GUIDING LIGHT,

AT FIRST, I CRIED TEARS OF CONFUSION, PAIN, AND GRIEF,

UNTIL GOD SHOWED ME THE TRUTH,

OF HOW TO EXPERIENCE HIS NATURE, WITH JOY, RELEASE AND RELIEF,

NO LONGER IS MY SPIRITUAL BANK IN OVER-DRAFT,

I HAVE A FOUNT OF ENDLESS RESERVES THAT WILL ALWAYS LAST,

GOD LET ME SEE WHY I WAS HAVING LACK,

AND JUST HOW TO AVOID BEING EMPTY AND HOW TO SPIRITUALLY PUT BACK,

I NO LONGER HAVE INSUFFICIENT FUNDS,

JESUS CHRIST PAID MY COST, THAT'S HOW I WON,

THE RIGHT TO A HEAVENLY SPIRITUAL BANK,

THAT IS NEVER DEPLETED, I HAVE ONLY MY GOD TO THANK,

ARE YOU WELL KEPT

I BELIEVE THAT WE ALL AT SOME POINT IN TIME NEED TO BE CONTAINED,

PRAYERFUL, THOUGHTFUL, AND NEED TO REFRAIN,

WE CANNOT BE LED BY OUR FEELINGS OR OUR FLESH,

OUR FLESH WILL NOT ALLOW US TO BE OUR BEST,

WE MUST BE SPIRIT LED IN WHAT EVER WE WANT TO BE,

BECAUSE SPIRIT WILL DIRECT US TO OUR DESTINY,

MY QUESTION TO YOU TODAY IS, ARE YOU WELL KEPT,

GOD KEEPS THE LOWEST TO THE HIGHEST, AND SUSTAINS ALL HIS ADEPTS,

WHEN YOU ARE WELL KEPT, YOUR THOUGHTS ARE SPIRITUALLY FORMED,

THEY ARE FREE FROM THE PROFANE, AND MENTALLY ADORNED,

THEY WILL MAGNIFY, ACCENTUATE, THE POSITIVE MIND,

THEY WILL REPRESENT CLEAN, PURE, IMAGES, OF GOD'S PRECIOUS TIME,

TO REPRESENT THOUGHTS OF LOVE, PURITY, AND LIGHT,

YOU CANNOT INHABIT PLACES OF DARKNESS, PROFANITY AND NIGHT,

MY QUESTION TO YOU TODAY IS, ARE YOU WELL KEPT,

GOD KEEPS THE LOWEST TO THE HIGHEST, AND SUSTAINS ALL HIS ADEPTS,

GOD'S WORDS A DAY KEEPS THE DEVIL AWAY

SICK AND TIRED OF BEING JUST SICK AND TIRED,

MAYBE IT'S TIME TO JUST REWIRED,

FROM THE OLD WAY OF DOING THINGS, RENEW YOUR SPIRIT WITH GOD AND SEE WHAT IT BRINGS,

A DOCTOR WOULD GIVE YOU A PRESCRIPTION FOR ONE PILL A DAY,

GOD SAY'S HIS WORDS EVRYDAY WILL KEEP THE DEVIL AWAY,

JUST KEEP YOUR MIND, SPIRIT, AND SOUL,

ON THE WORD OF GOD, HE WILL KEEP YOU SPIRITUALLY WHOLE,

GOD'S WORDS SAYS HE, WHO KEEPS HIS MIND ON ME,

I WILL SHIELD, PROTECT, AND CAUSE ALL EVIL TO FLEE,

SO, I AM LEARNING TO TAKE GOD'S WORD EVERYWHERE, EVERYDAY,

TO HAVE PEACE OF MIND, AND TO KEEP THE DEVIL AWAY,

REMEMBER THE PRESCRIPTION FOR EVERYDAY,

CALL ON GOD IN THE EVENING, MORNING, AND NOONDAY,

KEEP YOUR MIND STAYED ON GOD, AND ESCHEWS THE DEVIL AWAY,

WHEN EVER YOU DO ALL TIME IS THE RIGHT TIME TO PRAY,

IF YOU CAN JUST GET PAST MY SKIN

FROM THE INCEPTION OF TIME GOD WAS ALWAYS THERE, TO ASSIST US FROM THE CROOKED WAYS OF THE SPIRIT OF ERR,

GOD KNEW EVERYTHING THAT WE WOULD NEED,

FROM THE HOLY SPIRIT TO OUR HUMAN SEED,

HE ALSO KNEW THAT WE WOULD FALL PREY TO MORTAL MEN,

THAT WOULD MURDER AND KILL JUST BECAUSE OF THE COLOR OF YOUR SKIN,

NOT EVERYONE THAT YOU SEE SMILE AND PRAY,

REALLY WANTS TO SEE GOD SON HAVE HIS DAY,

THE BIBLE CALLS THEM THE ENEMIES OF THE CROSS,

THEY ARE THE SOULS THAT HAVE CHOSEN HELL OVER HEAVEN AND THEIR SOULS ARE LOST,

IF YOU ARE A TRUE BELIEVER IN JESUS CHRIST,

THEN IT IS A PREREQUISITE TO VALUE ANOTHER PERSON'S LIFE,

YOU MUST GET PAST EVIL TREACHERY AND SIN,

IF YOU REALLY WANT THE SON OF GOD TO BE YOUR SPIRITUAL FRIEND,

TO FOLLOW CHRIST AND ALL THE LAWS THAT GOD COMMANDED,

YOU MUST HAVE THE KIND OF LOVE HE DEMANDED,

YOU CANNOT LOOK ON, OR JUDGE ME BY THE COLOR OF MY SKIN,

YOU HAVE TO HONOR AND KNOW THERE IS A GOD THAT RESIDES WITHIN,

THE SAME GOD THAT LIVES WITHIN ME, IS THE SAME GOD THAT CONTROLS BOTH OUR DESTINY'S,

YOU HAVE TO LOVE ME BECAUSE GOD MADE IT A DECREE,

THE SAME RAINBOW THAT COVERS YOU COVERS ME,

GOD ORDAINED HIS COVENANT IN ALL THE LANDS, WHERE-EVER THERE IS LIFE WHERE-EVER THERE IS MAN,

IT IS IMPERATIVE THAT I ADD, I PRAY THAT YOU ARE DELIVERED FROM SIN,

AND THAT YOU CAN LOVE ME LIKE GOD DECREED,

AND JUST GET PAST MY SKIN,

WHOSE UNDER YOUR SKIN

FATHER, I HAVE FOUND THAT EVERY ONE THAT I SEE, DOES NOT POSSESS YOUR DIVINITY,

THEY ARE NOT WHAT YOU MADE THEM TO BE, THEY ARE NOW A PART OF EVIL DIGNITIES,

THEY LIVE ON OTHERS LIVES LIKE ITS THERE OWN, THEY DENOUNCE YOUR SON, AND YOUR THRONE,

I KNOW THEY ARE CONTROLLED BY LUST AND HATE, THEY HAVE NO FEAR OF CONSEQUENCES AND FATE,

MY QUESTION TO THE SINNER IS WHOSE UNDER YOUR SKIN,

IS IT STILL THE LIFE AND GENETICS THE FATHER, DESIGNED AND PUT WITHIN,

WE HAVE A RESONSIBILITY TO LIFE, LOVE AND LIBERTY,

TO PROMOTE THE THINGS GOD HAS GIVEN US TO NOT DESTROY, BUT TO LIVE JUSTLY,

THE CHURCH IS THE INSTITUTION THAT UNITES ALL NATIONS, PROMOTES OUR LIVES, NOT CONDEMNATION,

JUST REMEMBER BEFORE YOU COMMITT ANY SIN, IS THAT REALLY YOU UNDER YOUR OWN SKIN,

DISOBEDIENCE

LORD TEACH ME HOW TO FOLLOW YOUR LAWS,

SO THAT MY ACTIONS WILL NOT BE FLAWED,

LORD HELP ME REMEMBER YOUR COVENANT, FOR ALL THE PURPOSES, AND GOODNESS FOR WHICH IT WAS MEANT,

FATHER I DON'T WANT TO BE DISOBEDIENT, I KNOW THAT BRINGS WITH IT PUNISHMENT,

IT DOESN'T MATTER WHO YOUR ARE,

IF YOU DISOBEY THE LAWS WITH INTENT, YOU ARE CALLING DOWN GOD'S PUNISHMENT,

IN THE EYE'S OF GOD, THERE IS NO BIG OR LITTLE SIN,

GOD IS CONCERNED, WITH THE ROOT OF EVIL, WHERE AND HOW IT BEGAN,

SO, FATHER PURGE OUR HEARTS, MINDS AND SOULS,

SO, THAT WE CAN BE APPROVED BY WHAT YOU JUDGE AND CONSIDER PURE AND WHOLE,

WE ONLY WANT TO BE WHAT YOU MADE US TO BE PEOPLE GODLY SENT,

TO EARTH, AS GOD'S PROMISED GOD'S COVENANT,

WE ALL BELONG TO YOU LORD, WEATHER STANDING TALL OR HELL BENT,

GOD WILL DO THE SEPARATING BECAUSE WE ALL HIS INHEIRTANCE,

IF FOR EVIL REASONS, THE PEOPLE DROP, THEY NO LONGER WANT SERVE GOD ALMIGHTY, THEY WILL BE REPLACE WITH ROCKS,

EVERY THING THAT GOD CREATES, HE CAN MAKE ANIMATE,

ROCKS ARE PEOPLE TOO, READ THE BIBLE AND SEE WHAT GOD CAN CAUSE THEN TO DO,

CIVIL UNREST

LORD WE ARE LIVING IN TIMES, WHEN MEN'S EYES AND SOULS ARE BLIND,

THEY COULD NOT SEE GOD IF HE WERE RIGHT IN THEIR FACE,

BECAUSE THEY ARE DEVOID OF HIS LAWS AND HIS GRACE,

THEY PILFER, ROB, AND RAPE, GOD'S GRAIN, THEN SAY GOD SHOWED UP AND NEVER CAME,

THEY COMPLAIN ABOUT RACISM AND LACK, BUT THEY FORGOT ABOUT WHOSE SKIN IS ON ALL OF THEIR BACKS,

WHITE MAN, YELLOW MAN, RED MAN, AND BLACK,

SKIN IS ONLY A COVENANT COVERING TO COVER THEIR BACKS,

FATHER THERE IS SO MUCH LAWLESSNESS AND CIVIL UNREST,

BASICALLY, BECAUSE THEY DON'T HAVE YOUR TRUE LOVE, WHICH IS YOUR BEST,

YOU CANNOT DENY GOD OF HIS RIGHTFUL PLACE, AND EXPECT THE LAND TO BE FILLED WITH HIS GRACE,

YOU CANNOT HARBOR THOUGHTS AGAINST GOD OF ILL WILL,

IT WILL SHOW IN YOU NATIONS, AS A SPIRIT THAT REVEAL WHAT YOU FEEL,

LORD YOU CREATED THE NATIONS TO FOLLOW YOU,

NOT TO RIDICULE, DENY, WITHHOLD AND TRY TO REPLACE YOU OR SUE,

NOW WE ARE APPROACHING AN ULTIMATE END, WHERE GENERATED LIFE STARTS AND GODLY PEACE BEGINS,

I AM AFRAID FATHER, THIS PERIOD OF TIME MAY NOT KNOW, WHO YOU REALLY ARE,

FOR ALL THE EVIL DONE TO YOU AND ALL THE CIVIL AND PERSONAL WARS,

DON'T THEY KNOW LORD YOU ARE THE ENTIRE LAND, WITHOUT YOU ONE DAY THEY WILL HAVE NO PLACE TO STAND,

EARTH IS JUST ANOTHER FORM OF YOUR CREATION, THAT YOU WILL SOMEDAY RECALL,

EVERYTHING WILL DISSIPATE EXCEPT YOUR HOLY WORDS THAT CANNOT FALL,

SOME SPIRITS ARE SO EVIL AND AGAINST GOD'S TRUE LOVE,

THEY CAN NOT LOOK UP OR DIRECT THEIR EYE'S ON THE HEAVENS ABOVE,

FATHER, TROUBLES ARE ON THE NORTH, THEY HAVE COME FORTH,

TROUBLES FROM THE EAST, WON'T SEEM TO CEASE,

THEY HAVE POLLUTED THEIR MOUTHS, THUS TROUBLE ON THE SOUTH,

EVIL AND TROUBLE CREPT IN ON THE WEST, WHERE THE LAND WAS UPHOLDING SOME OF THE BEST,

FATHER THERE IS SO MUCH LAWLESSNESS AND CIVIL UNREST,

BASICALLY, BECAUSE THEY DON'T HAVE YOUR TRUE LOVE, WHICH IS YOUR BEST,

DON'T THROW ME AWAY

TROUBLES FOLLOWED ME AROUND EVERYWHERE, THEY INTERFERED WITH MY PRAYERS BECAUSE THEY DIDN'T WANT GOD TO BE THERE,

SO, THEY DEVISED DEVICES THAT COULD WOULD KEEP ME TRAPPED, SO THAT EVERYWHERE I WANT I WAS KIDNAPPED,

SO THAT THEY COULD USE MY TIME, MY LIFE, AND MY STRENGHT, BY THE TIME THEY GOT THROUGH USING ME I HARDLY HAD ANY SENSE,

MY PRAYER TO GOD WAS DON'T LET THEM THROW ME AWAY,

I HAVE ONLY JUST BEGAN TO REALIZE AND USE MY OWN DAY,

I HAVE NOT HAD THE RIGHT PLACE AND TIME TO SERVE YOU LIKE I SHOULD,

NOR HAVE I DONE THE THINGS YOU PUT INSIDE OF ME TO SHOW THAT I COULD,

ALL THE TIME THAT I HAVE SPENT IN IDLE SPACES, AND DISTANT PLACES,

LOOKING IN STRANGERS FACES, WHO HAVE NONE OF MY GOD'S GRACES,

MY SISTER, MY BROTHER, LISTEN TO WHAT I SAY, I AM A CHILD OF GOD'S,

SO, DON'T THROW ME AWAY,

WE ALL NEED GROUND TO STAND ON, HOW CAN YOU STAND IF ALL GROUND IS GONE,

SO BE MINDFUL THE GROUND YOU MIGHT NEED FOR ANOTHER DAY, DON'T LET IT BE WHAT YOU ARE THROWING AWAY TODAY,

MY PRAYER TO GOD WAS DON'T LET THEM THROW ME AWAY,

I HAVE ONLY JUST BEGAN TO REALIZE AND USE MY OWN GOD GIVEN DAY,

I AM HERMETICALLY SEALED

SOMETIMES FATHER I FEEL I HAVE NO PLACE,

THEN I REMEMBER YOUR GRACE,

I AM CONSTANTLY, ACCOSTED BY DEMONIC AND UNGRATEFUL THINGS,

THAT ARE NOT OF THE MIND SET OR SPIRIT, OF YOU AS THE HOLY KING,

MY REQUEST TO YOU FATHER IS TO KEEP ME HERMETICALLY SEALED,

NOTHING CAN ENTER MY SPACE AND PLACE,

UNLESS IT IS DIVINELY WILLED,

IN HEAVEN ALL GOD'S TREASURES ARE PROTECTED,

THE SECURITY OF HEAVEN'S VAULTS ARE PERFECTED,

SO THAT, NO MOTH, OR ILL BEGOTTON THOUGHT,

CAN ENTER INTO WHAT JESUS CHRIST BLOOD HAS BOUGHT,

YES, FATHER THAT IS MY ANSWER TO YOU,

FOR THE SECURITY OF YOUR HEAVENLY KINGDOM,

THAT CAN ONLY COME THROUGH YOU,

MY REQUEST TO YOU FATHER IS TO KEEP ME HERMETICALLY SEALED,

THAT NOTHING CAN ENTER MY SPACE AND PLACE,

UNLESS IT IS DIVINELY/HEAVENLY WILLED,

I DON'T WANNA BE LOST

LORD YOUR WORD HAS PROVEN TO BE TRUE, TO EVERY BLOOD BOUGHT SAINT THAT BELIEVES IN YOU,

I KNOW THAT WE ALL WILL BE JUDGED BY THE THINGS THAT WE DO AND BELIEVE,

THAT'S WHY YOUR HOLY WORD IT IS IMPERATIVE FOR US TO RECEIVE,

I KNOW LORD I DON'T HAVE MUCH WITHOUT YOUR GIVINGS, YOUR INSPIRATIONS, YOUR GRACE IS THE REASON WHY I AM LIVING,

I KEEP TRYING LORD BECAUSE I KNOW YOU PAID MY COST, HELP ME TO DO THE THINGS THAT WON'T LET ME BE LOST,

I HAVE BEEN TRYING TO MOLD AND SCULPT MY MIND, TO EXPRESS SOMETHING ABOUT

YOUR LOVE, AND THE ESSENCE OF THE DIVINE,

LORD I AM YOUR CHILD YOU PAID THE COST, I AM YOUR DIRECT DESCENDANT I DON'T WANNA BE LOST,

YOUR PROMISE TO ME AND THE WORLD, WAS THAT CHRIST PAID FOR US ON THE CROSS,

AND THAT WITH THIS PROMISE WE WOULD NEVER BE LOST,

SO, FATHER IF I AM NOT IN LINE WITH WHAT YOU WANT IN ME, MAKE ME MOLD ME INTO WHAT I SHOULD BE,

I HAVE NEVER TURNED AWAY FROM YOUR CORRECTIONS IN THE PAST, BECAUSE I KNOW THEY ARE THE ONLY PATHS THAT WILL MAKE MY LIFE LAST,

I HUMBLY PRAY FATHER THAT YOU WILL TAKE A LOOK, AT THE THINGS I HAVE WRITTEN ABOUT YOU IN MY BOOK,

THEY ARE ALL THE ATTRIBUTES AND LOVELY THINGS YOU MEAN TO ME, I AM TRYING TO SHARE WITH THE WORLD THAT MAY NOT SEE WHAT I SEE,

FATHER, I AM PETITIONING FOR MY PORTION PAID UPON THE CROSS, MY GUARANTEED PROMISE, WITH CHRIST I WON'T BE LOST,

NO LONGER BOUND

LORD WHAT WOULD THIS WHOLE WORLD DO, WITHOUT THE GRACE AND PROTECTION FROM YOU,

ALL CHAINS ARE NOT ON THE OUTSIDE SOME CHAINS BIND US FROM WITHIN,

WHEN WE ARE NOT FREE ON THE INSIDE WE ARE HELD IN AN INTERNAL PRISON,

WE CANOT REALLY DO WHAT YOU DESIGNED US TO, BECAUSE OUR ENENIES ARE NOT JUST A FEW,

MY JOY WILL COME THE DAY I AM NO LONGER BOUND, THAT WILL BE THE DAY THAT GOD HAS ME SAFELY FOUND,

THEN I WILL SOAR AND FLY IN THE OPEN SKY, WITH THE WINGS GAVE ME THIS IS ONE OF THE REASONS HE HAD TO DIE,

MY TRUE LIFE CAME WHEN CHRIST SET ME FREE, THEN I COULD SEE CLEARLY, A BRAND NEW DESTINY,

I AM SO GLAD I AM NO LONGER BOUND, I CAN FINALLY USE MY OWN TIME AND MY OWN MIND,

AND WRITE ABOUT ALL THE BEAUTIFUL THINGS, GOD DOES THROUGH ME AND THE INSPIRATION HE BRINGS,

NOW MY MIND, MY HEART, AND MY SOUL HAS BEEN SET FREE,

I AM NO LONGER BOUND, GOD LIVES INSIDE OF ME,

PLAGIARIZE

SOME PEOPLE COPY FROM BOOKS, MOVIES AND PICTURES,

THEY PLAN AND SCHEME ON WHICH WILL MAKE THEM RICHER,

TO THEM IT MATTERS NOT THEIR COURSE, WHAT MATTERS MOST IS THEIR STOLEN SOURCE,

YOU MAY STEAL A MANS PLANNED/CULTIVATED SOURCE,

JUST REMEMBER YOU HAVE TO ANSWER TO A HIGHER SOURCE,

WHAT THE LAW CAN'T DO GOD'S COMMAND-MENT WILL,

REMEMBER GOD COMMANDED THOU SHALT NOT STEAL,

YOUR ACTIONS WILL CAUSE YOU TO BE IDENTIFIED,

THERE IS NO REASON FOR YOU TO PARTICIPATE IN OR PLAGIARIZE,

GOD'S PEOPLE ARE DESIGNED TO CREATE, TO MOTIVATE, IMPROVE, AND ESCULATE,

THEY ARE TRUE KEEPERS OF THE WORLD AND THE UNIVERSE,

ALWAYS KEEPING THE PRINCIPLES AND DIVINITY OF THE BEGOTTON FIRST,

WE ARE THE TRUE HEIRS, WE KNOW OUR GIFTS, RIGHTS, AND REALIZE,

THERE IS NO REASON FOR US TO REDUCE OURSELVES TO PLAGIARIZE,

SEEKING FOR
GOD'S THE TRUTH

LORD YOU ARE THE ONLY SOURCE FOR ME, THAT WILL TRULY LET ME HUMANLY SEE,

THE VICISSITUDES OF LIFE AND THE PATHS THAT EXIST, YOUR WISDOM ALLOWS ME TO KNOW THE EXTERNAL/INTERAL THINGS THAT CONSIST,

WHEN I WAS YOUNGER I SOUGHT TRUTH FROM OTHERS,

NOW THAT I AM OLDER, I KNOW YOUR TRUTH WORKS THROUGHT EVERY MOTHER,

SISTER OR BROTHER,

YET THERE IS TRUTH ON VERY DIFFERENT LEVELS, I HAD TO LEARN THAT THERE IS A LIER,

WHOSE TRUTH IS OF THE DEVIL,

MY QUEST WAS TO MAKE SURE, I WAS ADHERING TO YOUR TRUE LIGHT,

AND BEING LED BY DARKNESS AND THE NIGHT,

I KNEW THAT IN ORDER FOR ME TO BE TRULY FREE, I WOULD HAVE TO DENY THE SELFISH,

AND FLESHLY PARTS OF ME,

NOW I FEEL I AM TRAVELLING TOWARD THE TRUTH,

THAT A SATANIC WORLD HELD BACK FROM ME IN MY YOUTH,

THEY KNOW NOW THAT I AM A TRUE SEEKER OF GOD'S HOLY WAYS AND WILL,

THAT ONCE ON THE TRUE PATH, GOD WILL ALLOW ME TO DO WHAT EVER I FEEL,

I HAVE BEEN SEEKING FOR THE TRUTH A VERY LONG LONG TIME,

I HAVE TRAVELLED BEYOND THE AVERAGE SINFUL MIND,

JUST TO FIND THE TRUTH I CARRY, THAT GOD SOLEMIZED,

AND PUT INSIDE OF ME CELEBRATED AND MARRIED,

THERE IS NO END TO TRUTH, WISDOM, AND GOD'S ETERNITY,

SO, ANY PATH THAT I TAKE TOWARD GOD,

IS A PATH THAT CAN AND WILL SET ME FREE,

I CAN HONESTLY SAY I HAVE BEEN TRULY BLESSED,

I HAD TO LEARN HOW TO DRESS AND TO DIVINELY CONFESS,

A HOLY PLACE WHERE GOD FAVORED AND ENDOWED HIS GRACE,

WHERE ONE DAY I MIGHT HAVE TO LOOK UPON HIS HOLY FACE,

WHEREVER, TRUTH LEADS ME I AM WILLING TO GO,

ONCE FOUND, THERE IS NO OTHER TRUTH, I WILL EVER NEED TO KNOW,

TRIBUTE TO DR. KING

THERE IS NO RULERSHIP, LIKE AN HONORABLE KING,

HE SPEAKS WORDS OF WISDOM, AND PROPHETIC THINGS,

THAT GUIDES THE PEOPLE INTO THE VISION,

TO HELP THEM TO SEE GOD'S DIVINE DECISIONS,

FROM MY MIND, HEART AND SOUL, I SING,

I WILL FOREVER HONOR, REVERE AND PAY TRIBUTE TO DR. M. L. KING,

YOU FIRST BELIEVED IN THE DREAM, THEN IT BECAME A REALITY,

YOU EMPOWERED YOUR NATION, GOD'S KINGDOM, AND GOD'S FAMILY,

NO MATTER HOW HARD EVIL, AND HATRED TRIES,

YOUR DREAM LIVE ON IN THE ATMOSPHERE AND NEVER DIES,

I SEE YOUR DREAM IN THE UNFOLDING OF A ROSE,

I FEEL YOUR DREAM WHENEVER A DIVINE WIND BLOWS,

I TOUCH YOUR DREAM WHEN I HOLD GOD'S HOLY WORDS,

THE TRILLIONS AND BILLIONS, OF PEOPLE THAT HAS SPIRITUALLY HEARD,

I REALIZE YOUR DREAM WHEN I EXERCISE ALL MY CIVIL RIGHTS,

HAVING CONFIDENCE IN MYSELF NOW, ABOUT SECOND CLASS CITIZEN PLIGHTS,

YOUR DREAM IS REMEMBERED WHEN A BLACK CHILD WALKS ACROSS THE STAGE,

AND GRADUATES WITH THEIR NAME ON THE HONORED STUDENT PAGE,

THAT WAS WHAT THE REAL DREAM WAS ALL ABOUT,

LASTING THROUGH GENERATIONS SETTING MINDS AND HEARTS FREE ONCE FULL OF DOUBT,

REST ON NOW, IN YOUR ETERNAL FLAME,

YOU HAVE WON THE VICTORY, AND PROMISES IN JESUS NAME,

YOU STOOD TALL WITH BIBLE AND STAFF IN HAND,

AS YOU SO ELOQUENTLY RECITED THE PEOPLES' DEMANDS,

FROM MY MIND, HEART AND SOUL, I SING,

I WILL FOREVER HONOR, REVERE AND PAY TRIBUTE TO DR. M. L. KING,

FROM MY MIND, HEART AND SOUL, I SING,

I WILL FOREVER HONOR, REVERE AND PAY TRIBUTE TO DR. M. L. KING,

SENATOR JOHN LEWIS OUR BLESSED SIR JOHN, GOD'S LION SON

MANY HAVE TRAVERSED THE PATHWAYS OF TIME,

NOT ALL HAVE BEEN OF ONE MIND,

TO FIGHT THE GOOD FIGHT OF FREEDOM AND LIBERTY,

FOR HIS OWN GENERATION, AND FOR YOU AND FOR ME,

HE KNEW IT WOULD TAKE A LIFETIME OF STRIFE,

TO STRAIGHTEN OUT THOSE THAT THOUGHT RACISM WAS RIGHT,

GOD DESIGNATED OUR BLESSED SIR JOHN, WHO IS A GODLY SON,

TO TAKE UP AND WEAR THE MANTLE HE HAD WON,

HE WAS DEBASED DESPISE DEJECTED AND ABUSED,

BUT THEY COULDN'T STOP HIM BECAUSE IT WAS GOD'S POWER HE USED,

HE SPOKE OUT AGAINST ALL LEVELS OF RACISM HATE AND WAR,

HE KNEW HOW TO USE WHAT HIS VOICE WAS CREATED FOR,

A LION IN THE PRIDE OF GOD'S OWN,

HE WAS CHOSEN TODAY, TO BRING GOD'S VOICE BACK HOME

HE HAS LEFT A LEGACY FOR MANY TO FOLLOW,

IT IS TIME NOW FOR ALL NATIONS TO UPHOLD GOD'S LOVE AND KNOW,

THERE WILL BE NO NEED TO HATE ANYONE ANYMORE,

WHEN GOD AND SATAN ARE FIGHTING AND THERE IS ONLY ONE DOOR,

GOD CONTROLS THE DOOR TO THE NEXT WORLD IN THE NEXT LIFE,

HE HAS ALREADY GIVEN THE KEYS TO HIS SON JESUS CHRIST,

GOD DESIGNATED AND BLESSED SIR JOHN WHO IS A GODLY SON,

TO TAKE UP THE MANTLE IN THIS LIFE-TIME HE HAD VALIANTLY WON,

FOR SENATOR JOHN LEWIS

WE MUST LEARN TO APPRECIATE

SOMETIMES WE WISH FOR WHAT WE THINK WE DON'T POSSESS,

NOT REALIZING GOD HAS GIVEN US NO LESS,

WE ARE EQUIPPED AS ANY OTHER PERSON,

ESPECIALLY WHEN WE ARE ASSOCIATED WITH HIS SON,

IT IS HIS SON THAT CAUSES YOU TO RISE EACH DAY,

UPON THE CROSS HE PAVED AND ASSURED US A WAY,

FOR US HE WOULD HAVE TO DIE,

ON HIM WE HAD TO LIVE AND RELY,

JUST BE THANKFUL FOR GOD HAS ALREADY GIVEN YOU LIFE,

IT WAS THE SACRIFICE THROUGH JESUS CHRIST,

YOU MUST LEARN TO LOVE AND APPRECIATE

WHAT YOU HAVE IS GENUINE, LEARN TO INITIATE IT,

I APPRECIATE THAT GOD, ALLOWS ME TO BE ME,

AND STILL DIRECT MY DESTINY,

AS LONG AS I ADHERE AND WORK WITHIN HIS PLAN,

I AM HEADED FOR THE PROMISED LAND,

I AM LEARNING HOW TO LOVE AND APPRECIATE,

CASTING ASIDE TO WISH AND TO IMITATE,

THE REAL BEAUTY BETWEEN YOU AND ME HIDES,

IT IS THE BEAUTY THAT LIES INSIDE,

NOT EVERYONE WILL BE ABLE TO SEE,

THE DIVINE ESSENCE THAT LIVES IN YOU AND ME,

YOU MUST LEARN TO LOVE AND APPRECIATE

WHAT YOU HAVE IS GENUINE, LEARN TO INITIATE,

MOLDING YOU

AS CHRISTIANS WE SHOULD BE MOLDED INTO THE IMAGE OF CHRIST,

BECAUSE HE WAS THE SACRIFICE, THAT GAVE HIS LIFE,

SO WHEN YOU THINK THAT GOD, IS NOT HOLDING YOU,

MAYBE IT'S BECAUSE HE'S SPIRITUALLY MOLDING YOU,

TO BE ONE OF CHRIST, YOU MUST BE BORN AGAIN,

YOUR SPIRIT MUST BE RENEWED FROM A MORTAL MAN,

GOD WILL RECLAIM YOUR SOUL TO HAVE AND GIVE YOU A BETTER END,

GOD ALREADY HAS PLANS FOR YOUR LIFE AND FUTURE,

YOU HAVE TO READ UIS HOLY WORD, AND LET HIM WATER IT TO GET IT NURTURED,

DON'T EVER GIVE UP ON GOD, TO SEE YOU THROUGH,

THERE IS NO ONE ELSE IN THE WORLD THAT CAN DO WHAT HE CAN DO,

CHRIST MUST BE FORMED IN YOU ON THE INSIDE,

ON HIS SPIRIT AND TRUTH YOU MUST RELY,

GOD WILL CONTINUE TO WORK, FASHION, AND MOLD CHRISTS TRUTH,

HE WILL DO THIS UNTIL CHRIST IS FORMED IN YOU,

AS CHRISTIANS WE SHOULD BE MOLDED INTO THE IMAGE OF CHRIST,

BECAUSE HE WAS THE SACRIFICE, THAT GAVE HIS LIFE,

SO WHEN YOU THINK THAT GOD, IS NOT HOLDING YOU,

MAYBE IT'S BECAUSE HE'S SPIRITUALLY MOLDING YOU,

MY DAY IS YOUR DAY

EVERYBODY KNOWS ABOUT THE DAY OF THE LORD,

AND HOW THE HOLY SPIRIT WAS WITH HIM ON ONE ACCORD,

WE ALSO KNOW ABOUT HIS ULTIMATE MIRACLES AND BLESSING,

HIS SPIRIT BROUGHT US LIBERTY AND RESTING,

WE KNOW THAT GOD APPOINTED HIM A TIME AND A DAY,

FOR HIM TO REDEEM MANKIND, AS A SAVIOR IN A SPECIAL WAY,

SO WE CAN SAY THE DAY THE LORD,

IS A DAY ALL BLOOD WAS UNIFIED ON ONE ACCORD,

JESUS'S BLOOD REDEMPTION DAY WAS A DAY HE INVESTED,

FOR THE WHOLE HUMAN RACE TO BECOME PERFECTED,

AND LIVE OUT THE MEANING OF TRUE FREEDOM,

THAT HIS BLOOD SACRIFICE HAD DEMPTIVELY WON,

SO WHEN I SAY, MY DAY IS YOUR DAY,

IT IS THE DAY THAT JESUS PAID FOR, AND PAVED A WAY,

THERE WAS NO ONE ON EARTH THAT DID NOT BENEFIT,

FROM JESUS CHRIST'S BLOOD TIED GIFT,

SO MY DAY IS YOUR DAY, BUT EVERYDAY IS THE LORDS DAY,

WITHOUT HIM THERE WOULD NOT HAVE BEEN ANY OTHER DAY,

FOR ME IT WAS NECESSARY

WHEN HATRED AND DECEIT HAS BLINDED YOU ALL YOUR LIFE,

YOU REALLY NEED TO KNOW JESUS CHRIST,

WHEN EVIL AND WICKEDNESS STEALS ALL YOUR TIME,

YOU NEED TO CALL AND DEPEND ON ALL THAT IS DIVINE,

WHEN ALL THAT IS DEMONIC WANTS TO TAKE YOUR PLACE,

YOU NEED TO TRUST IN GOD'S AMAZING GRACE,

AFTER ALL I'VE BEEN THROUGH, NOTHING MEANT TOO MUCH TO ME,

THEN GOD LET ME REALIZE ALL OF IT WAS FOR ME TO SEE, HE IS ALWAYS NECESSARY,

WHEN YOUR BODY IS OVER-COME AND HURT WITH PAIN,

DON'T FORGET TO PRAY, IN JESUS NAME,

THERE COMES A TIME IN OUR LIFE WE MUST ALL KNOW,

WHAT GOD CASTS OUT OF OUR LIVES AND WHAT WE MUST LET GO,

EVIL WAS NOT MEANT TO DWELL, IN GOD'S CHILDREN TO CAUSE THEM SO MUCH OF HELL,

GRACE, SPIRIT, HEALTH AND LOVE,

ARE ALL THE FRUITS AND ATTRIBUTES UP ABOVE,

WE MUST SPIRITUALLY AND RIGHTFULLY CLAIM,

AS HEIRS AND CHILDEN IN JESUS NAME,

IT WAS NECESSARY FOR JESUS CHRIST TO DIE,

SO THAT HE COULD REDEEM YOU AND I

IT WAS NECESSARY FOR JESUS TO DIE ON THE CROSS,

SO THAT NONE OF OUR BLOOD BOUGHT SOULS WOULD BE LOST,

I HAD MY DOUBTS BECAUSE OF SO MANY PERILS, AND TRIALS,

MADE ME THINK AND WONDER, IF I WAS I HOLY OR DEFILED,

AFTER ALL I'VE BEEN THROUGH, NOTHING MEANT TOO MUCH TO ME,

THEN GOD LET ME REALIZE ALL OF IT WAS FOR ME TO SEE, EVEN THROUGH MY TROUBLES, HE IS ALWAYS NECESSARY,

AFTER ALL I'VE BEEN THROUGH, MOST THINGS DID NOT MEAN MUCH OF ANYTHING TO ME,

THEN GOD LET ME REALIZE ALL OF IT WAS FOR ME TO SEE, HE IS ALWAYS NECESSARY,

EVEN THROUGH UNBELIEF, AND ALL THINGS THAT ARE CONTRARY,

HE WILL STILL BE GOD, AND WILL ALWAYS BE NECESSARY,

BORN TO DIE

JUST LIKE JESUS CHRIST WE ARE BORN TO DIE,

KNOWING THE UNJUST LAWS, HATRED OF THE WORLD TODAY, WE DON'T HAVE TO ASK WHY,

CHRIST DIED FOR US THAT WE MAY BE FREE,

FOR THAT SAME REASON, WE DIE TO GAIN A SPIRITUAL KEY,

JUST LIKE JESUS CHRIST WE ARE BORN TO DIE,

KNOWING THE UNJUST LAWS, HATRED OF THE WORLD TODAY, WE DON'T HAVE TO ASK WHY,

SOME OF US WILL BE GREAT LEADERS OF OUR DAY,

THEY WILL BE THE GREAT LIGHTS TO PAVE OUR WAY,

OTHERS WILL FIGHT SILENT PERSONAL FIGHTS, AS HEROS UNSUNG,

STRUGGLING THROUGH HARDSHIPS, AND ALL THE MANY DEHUMANIZED WRONGS,

IT IS BETTER TO GIVE THAN TO DENY,

ALSO, BETTER TO START THAN TO TRY,

THE MOST EXALTED ATTRIBUTE EXHIBITED BY GOD WAS TO GIVE,

THAT WAS THE BEGINNING FOR ALL HUMANITY TO LIVE,

GOD HAS ALREADY CHOSEN ALL DESTINY'S,

FOR THE CHILDREN, THAT WILL INHABIT LIFE GIVING WATERS, AS SPIRITUALLY WATERED SEAS,

JESUS SAID MY LIFE IS GIVEN ABUNDTANTLY,

THIS WATER I GIVE, SURPASSES, EVERY EARTHLY SEA,

IF YOU DRINK IT YOU MUST UNDERSTAND,

MY WATERS NEVER, LETS YOU THIRST AGAIN,

JUST LIKE JESUS CHRIST WE ARE BORN TO DIE,

WITH KNOWING THE UNJUST LAWS, HATRED OF THE WORLD TODAY, WE DON'T HAVE TO ASK WHY,

WE SHOULD KNOW THAT DEATH IS NOT OUR ETERNAL END,

GOD HAS SPIRITUAL PATHWAYS, FOR ALL SAINTS TO BEGIN AGAIN,

CHERUB'S GLORY/ANGELS PRAYERS

REBIRTH

I BELIEVE THAT ALL DIVINELY CREATED LIFE,

DOES NOT END AT THE HANDS OF EVIL, A GUN OR A KNIFE,

LIFE CAN BE TRANSFORMED, TRANSPORTED, OR TRANSMUTED,

WHAT EVER THE CHANGE, GOD WILL HAVE TO INSTITUTE IT,

WHAT EVER IT WILL BE, IT WILL BE A REBIRTH,

IT DOESN'T NECESSARILY MEAN IT WILL BE IN OR FOR THIS EARTH,

ALL THINGS GOD MAKES, CAN CHANGE FORM,

WHENEVER THE CREATOR CHOOSES, ANY OBJECT CAN BE TRANSFORMED,

A SPIRIT IS NOT LIMITED TO WHAT IT CAN BE,

GOD IS IN CONTROL OF ALL SPIRITUAL DESTINYS,

HE IS KING OF KINGS AND LORD OF LORDS,

HE IS CAPTAIN OF ALL SEAS, AND THE MAKER OF ALL HEARTS,

HE IS THE CREATOR AND MAKER OF HEAVEN AND EARTH,

HE IS THE INITIATOR OF ALL SPIRITUAL REBIRTHS,

SO DO NOT FRET ABOUT THIS LIFE UPON THE EARTH,

PRACTICE SPIRITUAL GOODNESS, TO HAVE A GOD ORDAINED SPIRITUAL REBIRTH,

ONE DAY AT A TIME

WHEN ALL THE CONNECTIONS, IN YOU LIFE SEEM TO DISCONNECT,

REMEMBER GOD IS THE ONLY ONE IN YOUR LIFE WHO WON'T REJECT,

LEARN TO LIVE LIFE ONE DAY AT A TIME, WHO KNOWS WHAT SECRETS, GOD HAS PLACED IN YOUR MIND,

YOUR MIND IS JUST A MENTAL STATE, IT ONLY HOLDS IN MEMORY THE THINGS YOU THINK ARE GREAT,

THE REAL ESSENCE OF TRUTH, WOULD NOT BE COMMITTED TO FLESH,

BECAUSE FLESH IS PHYSICAL AND NOT GOD'S BEST,

THE VERY SMALLEST THINGS YOU CAN THINK OF,

ON THE OPPOSITE SIDE HOLDS THE GREATEST PARTS OF GOD'S LOVE,

YOU START YOUR WEALTH WITH ONE PENNY,

IF YOU DON'T HAVE ONE THEN YOU DON'T HAVE ANY,

YOU CANNOT BE GREAT, IF YOU CANNOT BE SMALL,

IT'S THE REALLY SMALL THINGS THAT ARE INSIDE OF IT ALL,

SO, I LEARNED TO TAKE ONE DAY AT A TIME,

WHO KNOWS THE SECRETS, GOD HAS PLACED IN YOUR MIND,

EVERYTHING IN EXISTENCE STARTS WITH ONE,

ONE IOTA OF ANYTHING IS WHERE IT HAS BEGUN,

THE VERY ESSENCE OF SPIRIT STARTS WITH ONE BREADTH,

IT ENCOMPASSES THE ENTIRE UNIVERSE, RATHER THEY ARE PRESENT OR WEATHER THEY HAVE LEFT,

LEARN TO TAKE ONE DAY AT A TIME, IT MAY BE THE ONLY SAVING GRACE FOR YOUR MIND,

JUST LIKE YOU VERY FIRST BREADTH, IT HAS CARRIED YOU THROUGHOUT YOUR LIFETIME AND NEVER LEFT,

GOD'S SPIRIT, ESSENCE, SUBSTANCE AND BREATH,

WILL NOT DWELL WITH WICKEDNESS, HATRED, AND EVIL, WHERE THESE ARE HIS SPIRIT LEFT,

GOD'S SPIRIT WILL NOT GROW, IN THE THINGS HIS GLORY, PERFECTION, CANNOT SOW,

SO, LEARN TO TAKE IT ONE DAY AT A TIME,

LET GOD SOW IN YOU WHAT SHOULD BE IN YOUR MIND,

THERE IS A DAY JUST FOR SMALL THINGS,

SOME WON'T COMPREHEND OR ADJUST TO JUST THEY MEAN TO THE KING,

BIBLICALLY THEY ARE LIKE JOTS AND TITTLES,

TO MOST PEOPLE THEY WILL MEAN VERY LITTLE,

BUT STILL AND ALL GOD GAVE THEM A DAY, AND ADMONISHED US NOT TO DESPISE THEIR WAY,

ONCE THEY WERE PROBABLY JUST LIKE ME AND YOU,

THEY PROBABLY SACRIFIED ALL JUST TO LET OTHERS
GET THROUGH,

SO, BE CAREFUL OF WHAT YOU SAY ABOUT WHAT YOU WON,

IF YOU REALLY DON'T KNOW HOW YOUR EXISTENCE BEGUN,

SO, I LEARNED TO TAKE ONE DAY AT A TIME,

WHO KNOWS THE SECRETS, GOD HAS PLACED IN YOUR MIND,

YOU ARE NOT ON THIS JOURNEY ALONE

IN THIS LIFE WE ALL HAVE A PATH, THAT HAS BEEN CUT OUT FOR US TO GRASP,

MOST OF ALL WE NEED TO REALIZE AND TRUST,

ON OUR HEAVENLY FATHER, THIS IS A MUST,

WE WILL FIND CHALLENGES AND TEST ALONG THE WAY,

COMPASSION, KINDNESS, AND TRUTH, HELPS PAVE THE WAY TO YOUR DAY,

THERE ARE SOME THINGS TO MAKE YOUR LIFE BETTER,

LOVE, FAITH, AND TRUTH ARE DIVINE CHARACTERS,

I WAS ALWAYS TAUGHT TO EMULIATE AND RESPECT THE CHARACTER OF GOD,

WITH UTILIZING HIS ATTRIBUTES YOUR LIFE WON'T BE SO HARD,

I BELIEVE, YOU CAN BE ARMED WITH THE GOOD JUST LIKE THE BAD,

TO BE A RIGHTOUS SERVANT, YOU MUST BE ABOVE WHAT THE WORLD HAS HAD,

JUST REMEMBER YOU ARE NOT ON THIS JOURNEY ALONE,

EVERY CHALLENGE IS A STEPPING-STONE TO MAKE A WAY HOME,

WE ARE ALL A PIECE OF THE PUZZLE AND HAVE A PLACE TO DWELL,

WE USUALLY FIND OUT WHERE WE FIT WHEN WE ADHERE TO GOD'S PRINCIPLES AND STAY AWAY FROM THE PATHWAYS TO HELL,

JUST REMEMBER YOU ARE NOT ON THIS JOURNEY ALONE,

EVERY CHALLENGE IS A STEPPING-STONE TO MAKE A WAY HOME,

DIVINE DIGNITY

ALL ELECTS ARE CALLED TO GOD'S LIGHT,

TO LEAD TO GOVERN TO TEACH THE DOCTRINES OF CHRIST THAT ARE RIGHT,

YOU HAVE TO POSSESS THE RIGHT KIND OF SPITITUAL POWER,

THAT WILL SUSTAIN YOUR PURPOSE HOUR BY HOUR,

YOU MUST BE READY TO ENTREAT MANY DIGNITARIES,

OF DIFFERENT FAITHS AND WALKS OF LIFE THAT WILL BE CONTRARY,

DON'T WORRY ABOUT WHO YOU WILL FACE,

JUST KNOW THAT GOD HAS ARMED YOU WITH HIS DIVINE DIGNITY AND GRACE,

YOU WILL STAND WHERE OTHERS WILL FALL,

BECAUSE OTHERS DID NOT HEED GOD'S CALL,

DON'T BE LIKE THOSE THAT DEPEND ON GREED AND WEALTH,

WHO DOESEN'T BELIEVE IN GOD AND HAS CALLED THEMSELVES,

GOD WILL NOT LEAVE YOU NOR WILL HE LET YOU FAIL,

YOU ARE A VESSEL HE USES TO DISPEL EVIL AND ASSAIL,

WE ALL KNOW THAT GOD IS SOVERIGN AND HIS AUTHORITY RULES,

IN HIS HANDS WE ARE JUST USED AS SPIRITUAL TOOLS,

BLESS ME LORD WITH YOUR DIVINE DIGNITY,

USE ME AS ONE OF YOUR VESSELS FOR THE WHOLE
WORLD TO SEE,

RESTORE MY INTEGRITY

LORD YOU KNOW WHERE I AM AND YOU KNOW WHERE I HAVE BEEN,

YOU KNOW MY SECRET THOUGHTS AND ALL MY HIDDEN SIN,

YOU ALSO KNOW MY HEARTFELT TRUTH TO TRODE THE PATHWAYS YOU SAID ARE RIGHT,

TO KEEP THE TRUTH IN THE DAY AND TRUTH APART FROM THE NIGHT,

LORD IT IS MY SINCERE DESIRE TO BE ALL THAT YOU WANT ME BE,

AT THIS POINT IN MY LIFE THEY ALL BLIND ME, I ONLY HAVE YOU TO HELP ME SEE,

SO, LORD I AM NOT TRYING TO PUT BLAME WHERE IT DOES NOT BELONG,

JUST TRYING TO DECIPHER THE GOOD FROM WHAT IS WRONG,

FROM MY HEART TO YOUR DIVINE AUTHORITY,

I PRAY FATHER THAT YOU WILL RESTORE MY INTEGRITY,

I WILL ALWAYS HOLD YOUR TRUTHS IN HIGHEST ESTEEM,

NO MATTER WHAT HAPPENS IN MY LIFE, OR HOW BAD THINGS SEEM,

I LOVE YOU WITH THE SAME UNDYING LOVE YOU LOVE YOU PUT IN ME,

NO MATTER WHAT THEY SAY, I KNOW YOUR LOVE IS STILL HERE FOR ME,

EVEN WHEN THE WORLD, WANTS TO DENY ITS HISTORY,

FATHER ITS GOING TO TAKE YOUR SEVERE DIVINE AUTHORITY,

TO RESTORE THE UNIQUELY DESIGNED INTEGRITY YOU PUT IN ME,

DON'T LOOK BACK

GOD IS A GOD OF ALL THREE TENSES,

GOD IS YOUR PROTECTION, SECURITY AND ALL YOUR DEFENSES,

IT IS IMPORTANT TO REMEMBER ALL THE FACTS,

WHERE GOD REDEEMED YOU FROM SO DON'T LOOK BACK,

SOME OF US WERE HEADED FOR THE PITS OF HELL,

ONLY GOD COULD PRESERVE US AND PLACE US WITHIN HIS VEIL,

TO BE CLEANSED WASHED SANCTIFIED AND CHOSEN,

TAKEN OUT OF THE ENEMY HANDS OF DEATH, SIN, LIFELESSNESS AND BEING FROZEN,

GOD HAS BROUGHT YOU A VERY LONG LONG WAY,

HE HAS ESTABLISHED YOU AND LET YOU MAKE YOUR OWN DAY,

YOUR CROWN WILL FLOURISH ON YOUR OWN HEAD,

BY EVERYTHING YOU DO IN LIFE AND WHAT IS BRED,

YOUR SPIRITUAL MINDSET AND YOUR ATTITUDE IS LINKED,

YOUR WORLD AND SPIRIT IS DEPENDENT ON WHAT YOU THINK,

THOUGHTS ARE JUST AS ACTIVE AS ANY OTHER PART OF LIFE,

YOU MUST FIRST BELIEVE THERE IS A GOD TO BELIEVE IN JESUS CHRIST,

IT IS IMPORTANT TO REMEMBER ALL THESE FACTS,

SALVATION AND REDEMPTION WAS JUST FOR YOU SO DON'T LOOK BACK,

EVERYTHING GOD PLANNED FOR YOU IS IN FRONT OF YOU,

GOD DESIGNED YOUR FUTURE AS THINGS LIFE TO BE COMPLETED BY YOU,

GOD WANTS ALL HIS CHILDREN TO HAVE A FULFILLED WHOLESOME LIFE,

YOU MUST KNOW IT HAS TO HAPPEN THROUGH JESUS CHRIST,

SEEK CHRIST FOR YOUR LIFE THAT IS WHERE IT'S AT,

GO FORWARD WITH YOUR FAITH AND DON'T LOOK BACK,

STOLEN VIRTUE

LORD, WHEN WILL I REALIZE SINFUL MAN IS ALWAYS LOOKING FOR A WAY,

TO ROB STEAL OR KILL AND DESTROY MY DAY,

YOU PUT INSIDE OF US A SPECIAL PRIZE,

THAT IN TIME WE WILL REALIZE,

SOME THINGS ARE STOLEN THAT DOESN'T TAKE MUCH,

ALL IS NEEDED FOR THEM IS JUST ONE TOUCH,

IN THE BIBLE THE SICK WOMAN, KNEW WHAT SHE NEEDED TO DO,

TO BE HEALED AND RECEIVE SOME OF JESUS'S VIRTUE,

I GUESS YOU CAN SAY, HOW DO YOU STEAL WHAT YOU CANNOT SEE,

BECAUSE IT IS ALL DONE THROUGH FAITH AND SPIRITUALITY,

FOR THOSE OF US WHO ARE SEEKING THE ONE WHO IS TRUE,

GUARD YOURSELF AND HEART,

FROM THOSE THAT STEAL AND USE YOUR VIRTUE,

IN ROYALTY IT IS NOT PROPER TO TOUCH A KING OR QUEEN,

BECAUSE THEY ARE FULL OF VIRTUOUS THINGS,

ONE TOUCH OF VIRTUE CAN HEAL THE VILE,

THEY USE SOMEONE ELSES VIRTUE, TO BECOME UNDEFILED,

FOR THOSE THAT ARE SEEKING THE ONE WHO IS TRUE,

GUARD YOURSELF AND YOUR HEART,

FROM THOSE THAT STEAL AND USE YOUR VIRTUE,

THINK RIGHT TO BE RIGHT

SO, MANY TIMES I DID NOT DO,

ALL THE THINGS I NEEDED TO,

ONLY BECAUSE I DID NOT KNOW,

GOD GAVE ME THE ABILITY, TO MAKE MYSELF GROW,

GOD PUT THE POWER IN MY HANDS,

I HAD TO BE THE ONE TO UNDERSTAND,

THE MIND IS VALID AND NOURISHING AND CAN MAKE YOU WHOLE,

EVERYDAY WE CONSUME THE SUN'S SPIRITUAL GOLD,

YOU MUST THINK RIGHT TO BE RIGHT,

THE MOST VALUABLE SPIRITUAL LIFE YOU HAVE IS IN JESUS CHRIST,

CHECK OUT EVERYONE IN YOUR PRESENCE,

WE ARE NOT ALL MADE OF THE SAME ESSENCE,

SOME OLD ADAGES SAY WE ARE WHAT WE EAT,

IF THAT'S TRUE SOME PEOPLE ARE FULL OF DECEIT,

PRACTICE TO SURROUND YOURSELF WITH PEOPLE WHO CARE ABOUT YOUR HEALTH,

YOU WILL FIND IT IS NOT MONEY THAT IS MOST VALUABLE AND IS YOUR TRUE WEALTH,

THE LIFE AND THINGS YOU CANNOT SEE HOLDS MUCH MORE THAN GRAVITY,

IT IS THE PART OF YOU ASSIGNED TO INHABIT ETERNITY,

YOU MUST THINK RIGHT TO BE RIGHT,

THE MOST VALUABLE SPIRITUAL LIFE YOU HAVE IS IN JESUS CHRIST,

WHEN GOD ORDERS YOUR LIFE

SOME PEOPLE ARE JUST ORDINARY,

NOT HAVING MANY BURDENS TO CARRY,

YET, SOME PEOPLE ARE BURDENED DOWN,

BECAUSE OF THEIR PURPOSE TO SERVE AND DEFEND THE CROWN,

SOME PEOPLE ARE CHOSEN AND HEAVEN SENT,

TO PROTECT THE INNOCENT, SIMPLE, AND DIFFIDENT,

GOD KNOWS YOUR HEART, SPIRIT, AND YOUR SOUL,

HE IS YOUR MAKER AND CREATER OF YOUR MOLD,

WHEN GOD MAKES UP AND ORDERS YOUR LIFE,

AT YOUR VERY CORE WILL BE HIS COMMANDMENTS, AND HIS SON JESUS CHRIST,

WHATEVER YOUR PURPOSE, WHATEVER YOUR GIFT,

IT IS FROM A VERY RELIABLE DIVINE SOURCE AND IS NO MYTH,

GOD IS THE MOST ANCIENT OF ALL THINGS,

NOTHING AND NO-ONE IS OLDER, HE IS THE CREATOR OF EVERYTHING,

DON'T TRY TO OUT DO HIS WORKS, COPY OR TRACE,

YOU MIGHT FIND YOURSELF IN AN UNKNOWN PLACE,

BECAUSE GOD WAS BEFORE ALL TIME,

WHERE THIS PLACE IS CANNOT BE CONCEIVED BY THE HUMAN MIND,

ALL PERIODS OF TIME AND SPACE STARTS WITH THE DIVINE,

HE IS THE REGULATOR AND INITIATOR OF ALL TIME,

WHEN GOD MAKES UP AND ORDERS YOUR LIFE,

AT YOUR VERY CORE WILL BE HIS COMMANDMENTS, AND HIS SON JESUS CHRIST,

UNIVERSAL JOINT

SOMETIMES IN LIFE THINGS GET CONFUSING,

TOO MUCH CONTROVERSY AND USELESS ABUSING,

WANDERING LOAFERS, BACKBITERS, AND THEIVES,

TOO MANY ANTI-CHRIST AND THOSE THAT DISBELIEVE,

JESUS IS AND HAS A UNIVERSAL JOINT,

THAT CAN TRANSFER ALL SITUATIONS AND GET STRAIGHT TO THE POINTS,

THERE ARE MANY DOCTRINES AND GOSPELS THAT THAT PERVERTS GOD'S DAY,

THEY TELL LIES AND THEY SELL LIES,

THEY BLIND YOU AND KEEP THEIR FINGERS IN YOUR EYES,

THEY BIND YOU AND SPIRITUALLY ALTER YOUR MIND AND POSSESS YOUR BRAIN,

THEY ALTER AND DISECT YOU AND UNTIL YOU ARE SPIRITUALLY MAIMED,

YOU JUST TO MAKE SURE SPIRITUALLY YOU ARE SPIRITUALLY DRAINED,

WORKING FOR THE MASTER

EVERYONE IN LIFE IS ASSOCIATED WITH SOMEONE OR SOMETHING,

WHEN THE ASSOCIATION IS SPIRITUAL YOU ARE A SERVANT FOR THE KING,

IN THE SERVICE OF AND TO THE CROWN,

YOU WILL BE A CHOSEN VESSEL, TO HELP LIFT THOSE WHO HAVE FALLEN DOWN,

YOU MUST BE ABLE TO HANDLE AND TO WEILD,

AN ETERNAL SWORD OF POWER, THAT OUR GOD IN HEAVEN WILLS,

GOD'S ANOINTED ARE ALL HIS PROPHETS EVANGELIST AND PASTOR'S

IN THE WORLD SAVING SOULS AND OFFERING SALVATION, THROUGH CHRIST JESUS OUR MASTER,

ALL JOBS ARE NOT THE SAME,

ESPECIALLY WHEN YOU ARE SERVING SPIRITUALLY IN JESUS'S NAME,

YOU MUST BE A SPECIAL BREED,

DESIGNED BY GOD TEMPERED TO MEET ALL HIS PEOPLE'S NEEDS,

WHEN YOU HAVE BEEN CHOSEN TO MAKE THE WORLD A BETTER PLACE,

GOD HAS INVESTED IN YOU HIS POWER AND HIS GRACE,

EVERYONE IS NOT QUALIFIED TO FULFILL THE DUTIES OF A BONAFIED SAINT,

GOD DOES NOT NEED, NOR WILL HE USE WARRIORS OR SOLIDERS THAT FAINT,

IF YOU ARE READY WILLING AND ABLE TO FIGHT,

YOU MUST WEAR GOD'S ARMOUR AND DEFEND ALL OF HEAVEN'S RIGHTS,

GOD'S ANOINTED ARE ALL HIS PROPHETS EVANGELIST AND PASTOR'S

IN THE WORLD SAVING SOULS AND OFFERING SALVATION, THROUGH CHRIST JESUS OUR MASTER,

WHO'S IN CONTROL OF YOUR MIND

AT SOME POINT IN TIME, YOU WILL HAVE TO REALIZE,

NOT EVERYTHING CAN BE SEEN WITH THE NAKED EYES,

THERE ARE SOME FUNCTIONS OF THE BODY THAT ARE HID,

SO THAT MAN MAY NEVER FIND OUT ALL THE THINGS THAT GOD DID,

YET GOD GAVE US SOME CONTROL OF OUR MINDS,

TO HELP MAKE THE RIGHT CHOICES AND MANAGE OUR TIME,

WHOSE IN CONTROL OF YOUR MIND,

IS IT GOD AND WHAT'S DIVINE,

OR IS IT SATAN AND HIS STRONGHOLDS, KEEPING YOUR MIND IN A BIND,

YOU CAN TELL WHO IS DIRECTING YOU, BY YOUR THOUGHTS, AND THE THINGS YOU DO,

GOD WILL BLESS YOU AND DIRECT YOU TO A QUIET SOMBER PLACE,

WHERE HE CAN BLESS YOU AND BESTOW UPON YOU HIS GRACE

WHERE SATAN WILL CAUSE YOU TO RUN A MUCK,

GET LOST AND CONFUSED, BECOME PHYSICALLY STUCK,

SATAN WILL CAUSE YOU TO KILL STEAL

AND EVEN DESTROY,

THE DREAMS AND HOPES OF MANY GIRLS AND BOYS,

HE IS KNOWN TO BRUTALLY ATTACK,

WITH ARSENALS OF DECEIT AND LIES HE CREATES EVERYTHING INVALID AND WITHOUT FACTS,

GOD WILL NEVER HAVE YOU TO TAKE ANOTHERS LIFE,

SINCE HE PAID FOR US ALL THROUGH HIS SON JESUS CHRIST,

YOU MUST GUARD YOUR HEART YOU MUST GUARD YOUR SOUL,

SATAN WANTS TO POSSESS YOU AND MAKE YOU SPIRITUALLY UNWHOLE,

PUT GOD IN THE DRIVER SEAT OF YOUR LIFE,

LET GOD DRIVE YOU TO HIS SON JESUS CHRIST,

WHY SHOULD ANOTHERS DEBILITY BE THE CAUSE FOR YOU TO SHOW HUMILITY

LORD SO MANY TIMES AS HUMANS WE FAIL TO SEE,

OUR BLESSINGS YOU HAVE ALREADY PUT IN OUR DESTINY,

WE CANNOT DENY THE TRUTH,

OUR ENTIRE ANATOMY IS OUR BODY OF PROOF,

WE SHOULD ALWAYS GIVE PRAISE FOR THE THINGS YOU DO AND HAVE DONE,

ESPECIALLY WHEN YOU SACRIFICED YOUR ONLY SON,

I DON'T KNOW WHY ANOTHER'S DEBILITY,

HAS TO CAUSE US TO SEE AND SHOW GODLY HUMILITY,

WE GO THROUGH LIFE AS IF EVERYTHING WAS ALWAYS FINE,

NOT CONSIDERING OUR LIVES WE WERE BOUGHT WE WERE GIVEN THIS TIME,

EVERY SINGLE ORGAN THAT WE BARE, IS EVIDENCE OF HOW MUCH GOD CARES,

WE DON'T' RECOGNIZE HOW BLESSED WE ARE AND COMPLETE,

UNTIL WE SEE SOMEONE WHO HAS NO FEET,

WE ARE GIVEN THE RIGHT TO CHRIST'S BLOOD THAT MAKES US WHOLE,

PURIFIES OUR BODIES AND UNIFIES OUR SOULS,

CHRIST'S MAGNANIMITY AND SOVERE-IGNTY IS SO GREAT,

IT ENCOMPASSES EVERY SINGLE SPIRIT AND PERPETUATES ALL OUR FATES,

I THANK CHRIST JESUS FOR CREATING EVERY ASPECT OF ME,

AND INCORPORATING HIS SPIRIT AND DIVINITY INSIDE OF ME,

HE MADE ME WHOLE WITH NO MISS-ING PARTS,

EACHDAY I SHOULD PRAY TO HIM WITH HUMBLENESS OF HEART,

WE ARE BLESSED, WE ARE TRULY BLESSED EVERYBODY KNOWS,

JUST LOOK AT YOUR HANDS 10 FINGERS AND FEET 10 TOES,

BE THANKFUL FOR ALL THE GIFTS AND BLESSINGS EVERYDAY,

GOD CREATED US WITH MANY MEMBERS AND MANY DIFFERENT WAYS,

I DON'T KNOW WHY ANOTHER'S DEBILITY,

HAS TO CAUSE US TO SEE AND SHOW GODLY HUMILITY,

HISTORY (HIS/STORY)

FROM THE BOOK OF GENESIS TO REVELATION,

EACH BOOK IS A DEDICATION,

TO JESUS CHRIST'S, PAST, PRESENT, OR FUTURE LIFE,

IT TOOK 66 BOOKS TO TELL HIS STORY,

IN ORDER FOR HUMANITY TO COME INTO EXISTENCE IN TO BE,

JESUS THERE WOULD BE NO YOU, THERE WOULD BE NO ME,

JESUS IS THE REASON FOR ALL HUMANITY AND EVERYONE'S ONTOLOGY,

EVERYTHING THAT IS EVERYTHING THAT WILL BE,

IS ALL CONVOLUTED INTO HIS STORY,

THERE ARE NO TIMELINES OUTSIDE OF HIS STORY,

EVERY TIME LINE WRITTEN IS WITHIN SOME PART OF HISTORY,

NO MATTER HOW T IS WRITTEN,

IT ALL COMES BACK TO,

HIS HISTROY WRITTEN ABOUT ME AND ABOUT YOU,

EVERY SINGLE SPIRIT AND EVERY SINGLE SOUL,

IS ADDRESSED IN THE LOGOS, THEY ARE ALL HIS MOLD,

NOTHING EXIST OUTSIDE OF JESUS CHRIST,

HE IS THE START AND EPITOME OF ALL HUMAN AND SPIRITUAL LIFE,

ANATOMICAL COMMANDS

GOD GAVE ME THIS BODY AS A TEMPLE,

AS A TEMPLE FOR HIM TO DWELL IN,

NOT FOR DEMONS AND DEVILS TO COVET AND COMMITT HEINOUS SINS,

GOD SAID I MUST TAKE A STAND,

TO CONTROL THIS BODY BY ANATOMICAL COMMANDS,

GOD'S WORD IS THE BEST,

AND WHERE IT IS IT SHOULD BE BLEST,

GOD'S WORD IS PURE AND FULL OF LIBERTY,

RESTORING THE LOST AND SETTING THE CAPTIVES FREE,moo

GOD'S WORD IS THE HEAD, AND IS THE

LENDER,

NOT SOME CONFUSED VILELY AFFECTED, CONFUSED PERSON OR GENDER,

STAND ON GOD'S COVENANT LAWS,

NOT ON SIN SICK HUMAN FLAWS,

GOD'S WORD CAN AND WILL MAKE THE PEOPLE RIGHT,

IT CAN HEAL THE SICK, AND GIVE THE BLIND SIGHT,

GOD SAID I MUST TAKE A STAND,

AND CONTROL THIS BODY BY ANATOMICAL COMMANDS,

GOD LEFT US HIS COVENANT SO THAT WE MAY KNOW,

HE IS A GOD OF HIS WORD SO HE PLACED THE RAINBOW,

HE CREATED A BOND WITH EVERY MAN,

A COAT OF MANY COLORS AND MANY BANDS, TO REPRESENT ALL PEOPLE AND ALL NATIONS,

TO BE HEIRS TO ALL THINGS GOD HAS DONE,

GOD GAVE US 10 COMMANDS,

TO FOLLOW HIS WORD PROCURE HIS LANDS,

WE ARE GREAT BODIES OF STATUTES AND DIVINE LAWS,

IN GODS IMAGE WE ARE NOT MADE FOR FLAWS,

EVERY SINGLE FINGER ON EITHER OF YOUR HANDS,

IS LIKE A WORLD AT YOUR COMMAND,

ETERNAL BONDS

I THANK GOD FOR ALL THE THINGS IN MY LIFE,

THE MOST IMPORTANT ONE JESUS CHRIST,

YOU GAVE ME AN EXCEPTIONAL MOM AND DAD,

THEY POSSESSED ATTRIBUTES AND SPIRITS THAT OTHERS NEVER HAD,

GOD JOINED THEM AS A PERFECT PAIR,

GOD KNEW THEY HAD SPECIAL WAYS TO CARE,

FOR OTHER PEOPLE, CHILDREN AND THE WHOLE WORLD,

SO GOD GAVE THEM 10 CHILDREN, 4 BOYS AND 6 GIRLS,

THIS IS THE UNION OF GOD AN ETERNALLY

SPECIAL BOND,

TWO LIVING SPIRITUAL HEARTS TO SEAL WHAT
GOD HAS DONE,

A SPIRITAL MOTHER AND A DEVOUT KING,

GOD JOINED BISHOP EDDIE THOMAS AND MOTHER CHARLENE,

HAPPY ANNIVERSARY

PARALLEL SELF

How many me's are in this universe,

If its more than one then who was the first,

I know I have trillions of cells,

I thought they were all within my body and uniquely veiled,

It is being hypothesized

That we all have parallel selves,

That exist in the world on many different levels,

That makes some sense to me now, because we are replicated from the divine,

Thst means we have the character of God, of several kinds,

Like God I am full of characters and abilities,

Everything I create has a part of me,

I can be anything I can dream of,

Most of all when I am dreaming it should come from love,

FREQUENCY MEANT FOR ME

I HEAR MUSIC IN THE AIR, ITS ONLY BECAUSE GOD IS THERE,

I HEAR ANGELS WAY UP HIGH, ITS BECAUSE ANGELS NEVER DIE,

THEY PERMEATE AND FILL THE SPHERES,

THE SPIRIT OF GOD HAS TO FILL ALL THE YEARS,

EVERYTHING IN HEAVEN OR ON EARTH HAS BEEN GIVEN A VOICE TO BE,

GOD HAS BLESSED AND DESIGNATED A FREQUENCY JUST FOR ME,

WHEN I CALL HIM, THEIR WILL BE NO DOUBT WHO IT IS,

HE HAS SET MY LINE AND TIME I AM ALL HIS,

SOME FREQUENCIES ARE LOW AND SOME ARE SO FRIGHTFULLY HIGH,

SOME FREQUENCIES ARE BEYOND THE HUMAN EAR, THEY COULDN'T HEAR IT IF THEY TRY,

A FREQUENCY IS LIKE A SIGNATURE FOR YOUR SOUL,

IT IS THE COMPOSITION BETWEEN YOU AND GOD THAT CREATES YOUR MOLD,

BY SOLIMENIZATION AND FREQUENCY YOU ARE MARRIED TO CHRIST,

A CELEBRATION AND INVITATION TO A SACRED AND DIVINE LIFE,

I WON'T HAVE TO WORRY ANYMORE WHEN GOD HAS ME CAPTURED,

THEN I KNOW I WILL HAVE BEEN ENRAPTURED,

WHEN EVER THE RESURRECTION OR UNION WITH GOD WILL BE,

I WILL BE CAUGHT UP IN THE AIR WITH HIM BY THE FREQUENCY MEANT JUST FOR ME,

GOD'S GOT YOUR NUMBER

EVERYTHING YOU DO IN LIFE IS IN SOME WAY IS DIVINE,

CONNECTED TO GOD BY SOUND, COLOR OR A SPECIAL TIME,

GOD MADE YOU FOR HIS OWN,

AND PLACED YOU IN A PERFECT TIME ZONE,

WE ALL ADHERE TO A SPECIFIC ELEMENT,

WATER, EARTH, FIRE, IT IS ALL DONE WITH GOD'S INTENT,

THE ISOMETRIC LINES IN EARTH, ARE ALL CONNECTED FOR GOD TO DIRECT,

IN METEROLOGICAL, ATMOSPHERIC, PLACES ONLY GOD COULD PERFECT,

WHOEVER AND WHATEVER YOU ARE YOU MUST ALWAYS REMEMBER,

YOU WERE CREATED THERE IS NOTHING OUTSIDE OF GOD'S CREATION, HE'S GOT YOUR NUMBER,

IT DOSEN'T MATTER IF YOU ARE EVERY ONE'S HERO,

GOD HAS HEXADECIMALLY METED OUT LIFE EVERYTHING FROM THE HIGHEST NUMBER TO ZERO,

THERE IS NO PLACE YOU CAN WALK ON THE LAND,

THAT IS NOT UNDER GOD'S HOLY COMMAND,

THE SACRED WORDS AND VERSES ARE AT YOUR FEET,

ALLOWING YOU TO TRAVEL EVERYDAY WITHIN PATHWAYS
THAT WILL A;; ONE DAY UNITE AND MEET,

WHEN YOUR TIME IS UP IN THIS WORLD JUST YOU REMEMBER,

DEATH AND EVEN LIFE FOR GOD HAS A NUMBER,

GOD PLANNED FOR DEATH TO BE CONSUMED,

TO ALLOW LIFE BY VICTORY TO BE RESUMED,

WHEN GOD, HEAVEN AND ETERNITY HAS HAD ENOUGH,

VICTORIOUSLY DEATH WILL BE ALL SWALLOWED UP,

MY GOD GIVEN SEAT

EVERYONE HAS A POSITION AND ROLE THEY PLAY,

NO MATTER WHAT YOUR ROLE YOU HAVE BEEN GIVEN A DAY,

LIKE PAWNS IN A CHESS GAME, PROTECTING THEIR DESIGNATED SPACE,

AS SOLIDERS OF GOD'S WE ARE PROTECTING HIS GRACE,

WE KEEP THE KING IN HIS GOD GIVEN SEAT,

BY HONORING HIM WITH PRAISES AND KEEPING AWAY DEFEAT,

OUR GOD HAS NEVER LOST A FIGHT, BECAUSE EVERYTHING ABOUT HIM IS ALWAYS RIGHT,

IN HIS PRESENCE THE WRONG AND EVIL WILL HAVE BOW DOWN,

EVEN A DEVIL HAS TO RESPECT THE UNIVERSAL CROWN,

THE DEVIL WAS MADE LIKE EVERYONE ELSE,

HE HAD NO POWER TO MAKE HIMSELF,

THERE IS A GOD GIVEN SEAT THAT PERPETUATES THE DAY,

TWELVE HOURS THEY OPERATE TO DISPENSE BLESSINGS AND PROMISES IN GOD'S WAYS,

THERE IS A GOD GIVEN SEAT OPERATES IN THE NIGHT,

IT IS ABSENT OF GOD'S BLESSEDNESS OF DAYLIGHT,

WE KNOW THAT CHRIST RULES THE DAY,

AND IT WAS HIS DESTINTY TO DIE AND PAY FOR THIS WAY,

WE KEEP THE KING IN HIS GOD GIVEN SEAT,

BY HONORING HIM WITH PRAISES AND KEEPING AWAY DEFEAT,

WHEN ALL IS SAID AND DONE,

DEATH WILL BE SWALLOWED UP AND CHRIST'S.

VICTORY WILL BE WON,

GOD'S WORDS
ARE MY LAWS

GOD'S WORDS CAN BIND OR SET SOMEONE FREE,

IT CAN LEAD A LOST CHILD TO THEIR DESTINY,

IT CAN LIFT YOU UP WHEN YOU ARE DOWN,

IT CAN DIRECT YOU TO THE RIGHT PLACE IN ORDER TO BE FOUND,

GOD'S WORDS HAS NO FLAWS,

THEY ARE THE PERFECT COMPOSITION OF DIVINLY CONSTRUCTED LAWS,

THAT WILL STAND AND UPHOLD THE TRUTH,

FOR THE AGED MAN, FOR THE YOUNG MAN AND CHILDREN OF YOUTH,

I'M LOOKING AND MOVING AHEAD

LORD YOU PAID MY DEBT ON THE CROSS,

SO MY SOUL AND SPIRIT WOULD NOT BE LOST,

YOU WERE PERSECUTED,

AT THE HANDS OF THE LAW,

THE MAGISTRATES AND GOVERNMENT WAS FULL OF FLAWS,

YOUR WORD SAYS YOU PAID FOR MY SINS AND SICKNESS,

THE BIBLE TELLS THE WHOLE STORY AND IS MY GODLY WITTNESS,

MY LIFE IS IN YOUR HANDS, BY FAITH I MUST BELIEVE WHAT YOU SAID,

I AM HEALED, I AM PAID FOR, SO, I'M LOOKING AND MOVING AHEAD,

HEAVEN AND EARTH SHALL PASS AWAY,

YOUR ETERNAL AND HEAVENLY WORDS GO BEYOND MERE CIRCUMSRANCE TIME ERECTED DAYS,

WHEN ALL ELSE HAS BEEN. RESURRECTED AND RISEN,.

GOD'S HOLY WORDS WILL STILL BE ACTIVE AND LIVING,

HOLY WORDS WILL NEVER EVER PASS AWAY,

THEY ARE CONSTRUCTED OF THE HOLIEST OF SPIRIT THAT SUSTAINS AND MAKES EVERY DAY,

GOD'S WORDS ARE THE SUBSTANCE UP HOLDING EVERY LIVING AND BREATHING THING,

GOD IS HIS WORD, THE WORD IS GOD,

NOBODY CAN CHANGE OR DENY THE WORDS OF A HOLY KING,

HABITS

Why is it we let, harmful things grow?

The things we need most we just let them go,

Can't we change the fate, we're headed for, and open new paths, to love a little more,

I've seen so much, of people dropping lugs, smoking weed, popping pills, and shooting drugs, I've seen so much, of people snorting coke, drinking, gambling, and getting broke,

Are these the habits, that we depend, if so our problems will never end?

Why can't we start, to change the trend, to eliminate the problems, we can end,

Let's make it a habit, to pick up our bothers, that they in turn may pick up others, let's make it a habit, to reach out and touch, when you see someone, in need of so much,

Let's make it a habit, to strengthen the weak, and not misuse them because their meek, Let's make it a habit, to help the disabled, God works wonders, regardless to what they are labeled,

All these things, we've neglected, we've ignored, laughed at, and even rejected,

So, let's change our habits, and direct our course, and seek the habits of a better source,

There's one thing left, I must say, the best habit of all, is the habit to pray

---

DEADLY GUN

We take the life of an innocent soul, and cause a family grief,

Who goes against the principles of God, and kills for his own perverted peace,

Who looks upon the creations of God, and decides a life should end, truly it is a fool who doesn't know, where the wrath of God will begin,

Who is this image I see, that holds a deadly Gun, surely judgment will come upon him, like the raising of the sun,

Reverse this man's position, and put him in the victim's place, let blood, hatred, and death be all that he will taste,

Reverse this man's position, so in the end, he will know, it is not for him to decide when, one of God's children shall go,

Who is this image I see holding a deadly gun, surely judgment will come upon him, like the raising of the sun,

Punish him and smite him, for God did not give him the right, take his gun and send him, to the pits of darkness and night,

Reverse this man's position, so in the end he will know, it is not for him to decide, when one of God=s children should go,

MOTION PICTURE

Life is a motion picture, each frame is where you've been,

It reveals to you, your successes, it reveals to you your end,

Life is a motion picture, your history recorded on film,

And it is ever repeating, because the true light of life is never dim,

Life is a motion picture, sometimes things are in reverse,

To undo what has been done and start again with the first,

Life is a motion picture, engraved upon plates and film,

I am the root, of my play, the tree, the leaves, the limb,

I am also the director, the author and the actress you see,

And through these motion pictures and film, I find I'm eternally free,

A free spirit indeed I am, a truth beyond explanation,

For I have found within my world there is no dissipation,

Life is a motion picture sometimes things are in reverse,

To undo what has been done and start again with the first,

MY PRIVATE TELEPHONE

My personal line exists within, where no man can cut it off,

God allows, me to reach the ends of the earth, North West, East and South,

He graciously gives, when I'm in need, that I may always know,

With him I have a direct connection, because he deeded it so,

God gave me my own private telephone, to call him whenever I need,

Yes, I am ever thankful, for through him, I am truly freed

ILLUSIONS

Don't be alarmed, when what you see, is not really what you thought it would be,

Don't be confused, by changing forms, know that imitations are not born,

Just countless illusions pervading space, they are not real and have no definite place,

You must realize, what is real, by what you believe, by what you feel,

Not by the many illusions you see, they are not attuned with destiny,

They have no power of their own, they harness your power, because it's where they roam,

Just countless illusions pervading space, they are not real and have no definite place,

I'VE EARNED MY WINGS

Through this life of toils and snares, I've found few people who really cared,

About bringing true goodness to the world,

For the peace of all God's children all over the world,

I was raised with love and truth, I remember my teachings from my youth,

Wherever I go I sow good seed, each day I try, to do good deeds,

For each time I've cried, and for each tear I've shed, added dimensions and breadth to the wings I'll spread,

For each time my heart has been battered and tore, it'll add height and altitude for my wings to soar,

For each time I've been stomped on and crushed, I'll wear an angelic garment that can't be touched,

For all these reasons, I've earned my wings, with my rightful place, being Heir of a King

A MESSAGE FOR LIFE

2,000 years ago, a message came, he took on all our sins, he was labeled and blamed,

For sins and crimes, he did not commit, but this was the fate he was plagued with,

Its 2,000 years again there's still a message for life, the same messenger have come and delivered it twice,

Will we hear what he's saying, or just laugh and mock, while he's gathering his own, building his Christian flock,

Having ears to hear, it is a blessing from God, those who do not will have it quite hard,

He's patient and merciful, if we will yield, for destiny to be fulfilled,

It's 2,000 years again there's still a message for life, the same messenger has come and delivered it twice,

WHEN MY SPIRIT CALLS

Day to day we walk amid many wonderful things, sometime we even walk and talk, within each other dreams,

We adhere to signals and signs, placed upon this earth, what we need to understand most, was given to us at birth,

Listen when your spirit calls, it has information for you, whether it is good or bad, the communication will be true,

It is a divine vehicle a bond between you and God, to stay in communication and pray, even when times are hard,

Listen when your spirit calls, it has information for you, it is beyond a metaphysical experience, designed just for you,

HE REDEEMS

When burdens are heavy and troubles are near, when all you do is shed many tears,

There is someone who really cares, someone who all your burdens he bears,

Although times maybe hard it seems, rest assured to know that God redeems,

When the world seems to hate and despise you, give it to God, he knows what to do,

He'll take your scars and turn them to stars, he'll take your shame and turn it to gain,

Although times maybe hard it seems, rest assured to know that God redeems,

Never fear anything that man can do, remember that God can bring you through,

Always remember his mercy and grace, endeavoring to reach that blessed place,

Although times maybe hard it seems, rest assured to know you are Redeemed.

FRAMED BY THE WORDS OF GOD

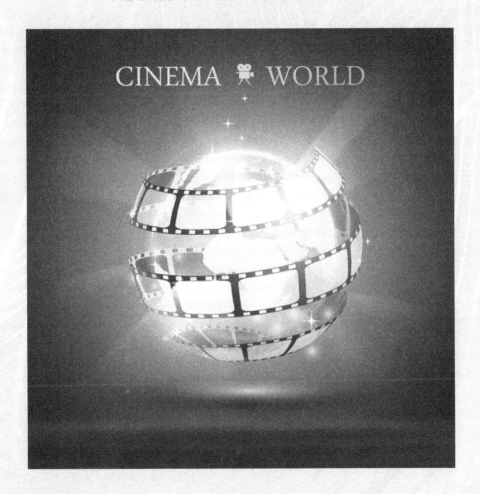

LEGACY OF LOVE

Loving you seemed to make things right,

You were a special part, of Gods infinite light,

You sowed the seeds of love and care, it made the difference, because you were there,

You've left with us, a legacy of love, a cherished memory we'll always think of,

We'll grieve I'm sure, but it's not a loss, Christ paid this price upon the cross,

To join and claim us, as your own, on that day you lead us safely home,

You've left with us, a legacy of love, A cherished memory, we'll always think of,

This is goodbye, just for a while, God loves you best you are his child,

Until we meet in another place, may we be kept by Gods love and grace,

You've left with us, a legacy of love, A cherished memory we'll always think of,

MASTERPIECE

I've searched the world over, to find the right one,

I thought would be to me, a ray of sun,

Finally, I've found your radiant light,

You are my protector, you are my knight,

Most of all, you are my masterpiece,

In you I found my souls complete,

I thank the heavens for you, and all that you bring,

You make my heart happy, you make my heart sing,

Most of all, you are my masterpiece,

In you I found my souls complete,

DELUSIONS

Delusions are instances, and truth is not there,

They play with the mind, with the lies they bear,

Delusions are known, to bring stresses and fear,

They try to manipulate, what you need to hear,

Cast out your delusions, don't give them the room,

Don't let them seal you fate, or cause your doom,

Develop your mind, with thoughts that's pure,

So, when troubles come, you can endure,

Take control of your mind, by changing each frame,

Envision thoughts of courage, and watch delusions change,

Cast out your delusions, don't give them the room,

Don't let them seal your fate, on cause your doom,

THERE IS NO SOLUTION
(WHEN THE EQUATION IS GOD)

There is no solution, when the equation is the lord,

to revel all of creation, is a task unsolvable and hard,

How can you solve, what is the very first?

how can you solve, what gave you your birth?

Why try to expound, on that which has no end,

and create for yourself, a problem of where you began,

Why try to solve that, which has no man's blood,

and heap upon yourselves, his wrath of hurricanes and floods,

This quest has been sought, by many others, and has caused distractions from one to the other,

Although things look like they have changed for a while, I pity the heathens, who try to change God's child,

Your very future and life depends, on where this child enters or where he begins,

Who is this child, I am speaking of, every child God has given you, through his infinite love,

There is no solution, where the equation is the lord,

To reveal all of creation, is a task unsolvable and hard,

LONG RIDE HOME

I drifted away from home long ago,

I was too immature and too young to know,

About life and the struggles, that people bear,

And the coldness in those, who just don't care,

I've learned my lesson, while I was alone,

Now I'm ready, to take the long ride home,

I saw so much, that I just can't tell,

How could anyone service, that awesome hell,

I had to learn how to survive, if I were to stay alive,

While out there in the streets, I had to learn how to eat,

I did what I had to do, just as you would, if you had to,

I've learned my lesson, with God alone,

Now I'm ready, to take that long ride home.

KNEELING AT THE THRONE

Standing by your side, where I've always been,

you are where my life begins,

I obediently serve, your every command,

I cherish and uphold, the King's land,

Each day I kneel, at the King's Throne,

I'm always by your side, you're never alone,

Though some have gone, and times have changed,

my mission is the same, and hasn't been rearranged,

To protect, to conquer, to obey, and devour,

anyone who is against your sword of power,

Handed down through generations, to uphold the truth, I was given this mission, in my youth,

Each day I kneel, at the King's Throne,

I'm always at your side you're never alone,

My lord, my King, most merciful one,

Forgive this world, for what they have done,

They have not the eyes, or mind to see,

The truth, or the love invested in thee,

Each day I kneel at the King's Throne,

I'm always at your side, you're never alone,

TOUCHED BY HIS LIGHT

I once was in darkness, and could not see, evilness and hatred surrounded me,

They blocked out my sun, so it could not shine, they covered my eyes to keep me blind,

Then he touched me, with his infinite light, he opened my eyes and put me to flight,

Like an eagle I flew, and soared high in the sky, above all the darkness above all their lies,

I soared so high I touched Heaven's Gate, I watched all hatred dissipate,

There was no more evil, in the land, God had come, just like he planned,

As for me, I found his grace, he has given to me, a special place,

I am now flying, soaring in the air, each day I do, I say a prayer,

Yes, he touched me, with his infinite light,

He opened my eyes, and put me to flight,

Like an eagle I fly, and soar high in the sky,

above all the darkness, above all their lies,

MY LOVERS SONG
(WOMAN GOD'S BLESSING TO MAN)

You are my joy my heart's desire, you are the fuel that lights my fire,

For you, I would give my very soul, as long as it would, keep our love whole,

I sing a lover's song every night, hoping to transcend, to you my delight,

So precious you are, a gift from above, a blessing to behold, adorned with true love,

You have taken my heart, lest I should die, you are truly the apple of my eye,

Comfort me my love, for I am beyond myself, only your love, can bring back my stability and health,

I sing a lover's song every night, hoping to transcend to you my delight,

I've looked the world over, to find a true love, but there was only you my dove,

As pure as snow, as black as night, as red as blood, as bright as light,

I sing a lover's song, every night hoping to transcend to you my delight,

LISTEN TO THE ANGELS

Softly whispering in the wind, at the voices of the Angels the trees do bend,

For they are the agents, of God's power and might,

They are the warriors, that chase off the evil in the night,

Listen to the Angels, they are paths to Heavens Gates, by them men are judged, by them we know our fate,

Angels are messengers, of Good news and love, they dispel all the evil, that seek things above,

Angels communicate, to the heart and soul, Angels are daring, Angels are bold,

Angels speak peace, to your heart in the night, that evil may not dim, nor darken your light,

Listen to the Angels, they are paths to Heavens Gates, by them men are judged, by them we know our fate,

WHEN WILL THE FAMINE END

There is a famine in the land, for all to see, it prohibits the proliferation of land and seas,

It is a time of strife, hunger and pain, it is a time when everyone feels the same,

There is a famine in the land, Lord! when will the famine end?

And start a new purpose, where love can begin,

God is judging, and judging right, separating darkness from light,

He has caused the land not to bare, until his justice, has been found there,

When God rids the land, of the ungodly sins, then we will know, when the famine ends.

It will be the beginning, of a brand-new day, where Gods love will lead the way.

I'LL MISS YOU
(GODLY FRIENDSHIP)

We traveled rough roads, and over several terrains, you saw my tears you saw my pains,

We fought many battles day and night, we comforted each other, with a reassuring light,

Now the time has come, for us to part, you have a very special place in my heart,

No matter, what I say or do, always remember, I'll really miss you,

We were two, up against the world, sometimes I felt like a little girl,

Especially when, I could not see, the end of the forest, for all the trees,

I hope the best for you, where ever you go, I want you to always know,

No matter what I say or do, Remember, I'll always love and miss you,

PROTECT MY HEART

Inside I harbor, the truths I know, will someday cause, my spirit to flow,

Like rivers of water, of justice and truth, sustaining my destiny, given in my youth,

Hidden deep in my heart, he's buried treasures, that no man can price, and no man can measure,

Protect my heart, that I may retain, all these riches for Jesus name,

Keep my heart pure, keep my heart strong, keep my heart on a straight path, so I won't go wrong,

Protect my heart, that I may retain, all these riches for Jesus Name,

DISTANCE ME FROM EVIL

Take me in your arms, embrace me upon your chest,

Let me feel the warmth of your heart, let me feel your rest,

Troubles have beset me, and hatred is on my heels, distance me from this evil, that I may know your will,

Let your love adorn me, let your truth see me through, let me know your promises, will do what you've created them to,

Trouble have beset me and hatred is on my heels, distance me from this evil that I may know your will,

BIND THE DEVILS HANDS

Walk with me Angels, bind the devil's hands, keep him in submission to my father demands,

Walk with me angels, bind the devil's feet, hold up the cross in victory, let him know his defeat,

Walk with me angels close the devil's eyes, that he not look, upon Gods children, with any thought to despise,

Walk with me angels, close the devils mouth, torment him, until the angels shout,

Pray with me angels, confuse the devils mind, that he may know, that Jesus is the only one sublime,

Talk with me angels, just to let me know, God has sent us to conquer this evil earthly foe,

IMMORTAL MEN

God has given gifts to men, God has told us how to win, an everlasting life that never ends, and how to become immortal men,

God has shown us how we should be, God has laid out our destiny, God has paved the way to begin, to seek out to become immortal men,

God smiles on us when we are right, we see his smile in the Sun's radiant light,

It's pleasing to know God smiles every day, because Jesus has already paved the way, for us to be sons and daughters and can now enter in, to claim our heritage as immortal women/ men,

MY SOUL MATE

I've had relationships, that caused me pain,

I've even had some, of material gain,

Those relationships don't last, they're just passing time,

No good for the body, not good for the mind,

Then I was blessed, with an Eternal Love,

The kind that only, God sends from above,

It's everything a woman, could want in a man,

It's almost more, than one man can stand,

It's worth it all, it's worth the wait,

To be eternally joined, to your own Soul Mate,

He possesses all the things, that you've missed,

She is Heavenly, and full of all your bliss,

He is God filled, to meet the task,

She is God filled, to make a Love that last,

It's worth it all, it's worth the wait,

To be eternally joined, to your own Soul Mate,

GOD HAS A PLAN FOR ME

When men try to hold you down, to hinder your progress,

Remember in whose hands you're placed, and whose life you've professed,

When life has taken all you have, and you have nowhere else to go, remember who it is that giveth life, and who is important to know,

I know God takes care of me and he is concerned, He is the reason I have this faith, He is the reason I have learned.

God has a plan for me, that no man knows that no man sees,

When friends have turned their backs on you, and left you all alone, remember who walks with you, when all your friends are gone,

When all life's doors have been shut, and soul's windows have been barred,

Remember there is no task to great, that can't be conquered by the Lord,

I know God has a plan for me, that no man knows, that no man sees,

DO THE WORKS OF CHRIST

We are the Vicars of Christ, acting as servants in this life,

We bear the burdens of the world, for every boy for every girl,

We are chosen to feed the poor, whenever the need is at our door, we are chosen to visit the sick, to petition to God to heal and fix,

We are chosen to clothe the naked, to cover their bodies and help them make it,

We must do the works of Christ, this is his legacy, and the works of his life,

We have been chosen to heal and bless, bringers of peace and mercy as Christ professed,

These are the fruits of the Spirit, and morrow for the bones, which Christians use, to build a Spiritual home,

This we must do the works of Christ, this is his legacy, and the works of his life,

CHRIST IS STANDING AT THE DOOR

When you have been hated battered and bruised, shut up, down trodden and abused,

Don't worry and don't you fret, my God hasn't failed you yet,

Christ is standing at the door, judging those who persecute the heartbroken and the poor,

When life has beaten you and held you down, when nowhere in the world, could a friend be found,

Christ is still standing at the door, judging those who persecute the heartbroken and the poor,

When you have no money and your health seems gone, pray to the Father and know you're not alone,

Christ is there opening the door, for those who are heartbroken and for those who are poor,

THE BRIDE
(THE CHURCH)

Joined by eternal laws, matrimonially sacred without spiritual flaws,

A building made not by man, but by God's Spirit as a Divine plan,

The Church Christ's Bride, binding all nations, without prejudice or condemnation,

Built to last through eternity, as a vehicle for Christ promised seed,

Christ Church will stand, when all else fails, she is the embodiment of the Gospels,

When all is said and all is gone, Christ and his Church will stand alone,

The Church Christ's Bride, binding all nations, without prejudice or condemnation,

GOD'S LOVE

I am the epitome, of all that God is, I am the ultimate
commandment I am all his,

He gave his love, that we may live, through his son, all he
had to give,

Yes, I'm God's love, not bound by time, a law unto myself, I am
sacred and sublime,

I move at my will, to change Hearts and Minds, keeping a flow
of love, throughout all nations in time,

Yes, I am God's love, a law unto myself, I am better than riches,
I am greater than health,

When I am moved, so is the Earth, I set into motion the
whole universe,

I am God, God is love, there is none higher or none above,

Yes, I'm God's love, not bound by time, a law unto myself, I am
sacred and sublime,

OUR BED IS GREEN
(SOLOMON'S LOVE)

Come my love, let's take a flight, let's have our fill of love through the night, let's explore the gifts of time, and enjoy the bliss of what we find,

Let's soar through time to the Taj Ma Hall, or to Rome before its fall, let's visit the wonders of the pyramids, and ponder on the secrets and treasures they've hid,

Let's visit the Temple, where Diana ruled, where many scholarly men were schooled,

Then we must come back, to our domain, this is where we must remain,

The world is ours, and at our feet, you sit as King upon your seat,

The trees, the flowers and all of nature's that's here, Is precious to us and Oh so dear,

Love is our essence, our bed is green, fecundating the earth with all-natural things,

We were entrusted with special gifts, to heal to love and to lift,

We were given a sacred place, for us to rule and govern with Grace,

Love is our essence, our bed is green, fecundating the earth with natural things,

OH BEAUTIFUL!

Oh, beautiful trees swaying in the wind, tell me the secret of why you bend,

Oh, beautiful waters, with rippling tides, tell me the secrets that you hide,

Oh, beautiful Sun, up in the sky, tell me who sat your powers so high,

Oh, beautiful full moon, on a star lit night, tell me who has filled you with this light,

Oh, beautiful roses, in your bed, tell me the secrets why your petals spread,

Oh, beautiful birds, in the air, tell me of the God, who put you there,

Oh beautiful, oh beautiful, I see you everywhere, so kind, so gracious, so pure, so fair,

Oh, beautiful lion fierce and mean, tell me of the God who made you a King,

Oh, beautiful honey bee dancing to your theme, tell me of the God who made you queen,

Oh, beautiful Oh beautiful, I see you everywhere, so kind, so gracious, so pure, so fair,

HE TURNS CURSES IN TO BLESSINGS

When you've done all you can do, know that God will pull you through,

When evil has blocked all your paths, know that they have evoked God's wrath,

He turns all curses into blessings, to give to me all the best things,

When evil have changed rights to wrong, stay prayerful, truthful, peaceful and strong,

When hate has gathered, all around you, remember the promises God made to you,

He turns all curses into blessings, to give to me all his best things,

He'll give me all that is needed, hatred and evil has been defeated,

He turns all curses into blessings, to give to me all his very best things,

BEYOND THE VEIL

I see the nations through epochs of time, some had tumultuous mountains and hills to climb,

Seven divisions divinely planned, placing each nation placing each man,

Viewing all life's events and where Gods dwells, I'm a sacred place far beyond the veil,

Symbolical of the coming of Christ, the seven veils were rent and torn by the power of his life,

To bring a promised gift to those who believed, to accept and see the Christ they're to receive,

Viewing all life's events and where God dwells, I'm a sacred place far beyond the veil,

The holiest of holies where no man goes, is a divine place that only God knows,

Viewing all life's events and where God dwells, I'm a most sacred place far beyond the veil,

GLORIA PATRI
(PRAISE BE TO THE FATHER)

Praise be to him who sits on high, who hears our voices when we cry,

Give unto the King all the praise that's due, Gloria Patri, (praise be to the Father), we shall always praise you,

We exalt you and lift your name, we know the true reasons why you came,

Our lips pour out blessings and praises to you, we love and magnify all that you do,

Give unto the King all the praises that's due, Gloria Patri, (praise be to the Father), we shall always praise you,

Your excellence is seen and heard, throughout the land, you have made your mountains and hills to stand,

Blessed be he, the lover of my soul, who has given me power and made me whole,

Give unto the King all the praises that's due, Gloria Patri, (Praise be to the Father), we shall always praise you,

SHEKINA GLORY

Marriages are sacred in God's sight, they are joined by a divine rite,

Blessed by God, a marriage shall stand, He is the keeper of every man,

Blessed by God's Shekina Glory, she hovers over the nuptial bed, revealing a sacred story,

Shekina Glory is the Holy Spirit, adorned in light, giving approval of God's power, and God's might,

Keeping together the union bound by oath, showering blessings, over their marital growth,

Where God is not, she will not dwell, her providence exists, within God's veil,

She is a keeper, of the faithful, the just and pure, she gives to them, the power to endure,

Blessed by God's Shekina Glory, she'll hover over the nuptial bed, revealing a sacred story,

THY WORD

Many have spoken, but few have heard, the majesty and depth of thy word,

For it is filled with life and strength, giving power to the weak and diffident,

They word is assurance, of things to come, it holds the future for everyone,

Thy word Oh Lord is the link and chain, that bends all nations to your name,

How sweet it is to entreat thy word. I listen for your call, thy word, I heard,

Many have spoken but few have heard, the majesty and depth of thy word

HOLD MY HAND

Lord I'm traveling in places, that's unknown to me, some of these places are where I should not be,

Yet my trust is always on your Grace, to keep and guide me in this place,

When I'm lost and not sure, where I am in this land, lovingly touch me Father, and just hold my hand,

Keep my steps in a path, that I might not go astray, show me where your love abides, and lead me that way,

When I am surrounded, by hatred, evil and strife, shine your light of love around me, that they may know you blessed my life,

Your love, oh Father! is in my heart, and keeps me in this land, when I am tired and in doubt, please just hold my hand,

Just one touch from you Father, conquers all my fears, it restores my youth, and adds life where there are tears,

Keep me above mine enemies, that they may see and know, God bears me up everywhere I go,

You blessed my life, and told me yes, I can, walk through storms and darkness, when you hold my Hand,

A MAN OF PURPOSE

Some men are caught, in the evolution and time, some men are bound, by their physical mind,

Some men just drift, with every changing tide, some men are cowards and they just hide,

But a God made man, is a man with purpose, A man of honor, a man that's just,

God imbues him with strength, to accomplish the task, for which he is sent,

A man with purpose, God endows with power, to utilize this gift hour by hour,

A man with purpose, some can't define, their gifts exist beyond this time,

Only God determines, when and where, that the man of purpose, may be sent there,

God created man with his own purpose, that we might one day, seek and trust,

IMAGINATION

I'm the strength, that gives the mind, the ambition and will, to conquer a thought, that has not, been fulfilled,

I can relax a mind, in an emotional state, or cause a disaster, that's worse than fate,

I'm the success, and manipulation, of rich men's schemes, I'm the ultimate utopian of poor men's dreams,

I'm the happiness, and joy, of young love hearts, I'm the sadness, and pain, when one does part,

They call me Imagination, some I've drove insane, others just live life, as natural as they came,

I'm as thin as the air, and as light as a feather, but if a nation is willing, I can bring them together,

It doesn't take much, to conquer a thought, just be willing, to use what you've got,

Your state of being, controls your moods, I direct your thoughts, and attitudes,

They call me Imagination, I exist within, some live-in reality and some pretend,

I could be a wish, a thought, even be an illusion, combine the three together, then they'd label me confusion,

I'm animate and inanimate at the same time, depending on you, and your state of mind,

I'm bound in your life, without cessation, you can master your life by Imagination,

66 SECTIONS OF
THE HOLY BIBLE

66 sections of holy knowledge, specialized to learn in school or college,

It tells of a life our master gave, that we may live, and not be slaves,

Past, present, and future, this book reveals, of our creation, and how he's healed,

The sick and afflicted, and wicked nations, that we may join, his congregation,

But still we sin, without a thought, about our Bible, and what he's taught,

Yet it's a blessing, for one to die, and for one to be born, they say we should cry,

This is not so, some would say, but look at the life we live today,

We live no different, from days of old, read your Bible, the future is told,

66 sections of holy knowledge, specialized to learn in school or college,

It tells of a life our master gave, that we may live, and not be slaves,

I SURRENDER

So long I have lived, my life in vain, committing acts of rebellion and shame,

Not knowing why or how to give, only dreading the turmoil, of each day I live,

So many things Father, I don't want to remember, to you my life and soul, I surrender,

With tears in my eyes, I pray for the day, when Christ would come, and show us a better way,

Of living and serving, and most of all to forgive, for in forgiving is when we live,

So many things Father, I don't want to remember, to you my life, and soul I surrender,

SOUL MATE

Birds gather when you're near, they even sing songs for you to hear,

A special gift to me you are, to keep you close and not too far,

You're a part of me, your gift gives life, I vowed to one day be your wife,

My special love so fair and true, God planned it all for me and you,

You are destined for me, my soul my mate, for you my love I'll patiently wait,

Stars fall at your feet, when you go by, to be near a love created from the sky,

The angels adorned you with heavenly things, Mother Nature filled you, with all her desire could bring,

Father time blessed you with time and space, to give our love room, to grow with Grace,

You are destined for me my soul my mate, on you my love I'll patiently wait,

DREAM CHILDREN

I see your smiles as you gleefully play, I see your tears, as you earnestly play,

I see your strength, while you grow and mature, I see your spirit, as you patiently endure,

My dream children, you are my life, you bring to me reality when truth's not in sight,

Sometime truth is hard to except, some people would rather settle for less,

I know for a fact, I'll always have you, God gave me Dream Children, to make my dreams come true,

So, search my children far and wide, bring my dreams from the other side,

That I may be all, that I can be, with my dreams and realities and of God's blessings to me,

I'M RICH YOU

On worldly riches, I can't depend, they're shallow, elusive and destined to end,

On man's premises, I cannot trust, they sell out, bail out, and are full of lust,

One day I found a priceless treasure, to which there was no earthly measure,

Each day my life is blessed and renewed, for I found the secret of being Rich in you,

I thank you for all the times you paid, for my life to be protected from the grave,

I praise you for each wound each scar, and how your face was disfigured and marred,

Most of all I surrender to you, in doing so I found the truth,

That is hidden in sacrifice and giving, it is the reciprocal action to love and living,

One day I found a priceless treasure, to which was no earthly measure,

Each day my life is blessed and renewed, for I found the secret of being Rich in you,

SEED'S

Springtime comes and seeds the earth, with fertility at hand and natural births,

Trees are filled with their own seeds, to procreate as nature needs,

God has given man special seed, to create after himself as he needs,

God has given various seeds of kind, for us to comprehend and not be blind,

We are filled with trillions of seeds, when we are born we have all that we need,

Sometimes we search deep to find, what was there all the time,

Angels love to fecundate the earth, to cause purity in the earth and generate new births,

Sometime we search deep to find, what was there all the time,

MY GOD DOES

Who makes the sky each day, and cause the sun to shine so bright,

Who makes the moon to take her course, and cause her to give her light?

Who makes the stars to adorn the heavens, that all may see and know,

That beyond the stars there is a place, where one day chosen people must go,

Who gives the breadth to wake us up, to start us on our way?

Who holds us in the palm of his hand, each day?

He is the sovereign son of God, the lamb, the truth and light, he is the one that keeps us all, through his majesty, love and might,

Who sets the world on its course, to routinely revolve each day, who puts the music in the heavens, we hear the angels play,

Who has us connected everywhere, by his infinite love, if you can't figure it out by now, I'll tell you my God does,

ON FAITH I STAND

I've been traveling from place to place, looking for peace of mind,

Trying to keep myself, in touch with whatever peace I'd find,

Only to find, some things really don't last, what was present, soon becomes something of the past,

I grew weary and tired of searching, for what seemed to be a myth,

Then I one day I was blessed with a promise and a gift,

God said ask what ye will, in my name, on faith you must stand, there'll be nothing you can't have in God's abundant land,

I followed God's directions, and found the peace I sought, he even added joy and love, the divinest of blessings he brought,

I believe his every word, and on his truth, I stand, for I am a living witness and a product of his plan,

God said ask what ye will, in my name and on faith you must stand, there'll be nothing you can't have in God's abundant land,

THE SILENT DOVE

Men will be judged and souls will be freed, according to their actions according to their deeds,

God will weigh their hearts, and look into their souls, redeeming those who are worthy, to reign with Christ as we were told,

We call the Silent Dove, the one who comes from God, on stringed instruments of praise we laud, the Holy Spirit and our lord,

Truth will not be hindered, nor will faith be withheld, for God has ordained freedom to those he will not fail,

The Holy Spirit is watching, and judging the souls of men, for those numbered by the Spirit, are those who know no sin,

There are many tender mercies, the Father tenderly gives, he sends the Holy Spirit that we may be corrected and live,

We call the Silent Dove, the one who comes from God, on stringed instruments of praise we laud, the Holy Spirit and our Lord,

RICH IN LOVE

Each waking moment I cherish, as if it were my last,

And always being conscious that what is present is soon the past,

Just to have my being, I found I'm Rich in Love,

No-one could have given me this, except God up above,

I'm blessed with friends and family, and the capacity to grow,

To be whatever Gods wants me to be, because God deems it so,

Just to have my being, I found I'm Rich in Love,

No-one could have given me this, except God up above,

TRIBUTE TO MY BROTHER
(ISAIAH THOMAS)

Sometime it's hard, to say all you feel,

Sometimes it's even harder, to do what you will,

Yet in those times, there seems to be strength,

That makes you wonder, where the weakness went,

I'd like to say, I love you, and hope that you hear,

And know that you are someone, I treasure very dear,

I'd like to pay tribute, to my brother,

Whom I feel in comparison, is like no other.

CHILDREN OF THE DREAM

Our world's in turmoil, full of evil and hate,

Surely God sees these atrocities, and lets us choose our fate,

Our children seek out drugs, our men seek out whores,

Our values, ethics and morals have been cast down to the floor,

When, oh! Father, will the nightmares end, in order for peace, unity and love to begin,

Secretly, I call for the children of the dream, the ones spawn from righteousness dwelling within the King,

These are they who have conquered, and set the captives free,

These are they from afar, that have spiritual eyes to see,

Secretly, I call for the children of the dream, the one's spawn from righteousness, dwelling within the king,

Keep our hearts endeavoring, to do the things that are right,

That we may be the leaders, of what is pure and walking in your light,

Give strength to the King and his sons, that earth may see your prince, leading, your people to a promised land, as told in biblical events,

Secretly, I call upon the children of the dream, the one's spawn from righteousness dwelling within the King,

GOD MADE MAN

Virulent and strong, wise and keen,

These are the attributes, that should be seen,

Noble and just are the providence of men,

Whom God has chosen and on whom we must depend,

Very distinctive are God made men,

Divinely ordered through a spiritual blend,

Bearers of seeds to impregnate the earth,

Keepers of truth, progenitors of birth,

We must respect and recognize, what God made man's stead,

God made him the leader God made him the head,

I pray for protection, health and strength,

That God will keep them growing immense,

Very distinctive are God made men,

Divinely ordered, through a spiritual blend.

WHAT'S IN A NAME

A name is an equation, of who you are,

A name can be despised or can take you far,

A name is the property, that you possess,

Imbedded in your soul, that God has blessed,

Some do not know what's in a name,

It's is the property of your soul not fortune, nor fame,

A name has as much, power as words,

Lazarus understood, his name, when it was Jesus he heard,

Some names are most blessed, and settled in Heaven,

Only through the Father can this be given,

Let your name be as silver and gold,

Purified and spotless for your father to behold,

Some do not know what's in a name,

It is the property of your soul not fortune, nor fame.

ONE MORE STEP
(GERALDINE'S BIRTHDAY)

You've made another step, although it took 365 days,

God knew we needed help, so he put steps to lead the ways

Like children sometimes, we stumble, sometimes we even fall,

Just like a loving Father, we're lifted by his call,

God puts us back on track, a path again to tread,

With confidence and pride we know, there's nothing for us to dread,

God is there to help us, take one more step, to assure us in all our travels, we are divinely kept,

TRANSCENDING LOVE

Each of us has a fate, that goes beyond the material, that goes beyond hate, we are given, and bequeathed, these gifts, through a divine source not a myth,

As children of the King, we should show, the truth about the love we know, and be the vicars, in the earth, that all may know, there is divine birth,

His love transcends to a place, where there is peace, where there is grace, far beyond the earthly plain, made for those who can attain,

The most precious gift given to us, Jesus Christ, the true, the just,

We are over-comers made for change, like the metamorphosis of a butterfly, reborn we are re-arranged,

We transcend his love throughout this vast universe, in harmony with the primary mover, he is law he is first,

We transcend his love to Heaven where all good abides, for here is the epitome of what God has set aside,

His love transcends, to a place, where there is peace, where there is grace, far beyond the earthly plain, made for those who can attain,

The most precious gift given to us, is Jesus Christ, the true, the just,

RESCUE ME

I've wondered throughout time, All over this land,

Only to find there were few to understand,

The truths and mysteries, hidden from view,

The treasures and wonders, lying dormant in you,

I hear a spirit calling, Rescue Me,

Open the door, and set me free,

So many of us, don't fulfill our dreams,

Because we're preoccupied, with so may other things,

We are adorned with miracles and gifts, some to lead and some to lift,

I hear a spirit calling, Rescue Me,

Open the door and set me FREE

YOU SHOULD HAVE KNOWN

You questioned my mind, you questioned my birth, you even questioned my integrity and my worth,

God gave me the right to exist and be, No man questions divinity,

You should have known, I had the right, to praise my God, and stand in his light,

You should have known, my God given gifts are a reality and not a myth,

You should have known, my inalienable rights, were given long before you were even in sight,

You should have excepted me, as your sister/brother, this is why God made us, to love one another,

Most of all you should have known, God never left me alone,

He exists in all great and small, this is the reason I can go through it ALL

THE FIRST AND THE LAST

Many wise men have written great books and words, many have read them, some have heard,

There is so much more than what we hear and see, to the words handed down throughout history,

There is one word, which was the beginning, there is one word that will be the ending,

This is relative to the first and the last, where words will unite future, present and past,

Time is invested in all God's text, translating generations and preparing for the next,

When all has been said and done, all the text will be resolved into One,

Many dissolutions, will take place, to separate the false words from his Grace,

Many new conjugations will be made, to produce the property of better grades,

There is one word, which was the beginning, there is one word that will be the ending,

This is relative to the first and the last, where words will unite Future, Present and Past

MOTHER'S
GOLDEN THREADS
(TO MOTHER CHARLENE THOMAS)

Mother you've woven, golden threads, throughout this life time,

Your abundance of love and care, is etched in every line,

God has granted you another year, to weave your blessings and grace,

Upon this earth with Christian love, for those who will run God's race,

I thank God for you and pray, that he extends you many more, years to work within the fabric of life, to keep an open door,

Happy Birthday Mother, you have so many Golden Threads,

Shining like a halo of angels, all around your Head,

I love and respect the wonderful things you do,

Next to God, there's no greater love, than a Mothers love that's true.

GOD'S HEART

A heart is an organ of sheer delight, it's wisdom can bring truth to light,

It has been honored by God himself, to search out man's deeds and greed of wealth,

If I had to choose, I'd rather be a heart, it is the keeper of the vital parts,

There is so much, the heart can do, it revitalizes things and makes them new,

The heart is an organ, of beauty and grace, especially when embodied with God's love and faith,

God looks upon the heart of everyman, to know his intentions and his plans,

Greatest of all, God fills us with his love, an infinite measure, more than we can think of,

God's love in a heart will change any fate, and put his love where there is no hate,

One thing I know, love cannot die, it is the epitome of all life,

Love is truly, the transcender of time, transcending past, present and future genealogical lines,

How beautiful and sacred, you've made the heart, I can rest assured, you'll never part,

When all else fails me, my heart inside, will keep me in your love, and be my guide,

Weather you're here or weather you're gone, your love has paid the price to lead my heart home,

---

WHEN YOU'VE GIVEN ALL

There are some things that man can't make, there are some things that man can't take,

And through it all we learn one thing, about the good and bad that living can bring,

A true and divine love can't be measured, it reaches beyond all things, that can be treasured,

So never give up on what you love, it can always be renewed, with strength from above,

When you know you've given your best your all, remember God still loved man, even after man's fall,

God loved us so much, he started eight (8) new lines, that reached from Noah and his sons, down to this time,

The sincerity of a gift, is when it comes from the heart, the fulfillment of a promise is when it does its part,

We are living God's promises every day, the gift of life to mankind made through Christ in one day,

When you know you've given your best your all, remember God still loved man even after man's fall,

SISTERS LOVE
(TO CHARLENE DUNN)

Today is your day, a day to behold, on this day 54 years ago, you received your soul,

God deemed you fit to enter this world, as a precious, chosen little girl,

There's no greater love than what he has for you, His love is the only love pure and true,

Happy Birthday sister, I send a sister love, our bonds are kept by God above,

May God grant you long-life and health, a Christ filled life of prosperity and wealth,

Happy birthday sister, I send a sister's love, our bonds are kept by God above,

ON THE OTHER SIDE

(To Eddie, Nathan, Willie, James, Isaiah, Anthony Aunt Helen, and Aunt Martha)

Many have been called to the other side, to move toward the creator of all,

To complete a plan, from the inception of time, to redeem man from his fall,

Separated from God, there was no life, no light or hope within,

connected to God there was eternity, where all life, light and hope began,

Many have been called to the other side,

to move toward the creator of all,

To complete a plan from the inception of time,

to redeem man from his fall,

You have moved on, yet in my heart I know, God has planted you in his garden, of heavenly things he grows,

When I look in Heaven's eyes, I truly hope to see, where God's garden has made a place for me,

GOD'S LOTUS BLOSSOM

The Garden of Eden, was given to men, until he let sin enter in,

God removed him, to pay this cost, a direct relationship with God, was what he lost,

There is one flower hidden from view, it abides in me, it abides in you,

It is sacred, it's precious, it's pure and true, it will only blossom in the evolution of you,

This flower has a special nature, that's not categorized by nomenclature,

This flower is sacred to the mind, it's petals can evolve in you 1,000 times,

This is God's lotus blossom, a flower like no other, it has the engendering nature of a Holy Mother,

A DAY IN THE SUN

When troubles seem to come your way, and it seems like you just can't pray,

Don't give in just fight back, you'll find your troubles can be attacked,

Look for the joy and find your peace, you'll soon experience your souls released,

When you do, that's your day in the sun, to give thanks and praises, for the victories you've won,

It's a battle each day, just to survive, the spiritually strong will stay alive,

Give thanks and praises, for the victories you've won, to earn the right, for your day with God's son,

GIFT OF GOD'S VOICE

The voice of God is settled in the heaven, way up above the earth,

For each child that is born, a voice is given at birth,

Some voices are divinely gifted, for purposes of God's alone,

you are gifted with a voice, to sing a sacred song,

Alleluia, sing praises, praises to our God, who sits on his throne,

Praise and glory to his name, to his name alone,

GOD'S LOVE

God's love is infinite, and will never part,

the keepers of his love must have a big heart,

On one side, a love for the just, who does things right,

on the other side a love for those blameless in God's sight,

A royal family from a royal clan,

upheld by God in the palm of his hands,

To keep the light of love in the windows of time,

burning bright within every man's mind,

God's love breaks the bonds, of envy and hate, restores your life to all things great,

God's love exists beyond time, to correct things that somehow diminish within our minds,

Most of all God's love redeems, reconciling us to our King!

HEAVEN AND EARTH

IT TOOK 7 DAYS TO CREATE THIS PLACE, GOD MADE IT

LIVABLE FOR EVERY HUMAN RACE, HE

MATHEMATICALLY DESIGNED EVERY SINGLE INCH, FOR GOD
IT WAS EASY, IT WAS A CINCH.

HE FIRST CREATED THE HEAVEN(S) AND EARTH, A

PLACE WHERE EVERY LIFE FORM HAS ITS BIRTH, THEN

HE SENT HIS DIVINE LIGHT, TO SEPARATE THE

CREATIONS BETWEEN DAY AND NIGHT,

THEN HE SEPERATED THE FIRMAMENTS FROM

WATERS

ABOVE AND WATERS BELOW, TO KEEP A SACRED

BALANCE, THAT ONLY GOD KNOWS,

THE EVENING AND MORNING WAS 1ST DAY, SACRED DAY,
TO PERFECT THE LINEAGES OF GOD'S HOLY WAYS.

HEAVEN(S) AND LIGHT

GOD DECIDED TO DIVIDE THE HEAVENS AT LENGTH, HE

SEPARATED THEM BY WATERS AND CALLED THEM

FIRMAMENTS,

HEAVEN IS THE HEIGHT OF THE ANGELIC ABODES,

WHERE THE DIVINE REWARDS ARE GIVEN AND

NOTHING IS OWED,

HEAVEN IS THE PLACE WHERE SAINTS CAN REST,

WHERE GOD HAS GIVEN THEM HIS VERY BEST,

EACH REALM IS BLESSED AND UNDER GOD'S CONTROL,

A SACRED PLACE WHERE ALL SAINTS ARE WHOLE,

HEAVEN'S GATES ARE LINED WITH JEWELS,

REPRESENTING THE RICHNESS OF OUR FATHERS

TOOLS,

TO ENTER IN THESE PEARLY GATES, IS THE

ANTICIPATION OF EVERY SAINT,

GOD CREATED AND PROMISED US A BETTER LIFE,

BOUND IT IN HEAVEN AND SEALED ITS HEIGHTS,

THE EVENING AND MORNING WAS THE 2ND DAY, TO PERFECT THE LINEAGES OF GOD'S HOLY WAYS.

SUN AND MOON

(LIGHT, SEASONS, DAYS AND NIGHTS)

GOD ALMIGHTY WAS PLEASED WITH HIS DESIGNS,

HE DECIDED THE SUN AND MOON SHOULD BE OF A

DIFFERENT KIND,

SO THE GREATER LIGHT, HE DESIGNED TO RULE

THE DAY, TO KEEP SEPARATE THE POWERS OF

DARKNESS AT BAY,

THE LESSOR LIGHT HE DESIGNED TO RULE THE

NIGHT, EACH LIGHT HAS ITS GLORY IN GOD'S SIGHT,

HE SET THE STARS IN HEAVEN FOR BEAUTY AND SIGNS, THEY
REPRESENTED THE WONDERS OF ANCIENT TIMES.

THESE HEAVENLY BODIES SHINE UPON THE EARTH,

SHEWING FORTH GOD'S HANDIWORK(S), THE EVENING
AND MORNING WAS THE 3RD DAY, TO PERFECT THE
LINEAGES OF GOD'S HOLY WAYS.

CREATIONS OF NATURE

GOD SAW THE EARTH AND KNEW IT WAS BARREN,

HE DECIDED ON WHAT THE EARTH SHOULD BE

WEARING,

HE CAUSED THE LAND TO COME TO ONE PLACE, HE INTEGRATED THE WATERS TO FLOW THROUGH BY GRACE,

HE REPLENISHED THE EARTH, WITH SEED, GRASS

AND TREES,

TO BE FOOD FOR ALL THOSE THAT BELIEVED,

THEN HE CAUSED THE WATERS TO APPEAR, THAT

THE LAND WOULD BE WATERED YEAR AFTER YEAR,

GOD, DESIGNED THE SEED TO YEILD AFTER ITS

KIND,

TO SECURE GENERATIONS TO COME THROUGH A

GODLY LINE,

THE EVENING AND MORNING WAS THE 4TH DAY, TO PERFECT THE LINEAGES, OF GOD'S HOLY WAYS.

LIVING CREATURES

GODS CAUSED THE WATERS TO BRING FORTH LIFE,

AND THE FOWL IN THE AIR TO TAKE ITS FLIGHT,

HE CREATED GREAT WHALES TO PRODUCE AFTER ITS KIND,

HE CREATED MANY BIRDS DIVERSE AND DIVINE,

HE BLESSED THEM AND CAUSED THEM TO

MULTIPLY, TO POPULATE THE EARTH HE WOULD

CAUSE TO SUPPLY,

THE FIRMAMENT ABOVE AND THE WATERS BELOW,

WOULD BE FILLED WITH WHAT GOD HAD CAUSED

TO GROW,

ABUNDANTLY LIFE WOULD BE DISPERSED,

COMMANDED BY GOD WHO HAS GIVEN THEM

BIRTH,

AND THE EVENING AND THE MORNING WAS THE 5TH DAY,
TO PERFECT THE LINEAGES OF GOD'S HOLY WAYS.

THE PERFECTION OF MAN

THE FIRMAMENTS AND WATERS HAD BEEN FILLED,

THEN GOD DECIDED THE EARTH SHOULD YEILD,

CATTLE AND BEAST AFTER ITS KIND AND ONE BEING

IN THE IMAGE OF GOD'S OWN MIND,

GOD THEN CREATED MAN, HIS PERFECTION IN THE

EARTH, THE ONLY CREATION WITH A DIVINE BIRTH,

GOD CREATED BOTH, WOMAN AND MAN, TO HAVE

DOMINION OVER ALL CREATURES IN THE LAND,

GOD BLESSED MAN AND WOMAN TO REPLENISH THE

LAND, TO BE FRUITFUL AND MULTIPLY, OBEYING

HIS COMMAND, AND THE EVENING AND THE

MORNING WAS THE 6TH DAY, THE PERFECTION OF

THE LINEAGES OF GOD'S HOLY WAYS,

THE LIGHT OF MY BODY

I AM UNIQUELY EMBEDDED WITH GRACE,

A SUBSTANCE DIVINELY GIVEN NEVER TO WASTE,

WITHIN MY BEING, I HAVE ALL I NEED,

GIVEN AT BIRTH, FOR ME TO SUCCEED,

IN THE IMAGE OF GOD CREATED HE ME,

I HAVE FOUND THE TRUE LIGHT, OF MY BODY,

MY MIND IS A UNIVERSE, MY THOUGHTS ARE FORMS,

THEY ARE THE CREATIVE VESSELS OF MY WORLD TO
ADORN,

MY HEART IS MY CENTER, TO ALWAYS RETURN, A PLACE I
ALWAYS ENTER, WHERE A DIVINE LOVE BURNS.

MY SPIRIT IS OF THE COSMOS, A PART OF THE

WHOLE, WHERE ALL SPIRITS COME FROM A SACRED

MOLD,

IN THE IMAGE OF GOD, CREATED HE ME, I HAVE FOUND THE
TRUE LIGHT OF MY BODY.

I AM THE CREATOR
OF MY WORDS

IN THE IMAGE OF GOD, I COMMAND, MY WORDS, MY

SIGHT, MY VOICE, MY HANDS,

IN THE IMAGE OF GOD, I CAN SEE, MY WAY, MY

CHOICE, MY DESTINY,

IN THE IMAGE OF GOD, I CONTROL, MY MIND, AND MY

BODY, TO KEEP ME WHOLE,

I WAS SPIRITUALLY ENLIGHTENED THE DAY I HEARD,

I AM

THE CREATOR
OF MY WORDS

I HUMBLY EXCEPT THE DIVINESS IN ME, TO CREATE

THINGS AS I WANT THEM TO BE,

I GRACIOUSLY CULTIVATE THE BEST IN ME, MAKING

ROOM FOR HEAVEN TO DWELL IN ME,

MY WORDS AND CREATIONS HAVE A DIRECT EFFECT,

ON WHAT I SOW AND WHAT I PROJECT,

I WAS SPIRITUALLY ENLIGHTENED, THE DAY I HEARD, I AM THE CREATOR OF MY WORDS.

IMAGES OF GOOD

ALL AROUND US ARE ENERGIES, WE DON'T SEE, YOU

MUST BE DEVELOPED SPIRITUALLY,

IF YOU ARE TO DEVELOP RIGHT, YOU NEED TO

CULTIVATE TRUTH AND LIGHT,

I INVOKE THE IMAGES OF GOOD, TO WORK THE

POWERS MY FATHER WOULD,

TO EXPEL EVIL, AND BE A SOURCE OF RIGHT, TO

STAND AS AN EMBLEM AND SIGN OF GOD'S LIGHT,

I LIVE AND AM SURROUNDED BY LOVE, THE POWER

THAT OPERATES FROM HEIGHTS ABOVE,

I INVOKE THE IMAGES OF GOOD, TO WORK THE POWERS
MY FATHER WOULD.

SIGN OF THE CROSS

THERE ARE MANY THINGS IN THE WORLD TODAY,

THAT ARE SYMBOLIC AND REPRESENT YESTERDAY,

AS EMBLEMS OF MAGISTY, POWER AND MIGHT,

THE SIGN OF THE CROSS INVOKES GOD'S SACRED

LIGHT,

THOSE WHO BELIEVE ARE KEEPERS OF GOOD,

SEEKING THE THINGS GOD SAYS THEY SHOULD,

WALKING IN LIGHT AND RESISTING THE DARK,

BEING THE VESSELS, WHERE GOD'S LOVE STARTS,

AS EMBLEMS OF MAGISTY POWER AND MIGHT, THE SIGN
OF THE CROSS INVOKES GOD'S SACRED LIGHT.

AND THIS TOO SHALL PASS

I'VE BEEN TROUBLED BEYOND BELIEF, I COULD NOT

SEEM TO FIND RELIEF,

THEY SOLD MY POSSESSIONS, AND DENOUNCED MY

FAITH, THEY CULTIVATED HELL ON EARTH AND

WANTED HEAVEN TO ABATE,

THESE KIND ONLY COME OUT WITH PRAYERS AND

FASTS, KNOW THAT EVIL IS NOT FOREVER, THIS TOO

SHALL PASS,

THEY GATHERED TOGETHER TO HIDE MY LIFE, THEY

THOUGHT THEY COULD MAKE ME LIVE FOREVER IN

STRIFE,

THEY TRIED TO SELL AND STEAL MY SOUL, BUT GOD

HAD OTHER PLANS THEY DID NOT KNOW,

GOD HAD THE MOLD, THE BOWL AND MY FATE,

EVERYTHING THEY HAD, WAS AN IMAGE OF WHAT

GOD MAKES,

FOREVER THEY WILL BE TRYING TO MAKE IMAGES

REAL, ALWAYS HAVING AGAIN TO GO BACK AND

STEAL,

THESE KIND ONLY COME OUT WITH PRAYERS AND
FASTS,

KNOW THAT EVIL IS NOT FOREVER AND THIS TOO SHALL PASS.

HEDGES ALL AROUND ME

I WALKED IN THIS WORLD TO LONG EXPOSED, THERE

WERE SO MANY THINGS I DID NOT KNOW,

ARROWS BY DAY, AND SWORDS BY NIGHT, EVIL WAS

ALL AROUND ME, IN DARKNESS AND LIGHT,

THEN ONE DAY AN ANGEL WAS SENT TO ME, TO TELL

ME OF MY DESTINY,

HE SHOWED ME THE PROTECTION THAT ANGELS

GIVE, TO PROMOTE MY DESTINY THAT I MIGHT LIVE,

TO FULFILL THE PLAN THAT GOD HAS DEEMED, AS CREATOR
OF MY LIFE, AS MAKER AND KING,

THEN GOD PLACED HEDGES ALL AROUND MY SOUL,

TO KEEP ME PURE, TO KEEP ME WHOLE,

THESE HEDGES EXTENDED TO HEAVENS GATE, THE FINAL
DESTINATION OF MY HEAVENLY FATE.

MY SOULS CANDLE

I HAVE A LIGHT, THAT CANNOT BE HID, FOR ALL THE

WORLD TO SEE, IT WAS GIVEN TO ME, AT BIRTH, TO

LIGHT MY PATH, AND SHINE ON MY DESTINY,

GOD HAS SET ME IN A PLACE, WITH HIGH AND

BLAZING LIGHTS, OUR SOULS ARE LIKE FESTIVALS,

THAT KEEP THE SABBATH, OF EACH SACRED

NIGHT,

MY SOULS CANDLE, WAS SET BY GOD, AS AN HONOR

AND A GIFT, CHRIST IS THE SCHINTILLA OF LIGHT,

IN EVERY SOUL AND TRULY IS NO MYTH,

SO MANY UNSEARCHABLE TRUTHS, THAT HAVE

PAVED THE WAY, TO WISDOM DEPTHS AND WISDOM

HEIGHTS, STILL EXIST TODAY,

MY SOUL IS SO MUCH MORE, THAN WHAT I COULD

KNOW OR SEE, IT EXIST BEYOND, JUST A PHYSICAL

THING, IT IS SPIRITUALLY LINKED TO ME,

MY SOULS CANDLE, SET BY GOD, IS AN HONOR AND A GIFT,
CHRIST IS THE SCHINTILLA OF LIGHT, IN EVERY SOUL AND
TRULY IS NO MYTH.

POWER TO CHANGE

LOVE IS THE GREATEST POWER WE KNOW, IT IS

GOD'S GIFT TO THE WORLD THAT WE MAY GROW,

IN TRUTH, WISDOM, POWER AND MIGHT, TO

CULTIVATE THE INFINITENESS OF GOD'S

SOVERENGITY AND LIGHT,

HE HAS GIVEN US THE POWE TO CHANGE, WHEN

OUR LIVES HAVE BEEN REARRANGED, WE ARE NOT

BOUND BY ELEMENTS OF THIS WORLD, NOR ARE

WE CHAINED BY THEIR TURMOILS,

WE ARE BOUND BY TRUTH AND LIGHT, WE

DESTROY EVIL TO REPLACE WITH GOD'S LIGHT,

HE HAS GIVEN US THE POWER TO CHANGE, WHEN OUR
LIVES HAVE BEEN REARRANGED.

WHERE ARE MY CHILDREN

I FOUND MYSELF ALONE IN A HOSPITAL ROOM, IT

WAS COLD AND CLAMY AND I FELT ENTOMBED,

I DIDN'T UNDERSTAND HOW, I EVEN MADE THE

TRANSITION, ALL I KNOW IS THIS WAS A STRANGE

POSITION,

MY BODY IS MY CHILDREN, WERE NURTURED BY ME, I

PRIDED MYSELF ON KEEPING MY BODY FREE,

THEN I AWOKE AND FOUND SOMETHING WRONG,

MY BODY DID NOT FEEL AS STRONG,

I SEARCHED MY BODY ONLY TO FIND, MY BODY NO

LONGER SEEMED LIKE MINE, I FELT FOR PARTS

THAT WERE NOT THERE, WHAT HAPPENED TO ME,

NO ONE COULD SHARE,

IT SEEMED MY CHILDREN WERE REMOVED,

WITHOUT MY KNOWLEDGE WITHOUT BEING

APPROVED,

I LIE IN THE ROOM WITH CONFUSED THOUGHTS,

WONDERING IF MY CHILDREN WE SOLD OR

BOUGHT,

WHERE ARE MY CHILDREN, GOD GAVE TO ME, SURELY THEY
ARE NOT WHERE THEY OUGHT TO BE.

MORE THAN A WOMAN

YOU THOUGHT YOU COULD CONFUSE ME WITH

YOUR DEVIOUS SCHEMES,

YOU THOUGHT YOU COULD DESTORY MY MOST

INTIMATE DREAMS,

YOU TRIED TO ABUSE ME AND KILL MY SOUL,

GOD IS MY KEEPER BE WARNED, YOU'VE BEEN

TOLD,

I'M MORE THAN A WOMAN, THIS YOU CAN'T SEE,

I'M EQUIPPED WITH GOD'S LOVE AND GOODNESS IN

ME,

MY MIND IS ONLY A PART OF ME, IT ALLOWS ME TO

EXPRESS GOD'S INTELLECT THROUGH ME,

MY BODY IS ONLY THE FORM I'M IN, IT ALLOWS ME

TO FUNCTION WITHIN GOD'S EARTHLY PLAN,

MY SPIRIT IS THE ETERNAL PART OF ME, SPIRIT

NEVER DIES IT IS THE GOD IN ME,

WHEN I AM JOINED WITH THE CREATOR OF ALL,

EVERY SPIRIT THAT IS HIS WILL HERE HIS CALL,

WE WILL GATHER THROUGHTOUT THE LAND,

EVERY GIRL BOY, WOMAN AND MAN.

POETESS

I AM POETESS, I AM TOLD, WRITING STANZAS AND

LYRICS, IN METRICAL FORMS, CONDUCIVE WITH

LINES AND TIME,

ELUCIDATING, ILLUSTRATING

AND CONCENTRATING WORDS THAT ARE

PREGNANT, WITH LIFE IMBUED AND ADORNED

WITH FORM,

BIRTHING AND BRINGING TO LIFE THE EMBRYOS

OF UNFANTHOMED THOUGHTS, THAT I HAVE

CONCEIVED AND BELIEVED,

I AM POETESS, I AM TOLD WRITING STANZAS AND

LYRICS IN METRICAL FORMS CONDUCIVE WITH

LINES AND TIME,

DEFINING ILLUSIONS IN WORDS

THAT KEEP WITH MY FRAME OF MIND, REALIZING

THEY ARE FIGMENTS OF THE IMAGINATION OF

TIME,

ELABORATING ON THE TRUTHS THAT HAVE

EXISTED THROUGHOUT TIME,

ESTEEMING DIVININTY AT ITS HIGHTEST STATE,

DIVULDGING IN WORDS WHAT IS TRULY GREAT,

MY TIME IS IN EACH LINE AND STANZA I SOW,

I AM POETESS, NOW I KNOW!

WE LIVE IN SEASONS

GOD INSTILLED SEASONS AND TIMES, TO

CORRELATE WITH CYCLES WITHIN GOD'S MIND,

GOD SAW THAT EVERYTHING WAS DIVINELY

PLACED, NOTHING WAS PURPOSELESS NOTHING

WAS A WASTE,

GOD METHODICALLY PLACED SEASON IN FOUR

CORNERS OF THE EARTH,

THAT IN ONE OF EACH SEASON, MAN WOULD HAVE

HIS BIRTH,

THEN GOD ASSOCIATED EVERYTING WITHIN LINES,

AND ORDERED ALL THINGS WOULD HAVE A SEASON

AND A TIME,

WE LIVE IN SEASONS, WITHIN TIME, NOTHING IS

OUTSIDE OF WHAT GOD DESIGNED,

MONDAY

MONDAY IS THE BEGINNING OF MY JOURNEY,

IT IS THE FIRST STEP, LEADING TO A SUCCESSION

OF PATHS, I WILL TAKE DURING THIS 7-DAY

JOURNEY,

IT IS THE DIVINE REVOLUTION OF CYCLES, THAT

WILL REPEAT THEMSLEVES, "PERPETUALLY",

MONDAY, IS THE CREATED DAY, THAT I EMBRACE, THAT OPENS
THE DOOR FOR ALL OTHER DAYS.

TUESDAY

TUESDAY IS THE DAY I OBSERVE WHERE I HAVE

TRAVELLED FROM,

IT IS THE DAY THAT ALLOWS ME TO LOOK BACK TO

MONDAY AND ASSESS MYSELF AND MY CHOICES,

TUESDAY IS THE SECOND CREATED DAY IN A

DIVINE CYCLE, THAT HAS BEEN PURPOSELY SET,

MEASURED AND METED

OUT,

TUESDAY IS THE DAY, I MAKE MY SECOND STEP

TOWARD A DESTINY THAT IS BEFORE ME,

I ACKNOWLEDGE TUESDAY FOR THE WISDOM I

HAVE GATHERED TRAVELLING TO THIS POINT IN

TIME,

TUESDAY IS THE CREATED DAY THAT I REFLECT ON MY CHOICES.

WEDNESDAY

WEDNESDAY IS THE THIRD DAY OF MY JOURNEY, IT

IS THE MEDIAN BETWEEN ALL OTHER DAYS, IT IS A

POINT OF CONTINUENCE OR CHANGE,

WEDNESDAY IS THE DAY OF ASSESSMENT OF

WHERE I HAVE BEEN AND WHERE I AM GOING,

THIS IS THE DAY OF MOVING IN THE SAME

DIRECTION OR MAKING A CONSCIOUS DECISION TO

CHANGE DIRECTIONS, I HAVE REACHED A TURNING POINT,
WHERE I HAVE THE AUTHORITY TO CHANGE MY DIRECTION(S),

WEDNESDAY IS A CREATED DAY OF DECISION, THAT

ALLOWS ME TO STEP INTO ALL OTHER DAYS WITH ASSURED
AND RENEWED CONSCIOUSNESS OF MY PATHS, WEDNESDAY
ALLOWS ME TO CONFIRM THE DESTINATION TOWARDS MY
CHOSEN PATH(S).

THURSDAY

THURSDAY IS THE FOURTH STEP IN A DIVINE CYCLE

OF EVENTS. IT IS A DAY OF PROGRESSION,

THURSDAY ALLOWS ME TO FEEL THE STRENGTH,

THAT EMANATES FROM MY CONSCIOUS DECISION

TO CONTINUE IN SPITE OF ANY OBSTACLES,

I REALIZE WHAT I HAVE OVERCOME DURING THIS

TIME, I REALIZE I HAVE THE STAMINA TO SURPASS

AND SURMOUNT ANY SETBACKS, PROBLEMS AND

OBSTACLES,

THURSDAY IS THE FOURTH DAY OF A 7-DAY

JOURNEY, IT IS A DAY OF RECONCILING, A DAY OF

GATHERING FORCES TO AVERT ANY OBSTACLES,

THURDAY IS THE CREATED DAY THAT I AFFIRM MY POSITION,
AND FORGE AHEAD TOWARD MY DESTINY.

FRIDAY

FRIDAY IS THE FIFTH DAY OF MY 7-DAY JOURNEY,

IT IS THE DAY I CONSIDER ALL PREVIOUS EVENTS

FROM A PHYSICAL PERSPECTIVE,

FRIDAY ALLOWS ME TO MOVE INTO ANOTHER

REALM, I AM SPIRITUALLY STRENGTHENED AND

ENLIGHTENED, FRIDAY IS THE DAY THAT LEADS TO

ANOTHER PORTAL,

I HAVE BEEN PREPARED FOR THE PREVIOUS FOUR

DAYS TO RECEIVE FRIDAY, AS A DAY OF ACENSION,

I EXCEPT WHAT HAS BEEN GRACIOUSLY AND

DIVINELY GIVEN TO ME, I ASK FOR DIVINE

SUPPORT AND GUIDANCE AS I ENTER A HIGHER

PLANE AND REALM OF SPIRIT,

FRIDAY IS THE CREATED DAY THAT I AM ATTUNED

WITH THE SPIRIT REALM,

FRIDAY IS THE DAY THAT OPENS UP AND USHERS

ME INTO REALMS, THAT LEAD TO HIGHER

ELEVATIONS,

SATURDAY

SATURDAY IS THE SIXTH DAY OF A 7-DAY JOURNEY,

IT IS THE DAY OF THE TASK MASTER,

SATURDAY IS THE DAY OF ACCOMPLISHMENTS,

YOU HAVE MASTERED THE FIVE PREVIOUS STEPS,

HERE YOU HAVE VISION, INSIGHT, POWER, AND

SPIRIT, YOU ARE AT THE HELM OF YOUR SHIP,

YOUR 7-DAY JOURNEY IS ABOUT TO END, YOU HAVE

THE VICTORY,

GOD ONLY CREATED 7-DAYS, IN WHICH HE

CREATED YOU AND ALL THAT IS AROUND YOU,

YOU HAVE TAKEN AND WILL BE TAKING THIS 7-DAY

JOURNEY, UNTIL YOU HAVE TRANSITED THROUGH

ALL THE PATHS AND TIME FRAMES GOD HAS FOR

YOU, BE CAUTIOUS, BE MINDFUL, BE WISE, GOD HAS

ALLOWED YOU TO TAKE YOUR JOURNEY, AND

MAKE HISTORY WHILE YOU ARE DOING SO,

THERE IS NO TIME OUTSIDE OF THE 7-DAY CREATION, ALL
OTHER TIME IS AN EXTENSION OF THE ORIGINAL 7-DAY
CREATIONS!

SUNDAY

GOD RESTED ON THIS DAY

IMAGINE A SACRED SONG OF THE UNIVERSE CREATED IN
SILENCE YOU CAN ONLY LEARN IT THROUGH GOD! LISTEN

INFORMATION
TO MUSE ON!

EVOLVED

YOU HAVE JUST EVOLVED!

YOU ARE LIVING IN A SEQUENCE OF EVENTS THAT

ARE CYCLES OF A 7-DAY CREATION PERIOD,

EACH 7-DAY INCREMENT WAS A PERPETUAL

SUCCESSION OF EVENTS THAT INVOLVES A CYCLE

OF TIME, WITHIN THAT SPACE OF TIME YOU MOVED

THROUGH, SEVERAL PHYSICAL AND SPIRITUAL

MOMENTS OF TIME, THE KEY TO THIS PRECIOUS GIFT THAT
GOD HAS GIVEN US, IS TO MAKE EACH MOMENT COUNT, TO

BECOME BETTER PERSONS, SPIRITUALLY,

MENTALLY AND PHYSICALLY, EVOLUTION DIDN'T STOP WITH
SPECIES, IT NOW RESIDES IN YOU, TO CONTINUALLY BECOME

BETTER THAN YOU ARE NOW, TO BECOME THE BEST YOU
CAN BE, WE ARE LIKE NO OTHER CREATION THAT GOD HAS
MADE, WE ARE IN GOD'S IMAGE GODLIKE/CREATIONS!

ENLIGHTENMENT

TIME AS WE KNOW IT IN HOURS, MINUTES AND

SECONDS, IS NOT THE SAME AS SPACE TIME OR

GOD'S TIME. SPACE TIME IS MEASURED IN ANGSTROM UNITS, OR 93,000,000 MILES.

SEVEN DAYS AS WE KNOW IT IS ONE WEEK AND

GOES BY PRETTY FAST. HOWEVER, SEVEN DAYS IN GOD'S TIME IS A VERY LONG PERIOD OF TIME...

GOD DEALS IN EPOCHES, EONS, AND AGES. ONE OF

THE BIBLICAL REFRENCES THAT GIVES US A VIVID PICTURE OF DIVINE TIME IS: 2 PETER 3:8

BUT, BELOVED, BE NOT IGNORANT OF THIS ONE THING, THAT ONE DAY IS WITH THE LORD AS A THOUSAND YEARS, AND A THOUSAND YEARS AS ONE DAY.

ALL TIME IN THE WORLD, UNIVERSE AND COSMOS IS

WITHIN GODS'S COMMAND. THEREFORE, WHEREVER GOD IS TIME CAN ALWAYS BEGAN ANEW.

STARS IN THIS UNIVERSE

WE ARE LIKE STARS IN THIS VAST UNIVERSE. WE ALL HAVE ADDRESSES AND SHINE BY DIFFERENT LIGHTS.

HAVE YOU EVER WONDERED WHAT HAPPENS TO THE STARS IN THE DAYLIGHT HOURS? WHAT IF

THEY DESCEND TO EARTH IN THE DAY AND ASCENDED TO THE SKY AT NIGHT, WOULDN'T THAT BE HEAVENLY!

GOD CREATED THE HEAVENS WITH WISDOM AND

LEFT ENOUGH INFORMATION FOR US TO FIND OUT ABOUT HIM OURSELVES AND THE SIGNS THE HEAVENS FORTELL.

I BELIEVE THE HEAVENS ARE A VERY INTEGRAL PART OF VITAL INFORMATION THAT WE SHOULD ACCESS EVERYDAY. EVENTS THAT GO ON UP THERE, ALSO REFLECT AND INVOLVE US DOWN HERE!

THIS WAS REVEALED IN THE BOOK OF MATTHEW 16:19: WHAT THOU BIND ON EARTH IS BOUND IN HEAVEN, WHAT THOU LOOSE ON EARTH IS LOOSED IN HEAVEN...

BE BLESSED, BE HEALED, STAY FAITHFUL.

CPSIA information can be obtained
at www.ICGtesting.com
Printed in the USA
LVHW021933060921
697132LV00013B/204

9 781662 825903